*Stalking the Wild Taboo*

About fifty years ago a study was made of the comparative readability of various colors of print and paper. Brown ink on tan paper proved best. One might suppose that the publishing trade, ostensibly dedicated to the dissemination of knowledge, would instantly respond to such a finding and change its technology. But no: black on white is still the invariable rule. One cannot but wonder: Why should an information-industry like publishing be so resistant to information relevant to its own operations? More important; what, if anything, can be done to rationalize its practices? Perhaps nothing; but we can try.

This book is concerned with the breaking of taboos, the altering of traditional practices. Symbolic of its goal, brown ink replaces black, and the paper is no longer white. These are only small matters, perhaps, but—who knows?—perhaps someday a respectable publishing house may go so far as to spell through *thru*, though *tho*, and quaintly *qaintly*. If the people who reject simplified spelling were consistent they would, like George Bernard Shaw, spell the name for the objects of Izaak Walton's passion *ghoti* (*gh* as in trough, *o* as in women, *ti* as in nation). . . . But enough of fantasy. Let us return to the feasible.

# GARRETT HARDIN

# Stalking the Wild Taboo

### Second Edition

William Kaufmann, Inc.     Los Altos, California

Library of Congress Cataloging in Publication Data

Hardin, Garrett James, 1915-
   Stalking the wild taboo.

   Includes bibliographical references and index.
   1.  Abortion--United States.  2.  Taboo.  I.  Title.
HD767.5.U5H37  1978      301.2'1      78-1976
ISBN 0-913232-40-8
ISBN 0-913232-41-6 pbk.

Copyright © 1978 by William Kaufmann, Inc.

                    WILLIAM KAUFMANN, INC.
                    One First Street
                    Los Altos, CA 94022.

# Contents

**PART THREE: TECHNOLOGY**

**PART FOUR: COMPETITION**

**PART FIVE: "NEED" AS SUPERSTITION**

*Preface*

I became a stalker of taboos by chance. In 1956 I published an essay on the "Meaninglessness of the Word *Protoplasm*," which earned me many friends and some opponents. It is natural for a scholar to feel anxious when someone points out that a word he views as essential stands, in fact, for no meaningful concept. He feels that his "rice bowl" is threatened; worse, his self-esteem is endangered, so long as he "identifies" with the word in question. It is a rare scholar who thanks you for trying to remove the blinders from his eyes. His defense is all too often, "Oh, that's only semantics!" Of course it's semantics: that's just the point. But why the word "only"?

Thinking about this "only semantics" defense opened my mind to some of the properties of taboo. In the words of the American Heritage Dictionary, a taboo is "a prohibition excluding something from *use, approach*, or *mention* because of its sacred and inviolable nature." (Italics added.) The "only semantics" ploy is an attempt to prevent approach to a subject. We in the Western intellectual community ordinarily use the word "taboo" only when discussing other cultures, but the excluding intent of "only semantics" shows that we too have our taboos. The word "sacred" often serves as the alarm-bell when one of our taboos is approached. Operationally speaking, a sacred element can be recognized by the aversive-evasive reaction it provokes, as for instance when someone says deprecatingly, "that's only semantics," and seeks to turn the discussion into other channels.

Observing other cultures we note that taboo can affect objects, actions, words, or thoughts. In our own culture the concept of the taboo may not be much needed for the first two classes. Few if any objects are taboo to touch in our society, and the forbidding of actions is adequately handled, for the most part, by legislation. When the law seems inappropriate we invent rules of "sportsmanship" and "good taste." These mini-taboos present only minor intellectual problems.

The third class of tabooed things—words—brings us face to face with a paradox. If we refuse to discuss a subject, how can we inform the unknowing what it is that is sacred? Even to delineate the sacred in words is to violate the taboo. A word-taboo is a sort of Chinese egg. Inside is the primary taboo, surrounding a thing that must not be discussed; around this is the secondary taboo, a taboo against even acknowledging the existence of the primary taboo.

A word-taboo held inviolate for a long time becomes a taboo on thinking itself (for how can we think of things we hear no words for?). Violating a word-taboo is bad taste, but he who is an *eccentric*—i.e., one who is out of the center of things—may ultimately hear a call to break the taboo lest his silence permit the final metamorphosis of word-taboo into thought-taboo—of repressed state into non-existence. When the vocation of the eccentric reaches this painfully insistent point, he shouts the word from the housetops. This is a dangerous moment; the time must be chosen carefully.

Altering the figure of speech we may say that the stalker of taboos, if he is to survive, must learn from the predatory animals, must adopt their tactics: long periods of quietness, a long profile, protective coloration, and the diversion of the quarry's attention to other matters until the propitious moment.

These essays show a progression from the first topic (abortion) in which the taboo is (or was until recently) almost wholly operative on words, to the last two (competition and "need") in which there is a considerable taboo on thinking itself. There is a rhythm to history and a taboo cannot be productively attacked until the time is ripe. Perhaps I am trying to force history in raising the issues of competition and need at this time: the reader must judge. Those who think the effort is not premature may want to join in the noble sport of taboo-stalking, that inquiry may be advanced. I hope so.

*Garrett Hardin*

# PART ONE: ABORTION

# 1

## *Tactics in Tackling Taboos*

There are, I suppose, some people who carefully plan their lives, moving step by calculated step into each new phase. Not me. Each significant transition in my life has been accomplished more or less accidentally; only afterwards, looking back, can I recognize a "point of no return" in my career. I have previously recounted[1]* the external events that brought me to the point of being an abortion activist:

> In 1954 the Planned Parenthood Federation of America decided the time had come to hold a conference on abortion. Forty-three men and women, mostly M.D.'s, were assembled at Arden House in New York for two lengthy conferences in 1955. The results, edited by Dr. Mary Steichen Calderone, were published in 1958.[2] The conference was a scientific and dramatic triumph. For the first time the true facts about modern abortion were made clear to the medical profession with a clarity that put them beyond dispute. They were resisted, of course. One of the most dramatic events of the conference was the confrontation of a retired professional illegal abortionist,

* Superscript numbers are keyed to references in the "Notes" at the end of the volume.

G. Lotrell Timanus, M.D., with his more legal and less daring colleagues. Even in cold print, the electric atmosphere of this meeting
can be sensed. It was one of those rare confrontations of adversaries
in which accused and accusor exchange places. It was worthy of a
Zola . . . Dr. Timanus has since appeared in a television documen-
tary, where it was obvious that he is everybody's kindly grandfather.
This is not the way we used to think of an "abortionist." It shakes
one's faith in black-and-white morality. If you can't believe in a ste-
reotype, what can you believe in?

The publication of Calderone's *Abortion in the United States* was
greeted with an almost absolute critical silence. A search of book
review indexes made by Fred Dietrich has failed to reveal a single
review of this book in either the medical or the popular literature;
among the semipopular magazines, only one reviewed it, namely
*Scientific American*. The January 1959 issue carried a long and sym-
pathetic account by James R. Newman. I think many students of
family planning trace their interest in abortion to a reading of Newman's review; I know I do.

At the time that I read Newman's review I was strongly opposed to
abortion. I am sure of this because I remember a conversation I had on
the subject, a conversation I can accurately date because of the attendant
personal circumstances (which are irrelevant to the present account). Yet
sometime between January 1959 and the spring of 1963 I changed my
opinion completely. Why the change? And why did the change require so
long a time?

I will take up only the second question; the answer to it is of the utmost
importance to all who aspire to stalk and destroy taboos. The answer is
connected with what I immodestly call "Hardin's Law":

*It takes five years for a person's mind to change.*

This law was discovered by introspection. There have been several
times in my life when I suddenly realized that my opinion about a fundamental matter had undergone a complete change in the recent past,
without my being aware of the process of change. When, on such oc-

casions, I have asked myself how long I had been in possession of all the facts needed for the change in my opinion, I have discovered that the answer was about five years. In areas of deep emotional meaning facts alone are not enough: there has to be a restructuring of the psyche, and this takes place with glacial slowness after all the facts are in.

Strictly speaking, I know this only for myself. I know, for sure, that I am very stupid when it comes to accepting significant new truths. The Law that generalizes my experience to mankind as a whole depends on the hidden assumption that *other people are as stupid as I am*. I can't prove it, but I find it comforting to think so.

True or not, the Law confers forensic wisdom on the person who believes it: it makes him patient with what he would otherwise regard as stupidity. Instead of expecting his finely honed logical argument to convince others instantly—an unrealistic expectation that would provoke him to raise his voice irritatingly—the believer in the Law says to himself: "There but for the grace of God go I," and settles back to wait an astronomical length of time for the slow chemistry of the psyche to have its effect.

I use the adjective "astronomical" advisedly. The following image may help. Suppose you were in communication with a passenger on the Centauri Cannonball, a spaceship circling the earth in an orbit 60 percent as far away as Alpha Centauri, our nearest star (after the sun). Communication is accomplished by laser beams, which travel at the speed of light, 299,793 kilometers per second. Suppose further that your correspondent is that unearthly creature, the perfectly rational man: given the necessary facts he changes his mind instantly. But because he is 24 trillion kilometers distant, it takes five years for your putatively perfect argument to reach him and for his acknowledgement of its effect to come back to you.

Given these facts, a reasonable earthling would be quite calm while awaiting the reaction of his distant discussant. Impatience would be irrational and unproductive.

In my experience, it is equally irrational to "lose one's cool" while awaiting a significant change of opinion in an earthly adversary. The spatial distance between two discussants on earth is nearly zero, but the "psychological distance" may be not much less than 24 trillion kilometers. It is as pointless in the latter case as in the former to lose one's temper while waiting for the change. Patience is clearly called for: and kindly consideration as well—which some prefer to call "love."

Moreover, there is yet one more consideration which should keep the temper down: the nagging suspicion that it may be *I* who is wrong. *I* may be the one for whom five years of patient waiting is needed.

From January 1959 to the spring of 1963 was nearly four and a half years—pretty close to the time predicted by Hardin's Law. The time may have been shortened somewhat by pressure to take a position. A student group asked me to lead a Tuesday evening discussion in a dormitory. About the only ground rule was that the topic should be controversial. It seemed to me that abortion was ideally suited to the occasion and I set about getting my thoughts in order. By this time a few organizations (e.g., the American Law Institute) had taken a cautious position in favor of abortions under highly restrictive conditions. I decided that all such tenth-way measures—they were certainly not half-way—were gravely wrong, and told the students I thought abortion-on-request was the only right answer. The arguments that followed were lively and productive.

A few weeks later a faculty committee asked me to give an all-campus lecture in the coming fall. I think it most unlikely that they had heard of the unpublicized dormitory bull session; they were probably expecting my topic to be evolution, or possibly overpopulation. I accepted the invitation, but at the moment did not let them know what they were in for.

It is essential that the reader recognize that abortion was a strongly tabooed topic in 1963. So much has the world changed in the past decade that this recognition takes a bit of imagination, but you can't understand history without imagination. Most newspapers in 1963 would not print the word "abortion"; even those that would avoided the subject if they could. It was no light matter for a professor in a state university—my situation—to take a public position against the prohibition of abortion.

I could easily have become a martyr, but I regarded martyrdom as a sign of failure. I took this as a matter of definition, a standard of judgment for evaluating every action under consideration. I know that many people do not accept this standard. I know also of the large (and sometimes inspiring) literature on martyrs. Had I ever known a great martyr personally I might have changed my opinion about the desirability of martyrdom. But I have known only minimartyrs, and these I have found, almost without exception, to be neither admirable nor effective.

The secret of gaining an audience without becoming a martyr is, I feel, to proceed by stages, alert to "feedback" at every moment. The dormitory meeting was an ideal first stage. Since it was not in a classroom no one could later charge me with having exploited a captive audience. *They* had invited *me*. Since the Tuesday evening bull sessions were advertized only by word of mouth it was unlikely that the public outside the academic walls would be aroused. If I made a mess of the presentation it would be a limited mess, and not disastrous. The lack of publicity allowed me to learn by doing, with minimum risk. I did learn; the public speech several months later benefitted greatly from the unpublicized dress rehearsal.

It was rather sneaky of me not to tell the faculty committee what the topic of my fall lecture was at the time I accepted the invitation. My justification is the following. It seemed to me quite possible that my colleagues might withdraw the invitation if I told them my subject immediately. They might be understandably fearful of a public outcry that could react adversely on our budget in subsequent years. So I waited several weeks until I felt they were psychologically "married" to the idea of my talking before I dropped the committee a note announcing my title. I waited for a reaction; but there was none—at least none that reached my ears.

(After it was all over in the fall I went to some trouble to find out what the reaction of the committee had been. Not surprisingly, I found that there had been a great deal of head-shaking; but in the end the committee decided against rescinding the invitation. Significantly, they made no move to get word of their doubts to me. To have so informed me would, in fact, have been to exert pressure against my speaking freely. In my view, the committee's behavior was admirable throughout, and worthy of a great university.)

Once the topic was accepted, my strategy, looking forward to the reception of my lecture in the fall, was one of complete openness. It seemed to me that if the lecture came as a surprise to newspaper editors their defensive response would be either to suppress the report or to attack the speaker. Immovable deadlines allow editors little time for deliberation. As a biologist I saw their situation as like that of any wild animal. Surprise an animal and it either flees or attacks. If you want to approach closely to it you must do so absolutely undetected, or else (depending on the species) slowly, with plenty of gentle warnings of your presence and your peaceful intentions.

I usually speak in public from brief notes only. I can think quickly on my feet, but this ability is not an unalloyed advantage because I don't always think well: I'm likely to make a quick wise-crack that affronts somebody needlessly. In dealing with a subject as "sensitive" as abortion was in 1963 my usual approach would have been dangerous, so I forced myself to write out my lecture months in advance. I read it to the family, and polished it until it had no detectable irrelevant offensiveness. Then I had several dozen copies mimeographed for the campus Public Relations Officer to distribute to the newspapers. This was a month in advance of the date of my public appearance. By minimizing the element of surprise I hoped to get the maximum press coverage since editors would have plenty of time to consider how to handle the hot potato. The strategy worked. One local paper printed one-third of the lecture, and the other almost as much. Each displayed it prominently, without editorial comment.

The lecture itself was successful. An estimated thirteen hundred people turned up at a hall that seated only nine hundred. This pleased 901 people—the last one being the lecturer, of course—even if not the other four hundred. Contrary to custom, I read my lecture word for word, in as unemotional a voice as I could muster. The interest was intense, and the questions from the audience afterward continued for a long time. Some of the points raised by the audience led to changes in subsequent lectures.

To the surprise of everyone, including me, there was almost no adverse reaction either to the lecture or to the extensive newspaper reports of it. Santa Barbara is a town much given to hate mail and vituperative phone calls. But, with one or two mild exceptions, I received only admiring comments. (Later in my career as an abortionist I was attacked more.) Eminently respectable women stopped me on the streets to tell me about their abortions. This was a new experience for me. (More grist for the lecture-mill.) Plainly, abortion-on-request was an idea "whose time had come." I had merely tapped riches ripe for the picking. This accidental discovery changed my life.

Late in the fall of 1963 I was asked to give a public lecture at the University of California in Berkeley, where I was to be a visiting professor in the Department of Genetics in the coming spring semester. Naturally I elected to talk on abortion, and a date was decided on: Wednesday, 29 April 1964. As it turned out, a worse date could hardly have been picked, but there was no way of knowing this six months in advance.

I reworked my Santa Barbara address and gave it a new title: *Abortion and Human Dignity*. The title was an improvement, I think, but on rereading the lecture now I don't think it is as good as my first one. It is a bit pretentious. This is too bad because the Berkeley speech is the one that was widely distributed. It was reprinted in two anthologies, in two magazines, and in mimeograph form I don't know how many times. I deliberately neglected to copyright it in order to encourage free reprintings. The greatest distribution was no doubt given to it as an offset pamphlet distributed in the thousands by the Society for Humane Abortion of San Francisco, headed by a dedicated hospital technician, Patricia Maginnis.

The magazine publications deserve a few words. A new literary quarterly was being hatched at Stanford during my term at Berkeley and I was asked to contribute to it. This seemed to me to be a good way to get the abortion lecture published in a form suitable for bibliographic citation (which an offset pamphlet hardly is) so I submitted the manuscript to Robin White, the editor, and he accepted it. It was published in Volume 1, Number 1 of *Per/Se*. White modified it somewhat, but in my judgment he was an excellent copy editor so I accepted the changes. *Per/Se* survived several years and then expired long before its majority, as most literary quarterlies do.

The other magazine was quite different: *Cavalier,* a *Playboy*-like monthly. Less successful than its model, its circulation was still some two orders of magnitude greater than that of a literary quarterly. But was it dignified? Certainly not; but if I was really in earnest about getting the message out was my personal dignity important? I decided not. (I could afford to make such a decision by this time: I was a full professor and beyond the reach of promotion committees.) I called the attention of the editors of *Cavalier* to the fact that the lecture wasn't copyrighted and that it was also scheduled for publication in a literary quarterly, but they rightly dismissed these facts as irrelevant to their commercial purposes. They even paid me some money, which salved whatever bruise my delicate sense of dignity might have suffered.

To get back to Berkeley, I have indicated that I unwittingly chose a poor date for the speech. The 29th of April fell on a Wednesday. Shortly before that time the University learned that the physicist Robert Oppenheimer was coming for a visit and would be willing to give two lectures. It had been, as I recall, fourteen years since he had last visited his spiritual home, and in the meantime he had been martyrized by Congressional witch-hunters. (See the published hearings entitled "In the Matter of J. Robert Oppenheimer.") The prodigal son was assigned two dates for his lectures: the Tuesday before mine and the Thursday afterward. As a comparative unknown I could hardly compete with "Oppie." There's only so much time for attending lectures; if I hadn't been giving the lecture on Wednesday I wouldn't have gone to Wheeler Hall myself on that night. Only about five hundred people attended. Realistically, I should not have expected more.

Because the material in the Santa Barbara and Berkeley lectures is covered better (in my opinion) in later papers neither lecture is included in this volume. But there are two paragraphs from the Berkeley speech that are worth reprinting here. Both of them were put in because of feedback from the women in the audience at the first speech. The more important of these paragraphs follows:

> Critics of abortion generally see it as an exclusively negative thing, a means of non-fulfillment only. What they fail to realize is that abortion, like other means of birth control, can lead to fulfillment in the life of a woman. A woman who aborts this year because she is in poor health, neurotic, economically harassed, unmarried, on the verge of divorce, or immature, may well decide to have some other child five years from now—a wanted child. The child that she aborts is always an unwanted child. If her need for abortion is frustrated, she may never know the joy of a wanted child.

The other addition was, I suspect, a mistake. I will quote it first, and then explain why I think the addition was injudicious. I began by calling attention to the fact that a rich woman could get a good medical abortion—a high priced illegal or quasi-legal one in this country, or a legal one in a foreign country to which she could afford to travel. A poor woman could not afford either. I asked, "Is such class discrimination good for society?" to which I answered:

> The evils of such discrimination are easy to demonstrate, but I must do so in two ways to meet the requirements of two different sets of

presuppositions. Some people believe that rich people are intrinsically better than poor people. Others believe that the only difference between poor people and rich people is that rich people have more money. It doesn't matter whether your beliefs are at one extreme or the other (or somewhere in the middle), you still must conclude that class discrimination in abortion is an evil. If you believe that rich people are better, how can you defend a system that increases the proportion of poor people generation by generation because abortion is denied to them? If you believe poor people are just as good as the rich, is it fair that poor women should be denied this privilege of the rich? And, looking at the problem in terms of knowledge and intelligence, is it good for society that ignorant (and possibly stupid) women have more children than knowing and intelligent ones? Is the child brought up by an ignorant, or poor, or unloving mother a better bet for the next generation?

What I intended was this: to cover all possibilities in a disputed area without taking sides in the controversy of rich vs. poor, nature vs. nurture, heredity vs. environment. I regarded this forensic approach as a sort of minimal, conservative one. Clearly it was not. As I presented it to the audience I could feel a wave of coldness wash back over me. No questioner subsequently revived this issue, but it was obvious I had lost the audience for a moment.

This well-meaning passage brushed against another taboo that is even stronger than any taboo on sexual discussion in our society: the question of innate human inequalities. I should have asked *only* "Is it fair that poor women should be denied the privileges of the rich?" Even raising the contrasting question, "Might the poor be in some sense inferior to the rich?" was to brand myself as the enemy. The question itself was taboo. Refusing to answer a tabooed question does not mitigate the sin of asking it.

Although I kept the offending paragraph in the printed version—tactically a mistake—I avoided the issue in subsequent speeches and articles (and the audience never raised it). The tactical moral is obvious, and must never be forgotten by the ambitious stalker of taboos:

*Never tackle more than one taboo at a time.*

# 2

# Semantic Aspects of Abortion

## (1967)

An increasing number of people are coming to believe that the prohibition of abortion, like the prohibition of alcohol, is a mistake. In recent years Japan, Poland, Hungary, Bulgaria, Yugoslavia, and Roumania[1] have done away with substantially all legal restrictions of this simple and safe medical operation—which is, in fact, only one-fourth as dangerous as a normal childbirth,[2] and promises to be made even safer by improvements in medical technology. Elsewhere I have briefly stated the case against prohibition laws in this field; longer statements have been made by others.[3] I will here assume the validity of the case against prohibition and explore some of the reasons for resistance to the idea of abortion, as revealed in the words of the defenders of the status quo.

In the course of lecturing for several years on the subject I have repeatedly encountered certain verbal stratagems used in the defense of prohibition. Some of the issues raised are profound, while others border on the ludicrous. Among the latter is the triumphant conclusion of a vituperative (and anonymous) letter sent to me following one of my lectures: "If your mother had had an abortion, where would *you* be today?"

From *ETC.*, 24:263–281. Copyright © 1967.

I must confess, I don't know. This question (which has been put to me several times) raises the most fascinating problems of being and nonbeing. A philosopher would no doubt discuss the question in the jargon of ontology. As a biologist, I prefer a different approach. I am reminded of the beginning of Lawrence Sterne's novel *Tristram Shandy* wherein the hero is discussing the circumstances surrounding his conception. As the critical moment approached Mrs. Shandy said to Mr. Shandy, "Pray, my Dear, have you not forgot to wind up the clock?"—"Good G--!" replied Mr. Shandy, "Did ever woman, since the creation of the world, interrupt a man with such a silly question?" It was, as young Tristram pointed out, an "unseasonable question at least."

Whether Mr. Shandy stopped what he was doing and went downstairs to wind the clock, Tristram does not record. Perhaps Mr. Shandy merely paused and shifted his position. It does not matter. The result, we can be sure, was the same; of the three hundred million spermatozoa Mr. Shandy released somewhat later, a different one led the pack, a different one reached the egg first, and a different Tristram was engendered. Put another way, the Tristram (or the Nancy) who might have been had not Mrs. Shandy asked about the clock—this Tristram never was, not then nor in any subsequent coming together of Mr. and Mrs. Shandy.

To reply to my correspondent, if my mother had had an abortion I almost certainly would not be here today. In fact, if my father had coughed at the crucial moment I would not be here today. . . . Perhaps he did cough. . . . Who am I, anyway?


## The Riddle of the Non-Beethoven

The same logic is involved in another argument that is often repeated whenever someone is urging the wisdom of aborting a woman who has had German measles and is hence likely to produce a deformed child. The author of the argument is unknown; in its classic form it runs as follows:

> Two physicians are talking shop. "Doctor," says one, "I'd like your professional opinion. The question is, should the pregnancy have been terminated or not? The father was syphilitic. The mother

was tuberculous. They had already had four children: the first was blind, the second died, the third was deaf and dumb, and the fourth was tuberculous. The woman was pregnant for the fifth time. As the attending physician, what would you have done?''

"I would have terminated the pregnancy."

"Then you would have murdered Beethoven."

The story has a terrific impact. Yet there's something wrong with it. Somehow logic has slipped a cog. Perhaps the most important counterpoint is this: after suitably altering the earlier details of the anecdote, one can quite legitimately substitute for the name ''Beethoven,'' the name "Hitler," or "Caligula," or "Genghis Khan." To deny that these are legitimate substitutions is to imply that there is something inherently excellent about syphilitic, tuberculous parenthood, that such parents should be actually encouraged to have many children in order that many Beethovens may be born. I have yet to hear an abortion-prohibitionist urge this.

I think we are disturbed by this story because it makes us realize that if Beethoven had never been born we would never have known the difference. We would never have missed him. "What a loss!"—or is it? Can we have a loss of which we are unaware? Beethoven's mother, like all women no doubt, started life with about 30,000 immature eggs in her ovaries. She produced only seven children. Therefore 29,993 eggs, all potential human beings, must have perished. Should we weep for this "loss?" And what about the 100,000,000 sperm his father produced every day of his mature years—say, some 1,000,000,000,000 in all. If certain technical problems had been solved, Mr. Beethoven senior could have populated the world 1,200 times over all by himself. Does the fact that his million, million sperm did not meet and fertilize an equal number of eggs constitute a loss in any meaningful sense? Considering our population problem it would be hard to defend this thesis.

It is plainly futile to make predictions of the nonexistent. Every child that is aborted (or not conceived) might have been a Beethoven—or, equally likely, a Hitler. Much more likely, it would simply have been another Caspar Milquetoast, of which the world already has an ample supply.

## The Promiscuity Issue

One of the two most widely urged reasons for not legalizing abortion is that to do so would be to invite promiscuous behavior among our young women. (Notice that our young men are almost never mentioned.) Does this argument imply that without easily available abortion, unmarried women will not indulge in coitus? Such an inference is hard to sustain in light of the frequently noted fact that at least 25 percent of our young brides are pregnant when they appear at the marriage altar. It surely cannot be maintained that fear of pregnancy is a *strong* deterrent to sexual intercourse.

However, neither can it be maintained that it is no deterrent whatever. More cogently, it should be pointed out that if we want the risk of pregnancy to be a deterrent to intercourse we should make it illegal for unmarried people to buy, possess, or use contraceptives. The minority of people who wish so to restrict contraceptives becomes smaller every day. Since we are not willing to control contraceptives in order to discourage promiscuity, we can hardly justify the prohibition of abortion on this ground.

In truth, it is not promiscuous behavior that produces unwanted babies so much as it is virginal behavior—or, more accurately, almost-virginal behavior. "Bad" girls don't get pregnant; neither do angels. It is "good" girls who get pregnant. Genuinely promiscuous girls know better. A statement made by the late Alfred Kinsey supports this contention:

> In regard to the unwanted pregnancies that come outside of marriage, in our experience these more often occur among the religiously devout who set out on a date with the determination that they are not going to be sinful and have coitus, and, with such a conviction in mind, will of course not carry contraceptives.[4]

Put bluntly, parents who, in the education of their daughters, lay great stress on the value of virginity thereby elect an *all-or-nothing* gamble. They may win, of course. Some have.

### The Semantics of Rape

Many who are unwilling to completely do away with abortion-prohibition urge that abortion be permitted in special cases, of which pregnancy caused by rape is usually one. To put this in perspective, it should be noted that such pregnancies are only a small fraction of the total unwanted pregnancies produced each year. The most careful estimate of the number of illegal abortions per year in the United States is that made by the Arden House Conference committee,[5] which decided that the true number lies between 200,000 and 1,200,000 per year. According to the F.B.I. there were 20,550 forcible rapes in the year 1964.[6] Christopher Tietze[7] has calculated that risk of pregnancy from a single unprotected coitus is not greater than one in twenty-five. Using these statistics as a base, we can calculate that the number of pregnancies produced by reported rapes probably does not exceed 800 per year. Further, we may conservatively say that of all unwanted pregnancies, fewer than one in a thousand result from rape. Permitting abortion in such cases would solve only a very small fraction of our problems.

Nevertheless, there is a large measure of agreement that the raped woman deserves relief. But the administration of a law that sets up rape as a general exception to abortion-prohibition is fraught with semantic difficulties. When discussing the criteria for permitting legal abortions, physicians almost always insist that they are best qualified to make the decision. When rape is involved, however, they usually shy away from responsibility—understandably. As one doctor testifying before a legislative committee said: "The doctor isn't in a position to ascertain whether or not she's been raped; any woman can say she's been raped. What is rape?"

The last question deserves to be recorded in bronze along with Pontius Pilate's "What is truth?" Who is to say what rape is? This is no idle question, as one news items shows.

> A 28-year-old Santa Barbara woman told police an intruder slipped into her house Saturday night, grabbed her as she was preparing to retire, and sexually assaulted her. She said the man grabbed her from behind in the kitchen and dragged her to the bedroom. He left early Sunday morning, she said.

> She told officers she was in a state of shock after the attack, but went to church yesterday morning. She then told an acquaintance, who called detectives. Police are investigating.[8]

Was she raped? Well . . . the tentative attitude indicated by the laconic "police are investigating" seems justified. This is the sort of thing that makes people hesitate to single out rape as a justification for abortion and avoid personally taking on the job of distinguishing genuine rape from reluctant consent. An extreme in suspiciousness was revealed in an article by a Catholic lawyer, Eugene Quay: "Actually there seems to be little likelihood of any pregnancy resulting from a rape by force or from any intercourse in which the woman's consent was *wholly* refused through-out."[9]

As a biologist I can tell you that there is not the slightest evidence for Mr. Quay's remarkable hypothesis that refusal is a contraceptive. On the contrary, when Mr. Quay italicizes the word *"wholly"* he unwittingly hints that he is promulgating a *panchreston*[10]—an "explain-all" hypoth-esis that fits all facts and is incapable of disproof. The implied hypothesis works like this: (*a*) if the woman resists the man throughout the act she will not become pregnant, and hence there will be no need for abortion; (*b*) if, however, she becomes pregnant this proves that her resistance was less than total, consequently she is not morally entitled to an abortion— and no change need be made in our prohibition laws. This is a lovely heads-I-win-tails-you-lose argument which violates the fundamental prin-ciple of science (indeed, of all rationality) that only falsifiable statements are admissible to discussion.[11] No observation could possible falsify the hypothesis implied by Mr. Quay.

If a woman says to me, "I was raped," how do I know she is telling the truth? The inescapable fact is I can never *know* this. No amount of vehemence, no wailing or weeping or tearing of the hair can possibly prove that her story is true. She may be only shamming. What is involved here is what philosophers call "the egocentric predicament." All that I really know of the world is what is in my mind. The classical attempt to resolve the predicament is known as "solipsism" and leads to statements of this form: "You do not exist; there is merely the mental construct of *you* which I choose, for some reason, to make in my mind." We need not admit the validity of this positive statement (most of us don't, most of the time) to grant the full validity of the egocentric predicament; namely, that there is no operational method whereby I can rigorously establish the *sincerity* of any other person. Solipsistic impotence is an anxious burden I can never lay down.

To decree that proved forcible rape is a justification for abortion which is otherwise generally prohibited would create logical and legal snarls impossible to resolve. Those called upon to judge would seldom be easy in their minds that they had judged rightly. That a judgment in a rape case may be necessary for other reasons is no excuse for creating this additional juridical burden.

Consider also what such a law would do to the raped woman. Is it not enough that her integrity had been violated by the rapist? Must society now violate it again by demanding that she beg and plead and put on a convincing theatrical performance before the judge will grant her a release from the hated burden of an unwanted child? *Who* wants this rape-engendered child anyway? The rapist? The raped? The judge? Certainly none of these. Let him who wants it, bear it. . . . But notice: "Him," the conventional pronoun for the unknown *who,* makes no biological sense. Men can't bear children. But they *can* make laws for women. They can; and they do. Unfortunately.

### "Therapeutic Abortion"—A Dangerous Euphemism

The great difficulty of instituting any deep-reaching reform in society is a constant temptation to reformers to take short-cuts, to temporize. Compromise is sometimes the wisest strategy. But it is often true that small reforms are the worst enemy of great reforms.

In respect to our present concern one of the visible dangers is the attempt of well-meaning reformers to label a proposed law, a "Therapeutic abortion law." The intention is clear—to institute a change in practice under the guise of "therapeutics." Therapeutics is medicine, and everybody is in favor of medicine. This verbal ruse is, however, dangerous.

In the first place, a therapeutic abortion is usually understood to be one that is required to save the life or, at the very least, the health of the mother. ("Health" is usually interpreted in a rather narrow physical—not mental—sense.) Such abortions are needed less and less each year. Diabetes and serious heart disease used to be ample excuse for a genuinely therapeutic abortion. They seldom are now; physicians can usually save both the mother and the baby.

Today, the quantitatively important reasons for abortion are to preserve the mental health of the mother, to reduce marital stress, and to make it possible for children to be born into families in which they are wanted. Abortion is needed to help minimize divorce, child-abandonment, child-neglect, and child-beating. In a word, what society needs is not therapeutic abortion, but *humane* abortion. It is significant that the most active reform group in the United States, which is in San Francisco, calls itself the Society for Humane Abortion.

Instituting reform under the aegis of "therapeutics" has another danger—that the ruse will be seen through by the opponents, thus discrediting the *bona fides* of the reformers. That this is no mere theoretical possibility is shown by the following exchange that took place in a public hearing of a California legislative committee:

> FATHER WILLIAM KENNEALLY: No one has the right to take the life of the child even in this therapeutic abortion, which is used as a euphemism. Therapeutic means to cure, and it doesn't cure anything, it kills somebody.
> CHAIRMAN O'CONNELL: It cures the mother.
> FATHER KENNEALLY: It may.
> CHAIRMAN O'CONNELL: I believe that's the origin of the term—
> FATHER KENNEALLY: It cures by killing. It's a kind of lynching in the womb.[12]

Father Kenneally's last remark shows an interesting and common semantic maneuver in discussion of this subject—the attempt to convince by the use of emotionally loaded terms. "Lynching in the womb" certainly sounds much more horrible than "killing in the uterus," though the latter phrase adequately summarizes the *facts* involved. However, the priest's statement does bring up a question of first importance: can killing ever be justified? This is without doubt the most important substantive issue in the whole controversy and will be discussed at length in a subsequent section. But first one more matter.

**The Tragedy of Malformations**

One of the most effective arguments in favor of abortion is that it could prevent the birth of many defective or malformed children. About 100,000 of these are born every year in the United States. It is not possible to give a precise figure for various reasons. The principal reason is the question of standards: How serious does the defect have to be before it is worth counting? In addition, should hereditary defects that develop many years after birth be counted (Huntington's Chorea, for instance)? And what about hereditary defects (like diabetes) that are medically controllable?

However large the figure may be, it is certain that only a small proportion of the hereditary defects are predictable before birth. Everyone knows about the "thalidomide babies" of the early 1960's. These babies, typically with pitifully embryonic or absent limbs, were deformed because the mothers had taken the tranquilizer thalidomide during the early months of pregnancy. About 5,000 such children were born, principally in Europe, before the cause was deduced and removed from the market. It takes little imagination to appreciate how these malformed babies must have blighted the lives of the families into which they were born.

Some thalidomide births were prevented by abortion; more could have been. But not all 5,000 could have been, because it simply was not possible to deduce, from a welter of conflicting facts, the true cause of the defects until many deformed babies had been born. It is noteworthy that animal experiments performed before the drug was approved for human use gave no hint of its dangerous potential. (The reasons for this technical failure are still being investigated.) We will never again be "caught" by thalidomide; but some new drug may again fool us. In the last analysis, a drug must finally be tested on human beings, some of whom may be called upon to pay a high price for its failure.

Taken all together, I think it is doubtful if more than 10 percent of the children born defective could ever be identified as defectives before birth—say 10,000 per year in the United States. Preventing 10,000 defective births per year—or even a tenth or a hundredth that number—would certainly be worth while. But, like rape-engendered births, defective babies present only a small fraction of the yearly need for abortion. We must keep our facts in perspective.

Whatever the number of predictable defective births per year, this proportion presents a disturbing problem to Catholic apologists. No one wants to speak in favor of defective births, but Catholic value theory prizes life itself so highly as to leave the spokesmen for the Church only a tortuous passage for escape from that unpopular position. At hearings of a California legislative committee,[13] the following statement was entered in the record by the St. Thomas More Societies (Catholic lawyers' guilds) of four cities: "We are not unmindful of extreme cases of hardship and have nothing but compassion for the mother faced with such difficult situations." Such urbane compassion reminds us of what Mark Twain once said: "It is easy to bear adversity—another man's, I mean."

The logical consequence of the official Catholic theory of value is shown in the testimony of Michael B. Flanagan, M.D.:

> German measles or Rubella occurring in the first 8 weeks of pregnancy may result in 10 to 15 percent deformity rate, of which about half are serious deformities. . . . 85–90 percent of these pregnancies therefore would result in normal healthy children. The destruction of these children constitutes a new slaughter of the innocents.[14]

Lest it be inferred that it is the "smallness" (!) of the risk that leads to this moral judgment, consider this statement by another Catholic physician, Dr. James Ravenscroft:[15] "Statistics show that serious fetal anomalies do occur in 15 to 40 percent of cases in which the mother has had proven Rubella during the first trimester of pregnancy. This is indeed a serious problem; but should one abort 60 percent of normal fetuses to save 40 percent of abnormal ones?"

The Catholic position rests on two ideas (or perhaps we should say, two aspects of one idea), one of which is amenable to rational discussion, and the other not. To take the latter first, it is asserted that abortion is wrong because it takes the life of an innocent child, and "Innocent human life is sacred," in the words of the eminent Catholic spokesman Norman St. John-Stevas.[16] The introduction of the words "innocent" and "sacred" takes the discussion out of the realm of rationality. No operational meaning—in Bridgman's sense[17]—can be given to these words, save perhaps this: "When I use the word 'sacred' that is my way of signaling to you that I won't discuss the matter further." Because the signaling is cryptic, the word "sacred" leads to deplorable heat, and no light, in discussion. That "sacred" does turn thoughts into nonrational channels is all too apparent in this statement by Austin O'Malley:[18] "An innocent fetus an hour old may not be directly killed to save the lives of all the mothers in the world."

The rational aspect of the Catholic view is that all lives have equal *value*. The rejection of the idea that a fetus (say, in an ectopic pregnancy) may be killed to save the life of the mother is based on belief in the equality of all human life, from the microscopic zygote to the adult in her most vigorous years. Only a few percent of the world's population hold this belief, as appears from the following analysis. Nominal Roman Catholics constitute less than 17 percent of the world's population. Abortion is reported to be the leading method of birth control in many nominally Catholic countries; for instance, Chile.[19] It is therefore not unreasonable to assume that belief in the equal value of mother and child is restricted to only a fraction of Roman Catholics—principally, no doubt, to celibate males.

A minority view is not necessarily wrong, however. (After all, the majority of the people once believed that the world was flat.) Pressed to defend their minority view, thoughtful Roman Catholics almost always come up with an argument similar to that of George H. Dunne, S.J.:

> The Catholic position is based upon respect for the individual human life, any human life; upon the principle that the direct and voluntary killing of any innocent human being, by the state or an individual, is murder; and upon the principle that the end, however good and desirable in itself, does not justify the means. Once these values are repudiated there is no *moral* limit to the crimes that can be committed against the human person. A rigorously logical path leads from abortion to euthanasia and the gas chambers.[20]

This is, of course, the well-known argument of "the camel's nose"—which says that if we let the camel put his nose in the tent, we will be unable to keep him from forcing his whole body inside. The argument is false. It is *always* possible to draw arbitrary lines *and enforce them*. We have speed limits for automobiles, and we enforce them. In the enforcement, the line becomes somewhat fuzzy—a policeman will not often make an arrest for infringing the law by one mile per hour—but indefinite escalation need not occur.

To take an example closer to the point at issue, let us look over the history of the reform of marriage laws in England a hundred years ago. At that time, it was against the law for a man to marry his deceased wife's sister—a strange prohibition which has, of course, no shred of biological justification, and only a tortured theological one. It took nearly a century of agitation to get this statute off the books. Some of the most decent people defended the status quo. Matthew Arnold, for example, thought that it would be quite dangerous to allow marriage to a deceased wife's sister because (he said) doing so would open the moral floodgates to other (!) forms of incest and then to bigamy and polygamy.[21] It has now been more than half a century since England permitted the camel's nose of marriage to deceased wife's sisters to enter the tent. The rest of the camel is still outside, contrary to Mr. Arnold's anticipations, and apparently permanently so.

## Are Blueprints Sacred?

We have arrived at the final and most crucial question involved in abortion: is abortion murder? This question is more complex than appears at first sight. It involves several semantically interesting issues.

It is often said that abortion cannot be tolerated by Christians because it violates the Sixth Commandment: *Thou shalt not kill.* The decisiveness of this point evaporates in the light of deeper Biblical scholarship. "Thou shalt not kill" is the wording in the King James version of the Bible. More recent editions, in which scholars have paid greater attention to exact translation (for example, the "Goodspeed Bible") render the commandment thus: *Thou shalt not commit murder.* This wording implies a semantic distinction between killing and murder. The distinction is obvious: murder is killing that is disapproved of. The meaning of the Sixth Commandment is this: some forms of killing are defined as "murder," and murder is forbidden. Other forms of killing may be permitted (though perhaps disapproved of), or even regarded as praiseworthy. Different societies, to varying degrees, have permitted or encouraged killing in war, killing by the state (capital punishment), killing in self-defense, or killing to save the life of an innocent victim of a murderous attack. In our society, opinions differ as to the acceptability of these various kinds of killing; but, with only rare exceptions, most people agree that killing is sometimes justified. When justified, it is not called murder, and the Sixth Commandment is not applicable. Do we want to *define* abortion as murder?

We are free to define it any way we like. Our definition should further what we regard as the good of society. What are the good effects of abortion? What are the evil? The good effects are obvious enough: to complete the system of birth control, to furnish a backstop method when all others have failed, and thus to make pregnancy truly a matter of free choice. Women want to have such freedom. The experience of the past two hundred years surely demonstrates the danger to society of having in it any class (race, sex, or what have you) that is unfree and perceives itself to be unfree.

Then what's wrong with permitting the killing of very young embryos? The position of those who define abortion as murder has been admirably revealed in this letter to the editor of a daily newspaper:

> If conscience allows the taking of human life at its inception and if abortion is to be made legal as some are proposing, why not wait until the baby is born and at that time suffocate the unfit? Surely the advocates of abortion should not consider killing at one stage of human life as fundamentally different than killing at another?[22]

The fascinating feature of this admirably brief letter is the second sentence. It is clearly intended to be a rhetorical question; but it is not a rhetorical question, for the answer is *yes*.

The problem can be restated in the traditional mode of general semantics by using index numbers as subscripts to indicate time. In general terms, is John Smith$_t$ the same as John Smith$_{t'}$, where $t$ and $t'$ indicate two different times? Is John Smith at age fifty the *same* person as John Smith at age twenty-five? In some respects he is clearly different, in some ways better, in others worse. Physically he has deteriorated. In judgment he has (we hope) improved. For better or for worse, his experiences have altered him; we may even say "He is a different man now." Yet for certain legal purposes we cannot tolerate the idea that John Smith$_{50}$ is not John Smith$_{25}$. Debts he incurred at twenty-five remain "his" debts, no matter how much he changes. The continuing, changing envelope of protoplasm we call John Smith is responsible for all the actions of the earlier states of this envelope. Rejecting this view would introduce a devastating amount of irresponsibility into the world.

Yet, even in law, we set limits to the fiction of sameness. John Smith$_{13}$ cannot incur debts that John Smith$_{25}$ will have to pay off. A child is not as fully responsible as an adult. When does childhood end and adulthood begin? Patently, no one can say for sure. Yet we must say; and so we create an arbitrary line at the twenty-first birthday. We don't fool ourselves when we do this; we know full well that a person 7,671 days old is not *demonstrably* different from one who is 7,670 days old. But there are real advantages in making a sharp, unambiguous distinction at some point, and so we give our free assent to an arbitrary line. *What* line does not matter much as long as there is *some* line.

No one would mistake a three-year-old child for an adult. Similarly, no one would mistake an embryo at three weeks of true age for an adult. As a matter of fact, one would not even recognize a three-week-old embryo as a human being. Given a collection of three-week embryos of man, gibbon, chimpanzee, gorilla, and countless other species, one could not, with the naked eye, tell which was *homo sapiens*. Even microscopically it would be very difficult to tell which was which. Is it right, then, to say that John Smith at twenty-one days of age is in some sense identical with John Smith at 7,938 days? Potentially, the former can develop into the latter. But is this *potential* important or valuable enough to justify damaging the unwilling mother's life by refusing to sacrifice the potential?

The question can be put another way. Those who refuse to permit abortion do so because they feel that the embryo is a human being. But is it? Modern biology has something to say in this matter. Consider the earliest stage of the developing human being, the fertilized egg. In structure, it bears not the slightest resemblance to a human being. Most of the material in this almost invisible cell is indistinguishable from the living material of any other animal cell. There is, however, a tiny bit of substance called DNA which "tells" the cell how to become a human being. The weight of this DNA is fantastically small—only 6 picograms. To put this in homely perspective: If all the DNA of all the fertilized eggs that produced the world's present population of 3,500,000,000 people had been gathered together in one lump, it would have weighed only one-third as much as one postage stamp. Yet this tiny amount of DNA contained the directions for producing all the people of the world. . . .

A fertilized egg is scarcely more than the blueprints for a human being. As development proceeds, the blueprints are gradually embedded in the structure of *Homo sapiens*. Value accrues. There is no sharp line at which life becomes objectively valuable. However, we can draw an arbitrary line, just as we do in the case of legal majority, and just as we do in the case of a speed limit. Good medical practice draws such a line at 12 weeks of pregnancy (in the United States) or 17 weeks in Sweden.

There is always resistance to the establishment of an arbitrary line. The psychological reasons for this are complex. Among these reasons is a fear that the line cannot be held because of a human tendency to push against the line. A process of slow escalation may take place—as we have seen in automobile speed limits, which have moved slowly upward over the past fifty years. But this escalation has taken place because people want to drive faster. The abortion problem is completely different. Women don't want to have their abortions later—they want to have them earlier. Only the impediments imposed by society (for example, time-consuming abortion committees in hospitals) create the need for late abortions.

What women really want is a very early abortifacient—a "morning after" pill, or a "sure period" pill. From an intuitive, personal point of view, as well as from the most broadly theoretical standpoint, it is recognized that all life is not equally valuable, and that the value of the life of a few-days-old embryo is only a tiny fraction that of the value of an adult life. Consider this equation:

$$\text{life}_{10\,\text{days}} = \text{life}_{8,000\,\text{days}}$$

Is it true? Certainly not. This must be explicitly said over and over again.

It is interesting and most encouraging to notice that this view of the variable value of life is beginning to appear in Roman Catholic literature. To a scientist, Catholic theology seems very much caught in a web of words that have only a tangential contact with the substantial world. However, the skill that has spun this web is apparently also available to cut through it. The appearance of the IUCD (intra-uterine contraceptive device), which may really be a covert abortifacient, and the threatened appearance of the morning-after pill have necessitated a hard look at the whole abortion problem by Catholic physicians. Among these, Dr. Ehrensing of Charlottesville, Virginia,[23] has produced an analysis of life as a blueprint which closely parallels the one stated here. In addition, he has tried to help those working with traditional verbal formulas by making a distinction between "human life" and "a human person." As he puts it: "The human fertilized ovum with the complete human chromosome pattern, the human genetic code, is very much 'human life' without necessarily being a human being."

The cautiousness of Dr. Ehrensing's phrase "without necessarily being" is no doubt necessitated by the fact that the author is subject to church discipline; he cannot dictate the correct semantics to his church, he can only suggest. Nevertheless, the earnestness and length at which he develops this suggestion gives one hope for the future.

# 3

# *Abortion—or Compulsory Pregnancy*

## *(1968)*

The year 1967 produced the first fissures in the dam that had prevented all change in the abortion-prohibition laws of the United States for three-quarters of a century. Two states adopted laws that allowed abortion in the "hardship cases" of rape, incest, and probability of a deformed child. A third approved the first two "indications," but not the last. All three took some note of the mental health of the pregnant woman, in varying language; how this language will be translated into practice remains to be seen. In almost two dozen other states, attempts to modify the laws were made but foundered at various stages in the legislative process. It is quite evident that the issue will continue to be a live one for many years to come.

The legislative turmoil was preceded and accompanied by a fast-growing popular literature. The word "abortion" has ceased to be a dirty word—which is a cultural advance. However, the *word* was so long under taboo that the ability to think about the *fact* seems to have suffered a sort of logical atrophy from disuse. Popular articles, regardless of their conclusions, tend to be over-emotional and to take a moralistic rather

From *Journal of Marriage and the Family,* 30:246–251. Copyright © 1968.

than an operational view of the matter. Nits are picked, hairs split. It is quite clear that many of the authors are not at all clear what question they are attacking.

It is axiomatic in science that progress hinges on asking the right question. Surprisingly, once the right question is asked the answer seems almost to tumble forth. That is a retrospective view; in prospect, it takes genuine (and mysterious) insight to see correctly into the brambles created by previous, ill-chosen verbalizations.

The abortion problem is, I think, a particularly neat example of a problem in which most of the difficulties are actually created by asking the wrong question. I submit further that once the right question is asked the whole untidy mess miraculously dissolves, leaving in its place a very simple public policy recommendation.

## Rape as a Justification

The wrong question, the one almost invariably asked, is this: "How can we justify an abortion?" This assumes that there are weighty public reasons for encouraging pregnancies, or that abortions, per se, somehow threaten public peace. A direct examination of the legitimacy of these assumptions will be made later. For the present, let us pursue the question as asked and see what a morass it leads to.

Almost all the present legislative attempts take as their model a bill proposed by the American Law Institute which emphasizes three justifications for legal abortion: rape, incest, and the probability of a defective child. Whatever else may be said about this bill, it is clear that it affects only the periphery of the social problem. The Arden House Conference Committee[1] estimated the number of illegal abortions in the United States to be between 200,000 and 1,200,000 per year. A California legislator, Anthony C. Beilenson,[2] has estimated that the American Law Institute bill (which he favors) would legalize not more than four percent of the presently illegal abortions. Obviously, the "problem" of illegal abortion will be scarcely affected by the passage of the laws so far proposed in the United States.

I have calculated[3] that the number of rape-induced pregnancies in the United States is about 800 per year. The number is not large, but for the woman raped the total number is irrelevant. What matters to her is that she be relieved of her unwanted burden. But a law which puts the burden of proof on her compels her to risk a second harrowing experience. How can she *prove* to the district attorney that she was raped? He could really know whether or not she gave consent only if he could get inside her mind; this he cannot do. Here is the philosopher's "egocentric predicament" that none of us can escape. In an effort to help the district attorney sustain the illusion that he can escape this predicament, a talented woman may put on a dramatic performance, with copious tears and other signs of anguish. But what if the raped woman is not an actress? What if her temperament is stoic? In its operation, the law will act against the interests of calm, undramatic women. Is that what we want? It is safe to say also that district attorneys will hear less favorably the pleas of poor women, the general assumption of middle-class agents being that the poor are less responsible in sex anyway.[4] Is it to the interest of society that the poor bear more children, whether rape-engendered or not?

A wryly amusing difficulty has been raised with respect to rape. Suppose the woman is married and having regular intercourse with her husband. Suppose that following a rape by an unknown intruder she finds herself pregnant. Is she legally entitled to an abortion? How does she know whose child she is carrying anyway? If it is her husband's child, abortion is illegal. If she carries it to term, and if blood tests then exclude the husband as the father, as they would in a fraction of the cases, is the woman then entitled to a *delayed* abortion? But this is ridiculous: this is infanticide, which no one is proposing. Such is the bramble bush into which we are led by a *reluctant* consent for abortion in cases of rape.

### How Probable Must Deformity Be?

The majority of the public support abortion in cases of a suspected deformity of the child[5] just as they do in cases of rape. Again, however, if the burden of proof rests on the one who requests the operation, we encounter difficulties in administration. Between 80,000 and 160,000 defective children are born every year in the United States. The number stated depends on two important issues: (a) how severe a defect must be before it is counted as such and (b) whether or not one counts as birth defects those defects that are not *detected* until later. (Deafness and various other defects produced by fetal rubella may not be detected until a year or so after birth.) However many defective infants there may be, what is the prospect of detecting them before birth?

The sad answer is: the prospects are poor. A small percentage can be picked up by microscopic examination of tissues of the fetus. But "amniocentesis"—the form of biopsy required to procure such tissues—is itself somewhat dangerous to both mother and fetus; most abnormalities will not be detectable by a microscopic examination of the fetal cells; and 96 to 98 percent of all fetuses are normal anyway. All these considerations are a contra-indication of routine amniocentesis.

When experience indicates that the probability of a deformed fetus is above the "background level" of 2 to 4 percent, is abortion justified? At what level? 10 percent? 50? 80? Or only at 100 percent? Suppose a particular medical history indicates a probability of 20 percent that the baby will be defective. If we routinely abort such cases, it is undeniable that four normal fetuses will be destroyed for every one abnormal. Those who assume that a fetus is an object of high value are appalled at this "wastage." Not uncommonly they ask, "Why not wait until the baby is born and then suffocate those that are deformed?" Such a question is unquestionably rhetorical and sardonic; if serious, it implies that infanticide has no more emotional meaning to a woman than abortion, an assumption that is surely contrary to fact.

### Should the Father Have Rights?

Men who are willing to see abortion-prohibition laws relaxed somewhat, but not completely, frequently raise a question about the "rights" of the father. Should we allow a woman to make a unilateral decision for an abortion? Should not her husband have a say in the matter? (After all, he contributed just as many chromosomes to the fetus as she.)

I do not know what weight to give this objection. I have encountered it repeatedly in the discussion section following a public meeting. It is clear that some men are disturbed at finding themselves powerless in such a situation and want the law to give them some power of decision.

Yet powerless men are—and it is nature that has made them so. If we give the father a right to veto in abortion decisions, the wife has a very simple reply to her husband: "I'm sorry, dear, I wasn't going to tell you this, but you've forced my hand. This is not your child." With such a statement she could always deny her husband's right to decide.

Why husbands should demand power in such matters is a fit subject for depth analysis. In the absence of such, perhaps the best thing we can say to men who are "hung up" on this issue is this: "Do you really want to live for another eight months with a woman whom you are compelling to be pregnant against her will?"

Or, in terms of public policy, do we want to pass laws which give men the right to compel their wives to be pregnant? Psychologically, such compulsion is akin to rape. Is it in the public interest to encourage rape?

### "Socio-Economic"—an Anemic Phrase

The question "How can we justify an abortion?" proves least efficient in solving the real problems of this world when we try to evaluate what are usually called "socio-economic indications." The hardship cases— rape, incest, probability of a deformed child—have been amply publicized, and as a result the majority of the public accepts them as valid indicators; but hardship cases constitute only a few percent of the need. By contrast, if a woman has more children than she feels she can handle, or if her children are coming too close together, there is little public sympathy for her plight. A poll[5] conducted by the National Opinion Research Center in December, 1965, showed that only 15 percent of the respondents replied "Yes" to this question: "Please tell me whether or not you think it should be possible for a pregnant woman to obtain a legal abortion if she is married and does not want any more children." Yet this indication, which received the lowest rate of approval, accounts for the vast majority of instances in which women want—and illegally get—relief from unwanted pregnancy.

There is a marked discrepancy between the magnitude of the need and the degree of public sympathy. Part of the reason for this discrepancy is attributable to the emotional impact of the words used to describe the need. "Rape," "incest," "deformed child"—these words are rich in emotional connotations. "Socio-economic indications" is a pale bit of jargon, suggesting at best that the abortion is wanted because the woman lives by culpably materialistic standards. "Socio-economic indications" tugs at no one's heartstrings; the hyphenated abomination hides the human reality to which it obliquely refers. To show the sort of human problem to which this label may be attached, let me quote a letter I received from one woman. (The story is unique, but it is one of a large class of similar true stories.)

I had an illegal abortion 2½ years ago. I left my church because of the guilt I felt. I had six children when my husband left me to live with another woman. We weren't divorced and I went to work to help support them. When he would come to visit the children he would sometimes stay after they were asleep. I became pregnant. When I told my husband, and asked him to please come back, he informed me that the woman he was living with was five months pregnant and ill, and that he couldn't leave her—not at that time anyway.

I got the name of a doctor in San Francisco from a Dr. friend who was visiting here from there. This Dr. (Ob. and Gyn.) had a good legitimate practice in the main part of the city and was a kindly, compassionate man who believes as you do, that it is better for everyone not to bring an unwanted child into the world.

It was over before I knew it. I thought I was just having an examination at the time. He even tried to make me not feel guilty by telling me that the long automobile trip had already started a spontaneous abortion. He charged me $25. That was on Fri. and on Mon. I was back at work. I never suffered any ill from it.

The other woman's child died shortly after birth and six months later my husband asked if he could come back. We don't have a perfect marriage but my children have a father. My being able to work has helped us out of a deep financial debt. I shall always remember the sympathy I received from that Dr. and wish there were more like him with the courage to do what they believe is right.

Her operation was illegal, and would be illegal under most of the "reform" legislation now being proposed, if interpreted strictly. Fortunately some physicians are willing to indulge in more liberal interpretations, but they make these interpretations not on medical grounds, in the strict sense, but on social and economic grounds. Understandably, many physicians are unwilling to venture so far from the secure base of pure physical medicine. As one Catholic physician put it:

> Can the patient afford to have another child? Will the older children have sufficient educational opportunities if their parents have another child? Aren't two, three or four children enough? I am afraid such statements are frequently made in the discussion of a proposed therapeutic abortion. [But] we should be doctors of medicine, not socio-economic prophets.[6]

To this a non-Catholic physician added: "I sometimes wish I were an obstetrician in a Catholic hospital so that I would not have to make any of these decisions. The only position to take in which I would have no misgivings is to do no interruptions at all."[7]


### Who Wants Compulsory Pregnancy?

The question "How can we justify an abortion?" plainly leads to great difficulties. It is operationally unmanageable: it leads to inconsistencies in practice and inequities by any moral standard. All these can be completely avoided if we ask the right question, namely: *"How can we justify compulsory pregnancy?"*

By casting the problem in this form, we call attention to its relationship to the slavery issue. Somewhat more than a century ago men in the Western world asked the question: "How can we justify compulsory servitude?" and came up with the answer: *"By no means whatever."* Is the answer any different to the related question: "How can we justify compulsory pregnancy?" Certainly pregnancy is a form of servitude; if continued to term it results in parenthood, which is also a kind of servitude, to be continued for the best years of a woman's life. It is difficult to see how it can be argued that this kind of servitude will be more productive of social good if it is compulsory rather than voluntary. A study[8] made of Swedish children born when their mothers were refused the abortions they had requested showed that unwanted children, as compared with their controls, as they grew up were more often picked up for drunkenness, or antisocial or criminal behavior; they received less education; they received more psychiatric care; and they were more often exempted from military service by reason of defect. Moreover, the females in the group married earlier and had children earlier, thus no doubt tending to create a vicious circle of poorly tended children who in their turn would produce more poorly tended children. How then does society gain by increasing the number of unwanted children? No one has volunteered an answer to this question.

Of course if there were a shortage of children, then society might say that it needs all the children it can get—unwanted or not. But I am unaware of any recent rumors of a shortage of children.

## Alternatives: True and False

The end result of an abortion—the elimination of an unwanted fetus—is surely good. But is the act itself somehow damaging? For several generations it was widely believed that abortion was intrinsically dangerous, either physically or psychologically. It is now very clear that the widespread belief is quite unjustified. The evidence for this statement is found in a bulky literature which has been summarized in Lawrence Lader's *Abortion*[9] and the collection of essays brought together by Alan Guttmacher.[10]

In tackling questions of this sort, it is imperative that we identify correctly the alternatives facing us. (All moral and practical problems involve a comparison of alternative actions.) Many of the arguments of the prohibitionists implicitly assume that the alternatives facing the woman are these:

*abortion——no abortion*

This is false. A person can never do nothing. The pregnant woman is going to do something, whether she wishes to or not. (She cannot roll time backward and live her life over.)

People often ask: "Isn't contraception better than abortion?" Implied by this question are these alternatives:

*abortion——contraception*

But these are not the alternatives that face the woman who asks to be aborted. She *is* pregnant. She cannot roll time backward and use contraception more successfully than she did before. Contraceptives are never foolproof anyway. It is commonly accepted that the failure rate of our best contraceptive, the "pill," is around one percent, i.e., one failure per hundred woman-years of use. I have earlier shown[11] that this failure rate produces about a quarter of a million unwanted pregnancies a year in the United States. Abortion is not so much an alternative to contraception as it is a subsidiary method of birth control, to be used when the primary method fails—as it often does.

The woman *is* pregnant: this is the base level at which the moral decision begins. If she is pregnant against her will, does it matter to society whether or not she was careless or unskillful in her use of contraception? In any case, she is threatening society with an unwanted child, for which society will pay dearly. The real alternatives facing the woman (and society) are clearly these:

*abortion——compulsory pregnancy*

When we recognize that these are the real, operational alternatives, the false problems created by pseudo-alternatives vanish.


**Is Potential Value Valuable?**

Only one weighty objection to abortion remains to be discussed, and this is the question of "loss." When a fetus is destroyed, has something valuable been destroyed? The fetus has the potentiality of becoming a human being. A human being is valuable. Therefore is not the fetus of equal value? This question must be answered.

It can be answered, but not briefly. What does the embryo receive from its parents that might be of value? There are only three possibilities: substance, energy, and information. As for the substance in the fertilized egg, it is not remarkable: merely the sort of thing one might find in any piece of meat, human or animal, and there is very little of it—only one and a half micrograms, which is about one twenty-billionth of an ounce. The energy content of this tiny amount of material is likewise negligible. As the zygote develops into a embryo, both its substance and its energy content increase (at the expense of the mother); but this is not a very important matter—even an adult, viewed from this standpoint, is only a hundred and fifty pounds of meat!

Clearly, the humanly significant thing that is contributed to the zygote by the parents is the information that "tells" the fertilized egg how to develop into a human being. This information is in the form of a chemical tape called "DNA," a double set of two chemical supermolecules each of which has about three billion "spots" that can be coded with any one of four different possibilities, symbolized by *A, T, G,* and *C.* (For comparison, the Morse code offers three possibilities for coding: dot, dash, and space.) It is the particular sequence of these four chemical possibilities in the DNA that directs the zygote in its development into a human being. The DNA constitutes the information needed to produce a valuable human being. The question is: is this information precious? I have argued elsewhere[12] that it is not:

> Consider the case of a man who is about to begin to build a $50,000 house. As he stands on the site looking at the blueprints a practical joker comes along and sets fire to the blueprints. The question is: can the owner go to the law and collect $50,000 for his lost blueprints? The answer is obvious: since another set of blueprints can be produced for the cost of only a few dollars, that is all they are worth. (A court might award a bit more for the loss of the owner's time, but that is a minor matter.) The moral: *a non-unique copy of information that specifies a valuable structure is itself almost valueless.*
>
> This principle is precisely applicable to the moral problem of abortion. The zygote, which contains the complete specification of a valuable human being, is not a human being, and is almost valueless. . . . The early stages of an individual fetus have had very little human effort invested in them; they are of very little worth. The loss occasioned by an abortion is independent of whether the abortion is spontaneous or induced. (Just as the loss incurred by the burning of a set of blueprints is independent of whether the causal agent was lightning or an arsonist.)
>
> A set of blueprints is not a house; the DNA of a zygote is not a human being. The analogy is singularly exact, though there are two

respects in which it is deficient. These respects are interesting rather than important. First, we have the remarkable fact that the blueprints of the zygote are constantly replicated and incorporated in every cell of the human body. This is interesting, but it has no moral significance. There is no moral obligation to conserve DNA—if there were, no man would be allowed to brush his teeth and gums, for in this brutal operation hundreds of sets of DNA are destroyed daily.

The other anomaly of the human information problem is connected with the fact that the information that is destroyed in an aborted embryo *is* unique (unlike the house blueprints). But it is unique in a way that is without moral significance. A favorite argument of abortion-prohibitionists is this: "What if Beethoven's mother had had an abortion?" The question moves us; but when we think it over we realize we can just as relevantly ask: "What if Hitler's mother had had an abortion?" Each conceptus is unique, but not in any way that has a moral consequence. The *expected* potential value of each aborted child is exactly that of the average child born. It is meaningless to say that humanity loses when a *particular* child is not born, or is not conceived. A human female, at birth, has about 30,000 eggs in her ovaries. If she bears only 3 children in her lifetime, is there any meaningful sense in which we can say that mankind has suffered a loss in those other 29,997 fruitless eggs? (Yet one of them might have been a super-Beethoven!)

People who worry about the moral danger of abortion do so because they think of the fetus as a human being, hence equate feticide with murder. Whether the fetus is or is not a human being is a matter of definition, not fact; and we can define any way we wish. In terms of the human problem involved, it would be unwise to define the fetus as human (hence tactically unwise ever to refer to the fetus as an "unborn child"). Analysis based on the deepest insights of molecular biology indicates the wisdom of sharply distinguishing the information for a valuable structure from the completed structure itself. It is interesting, and gratifying, to note that this modern insight is completely congruent with common law governing the disposal of dead fetuses. Abortion-prohibitionists generally insist that abortion is murder, and that an embryo is a person; but no state or nation, so far as I know, requires the dead fetus to be treated like a dead person. Although all of the states in the United States severely limit what can be done with a dead human body, no cognizance is taken of dead fetuses up to about five months' prenatal life. The early fetus may, with impunity, be flushed down the toilet or thrown out with the garbage—which shows that we never have regarded it as a human being. Scientific analysis confirms what we have always known.

## The Management of Compulsory Pregnancy

What is the future of compulsory pregnancy? The immediate future is not hopeful. Far too many medical people misconceive the real problem. One physician has written:

> Might not a practical, workable solution to this most difficult problem be found by setting up, in every hospital, an abortion committee comprising a specialist in obstetrics and gynecology, a psychiatrist, and a clergyman or priest? The patient and her husband—if any—would meet with these men who would do all in their power to persuade the woman not to undergo the abortion. (I have found that the promise of postpartum sterilization will frequently enable even married women with all the children they can care for to accept this one more, final pregnancy.) If, however, the committee members fail to change the woman's mind, they can make it very clear that they disapprove of the abortion, but prefer that it be safely done in a hospital rather than bungled in a basement somewhere.[13]

What this author has in mind is plainly not a system of legalizing abortion but a system of managing compulsory pregnancy. It is this philosophy which governs pregnancies in the Scandinavian countries,[14] where the experience of a full generation of women has shown that women do not want their pregnancies to be managed by the state. Illegal abortions have remained at a high level in these countries, and recent years have seen the development of a considerable female tourist trade to Poland, where abortions are easy to obtain. Unfortunately, American legislatures are now proposing to follow the provably unworkable system of Scandinavia.

The drift down this erroneous path is not wholly innocent. Abortion-prohibitionists are showing signs of recognizing "legalization" along Scandinavian lines as one more roadblock that can be thrown in the way of the abolition of compulsory pregnancy. To cite an example: on 9 February 1966, the *Courier,* a publication of the Winona, Minnesota Diocese, urged that Catholics support a reform law based on the American Law Institute model, because the passage of such a law would "take a lot of steam out of the abortion advocate's argument" and would "defeat a creeping abortionism of disastrous importance." [15]

Wherever a Scandinavian or American Law Institute type of bill is passed, it is probable that cautious legislators will then urge a moratorium for several years while the results of the new law are being assessed (though they are easily predictable from the Scandinavian experience). As Lord Morley once said: "Small reforms are the worst enemies of great reforms." Because of the backwardness of education in these matters, caused by the long taboo under which the subject of abortion labored, it seems highly likely that our present system of compulsory pregnancy will continue substantially without change until the true nature of the alternatives facing us is more widely recognized.

# 4

## *Reformers are Repeaters*

The careful reader—heaven forbid that there be any other—will have noticed, and perhaps be annoyed by, a certain repetitiousness in the two preceding essays. I apologize. Before I was through with abortion I wrote for many publications and I did quite a bit of repeating, particularly of the DNA-as-blueprints argument. Some of my readers were moved by the argument but many were not. I'm afraid it takes a good deal of sophistication about science to fully appreciate what is involved in this argument.

There are basically three different aspects to the phenomena of the world: matter, energy, and information. The foundation for the analysis in terms of matter was laid about the first of the nineteenth century, with the work of Dalton and Lavoisier. Energy began to be understood when the first and second laws of thermodynamics were enunciated around 1850. But it was not until about the middle of the twentieth century—a scant generation ago—that information was scientifically understood. It will take some time for an "instinctive" feeling for this modality to become widespread in the general public. However this understanding is needed right now if we are to look at the abortion problem rationally.

I brought up this problem once more in a footnote to my book *Exploring New Ethics for Survival*[1]:

> In law, there is no person until a living child is born; at this point it
> has retrospective rights and can sue for damages *in utero*, e.g., by
> industrial X-rays. No live birth, no child—no human being . . .
> Whether a fetus of *Homo sapiens* is or is not a human being is not a
> scientific question. It is nonetheless gratifying to report that scien-
> tific practice is consonant with law. In all of biology, embryos and
> fetuses are specifically distinguished from the definitive, more com-
> pletely formed stages. An acorn is not an oak tree, an egg is not a
> hen, a human fetus is not a human being or person. Smashing acorns
> is not deforestation, scrambling eggs is not gallicide.

And abortion is neither homicide nor murder.

The passage quoted raises an interesting question in tactics. To be useful, an argument must do more than "preach to the converted"; the language must have a favorable impact on those of another opinion. Then what about that sentence. "Smashing acorns is not deforestation"? Does "smashing" evoke too brutal an image? It may. Yet one wants somehow to get people to give their deepest attention to the true nature of *in*forma-tion—literally *non*-formation, which is the primitive meaning of the word "inform". That which is mere "information" is a non-form of that to which its name is given. The information-for-a-house is not a house; the information-for-a-person is not a person. How can one get people to pay attention to this profound logical point?

If it is a new point—as it certainly is to the vast majority of mankind—repetition is indispensable. C. M. Child, an old professor of mine, in-sisted[2] that "one publication of an idea is not enough. It must be pre-sented again and again and so far as possible illustrated by different results." Esthetically, this is unfortunate; or so it seems to most scientists who cherish the story of Willard Gibbs' famous speech to the Yale fac-ulty. This great 19th century physical chemist (who no doubt would have won the Nobel Prize had he worked in the 20th) was said to have spoken up only once in faculty meetings. The subject was the perennial one of language requirements, and there were those who were trying to get mathematics accepted as an alternative to foreign language. The discussion became heated. Finally Gibbs rose and delivered his only speech to the faculty: "Mathematics *is* a language." Just four words: no repeating. More laconic, no doubt, than anything ever said in classical Sparta (Laconia).

Esthetically admirable though Gibbs' speech may be such laconic presentations do not get the work of reform done. The would-be reformer must repeat his arguments many times over, in many different dialects, for many different audiences. The reformer knows at the outset that he does not live in Utopia (hence his activities); he also must adjust to the fact that he does not live in Laconia.

# 5

## *Abortion in Anthropological Perspective*

### *(1969)*

Taboo is far more effective than censorship. A censor is an external agent, who seeks to prevent overt, public expression. We can still think about those things the censor forbids us to write about; and we delight in outwitting him. But taboo, the internalized equivalent of the censor, is **myself** indeed. How can I think of outwitting myself? Taboo not only prevents overt expression, it prevents thinking itself. If the much overused word "unthinkable" has any meaning at all, it refers to those subjects that are under taboo. Abortion was unthinkable to a large proportion of the population in the western world until only a few years ago.

To how large a proportion? For a long time I assumed that the great majority of our people were incapable of thinking about abortion—until my eyes were suddenly opened to an anthropological fact I had not been aware of. My education began when a middle aged woman was telling me about getting an abortion in Spain, where she had been living at the time.

"And what did your husband think of it?" I asked.

"My husband?" she said in some surprise. "You don't think I told him, do you? It was none of his business."

I was amused, but thought no more of the matter until a few weeks later when I was told of a strikingly similar event that took place in Italy.

"And what did you tell your husband'?" I asked the woman.

"Nothing," she replied calmly. "He's much too immature to think about such things."

Suddenly I remembered something I had read about the Rif tribes of northern Africa.[1] Among these people abortion is a very serious offence. If a husband were certain that his wife had had one he would, at least, divorce her; and he might kill her, with the approval of his friends. Does this mean that abortions do not occur among the Rifs? Not at all! In addition to the general market, the women have a market place of their own to which men are forbidden to come. The women's market specializes in the needs of women, including contraceptives and abortions. Since men can never enter, they can never really know what goes on. No doubt they have their suspicions, but they probably learn not to voice them. Even in a primitive society whose women are in a very subservient role wives still have means of enforcing a minimum of civility among their menfolk. They can always put more pepper in the soup, if nothing else.

In other words, the intolerable laws promulgated by men in this society were tolerated simply because women lived in a different culture—or more exactly, subculture. The Rif situation shows this up particularly well; but, once seen, the same arrangement can be recognized all over the world. In Europe, for many centuries, the specifically female needs of women were taken care of by other women—mothers, mothers-in-law, grandmothers, and midwives (female). Methods of contraception—often not very good, it is true—were passed down from mother to daughter, from midwife to wife. Abortions were performed by midwives, with husbands ("too immature," or its medieval equivalent) generally left out of the confidence. The separation of the two subcultures permitted an oceanic separation of theory and practice.

Consider Italy. A Roman Catholic country, its official face is set solidly against all abortions; but it is generally estimated that the abortion rate is equal to the live birth rate,[2] which makes Italian abortions four times as common as American. Italian men write the laws of Italy, and men write books on theology; women have the abortions and the children, with scarcely a glance at the literature of the other subculture. For a long time the male subculture has been literate and theoretical, the female subculture nonliterate and practical. The written analysis of sexual problems has been carried out by males who certainly never had the experience of having children; many of them did not even have the experience of living and sharing with the child-bearing subculture. With such a separation of experience and theory-construction it is scarcely to be wondered at if male theories often bore little relationship to reality. Those who are trained in the sciences know how essential it is to keep theorizers close to the growing edge of experience. It is hard for scientists to take seriously the vast bulk of theological writings on motherhood. Women have children, and men write books on theology. . . . When men take over the bearing and day-to-day raising of children, perhaps then women, seeking the ineffable they have lost, will take to theologizing. (That will be the day!)

In the meantime we are in trouble because the centuries-old separation of the two subcultures is breaking down. Women have become literate and are taking up men's occupations. Women midwives are disappearing in Europe (and are almost nonexistent in America). Their place is being taken by men physicians who try to enforce the mores of the male subculture, seldom realizing that there is any other. Women, the rising but subservient class, tend to adopt the standards of the class they are rising into. This is orthodox sociology; ambitious Negroes adopt the standards of the white class they seek to join. In reaction to this, some Negroes have recently pushed for greater psychological and sociological separation under the banner of "Black Power." Perhaps the revolutionaries are wise. Perhaps we also need a Woman Power movement to preserve the traditional moral standards of the female subculture in the face of repressive male power.

# 6

## If Right-to-Lifers Have Their Way

### (1974)

[On 22 January 1973 the U.S. Supreme Court ruled that all medically performed abortions are legal in the first trimester of pregnancy, but that the states could regulate—in ways not specified—the performance of later abortions. The clarity and near unanimity of the decision (by a 7-to-2 majority) were unforeseen by disputants on both sides. Opponents of abortion, under the generic banner of "Right to Life," soon rallied, greatly expanding their efforts. Many bills were introduced into Congressional committees aimed at creating amendments to the Constitution that would define all stages of the developing embryos as "human", within the meaning of the law, and thus protected by all the statutes that protect human life. Immense pressures were put on the committees to vote these bills out and onto the floor, but without success in the 93rd and 94th Congresses (through the fall of 1976).

The danger that such an amendment might be passed seemed to me to be not inconsiderable, because Right-to-Lifers were operating within a mainstream of western civilization. In the past two hundred years we have steadily extended legal rights to larger populations, first to former slaves and then to women and children. What more logical than to extend these rights back into the prenatal period, all the way to the zygote? How can anyone defend an arbitrary line drawn at any later time? (The word "arbitrary" is itself prejudicial: label an act "arbitrary" and all support of it vanishes.)

The defense of the arbitrary can best be made by showing the possible consequences of refusing to set an arbitrary line. Most people would feel happiest setting the beginning of legal personhood at the time of viability of the fetus, i.e., at the earliest point at which an individual could be kept alive if born (or delivered) prematurely. But this point is a function of the state of the science of medicine; it is steadily moving backward to earlier and earlier stages. Before we adopt viability as the criterion of personhood, rather than an arbitrary point in time, we should try to imagine the practical consequences of this decision when science has made the ultimate advance. A good way to mobilize the necessary imagination is by way of science fiction, and this I attempted to do in two chapters of a small book, *Mandatory Motherhood. The True Meaning of Right to Life.*\* I tried to picture what might happen if Right-to-Lifers succeed in passing a Twenty-Eighth Amendment to the Constitution, giving the zygote all the rights to existence enjoyed by an adult.]

"Your Honor. My client has been accused of murder under the Twenty-eighth Amendment to the Constitution of the United States. There is no argument as to the facts, so I ask that the Court look deeper into the meaning of those facts.

"My client, Dr. Samaritan, is a profoundly compassionate man. His behavior on the witness stand, I am sure, convinced everyone of this. As Margaret's physician he was deeply touched when this unfortunate woman came to him with her problem. Six children already; and now impregnated with a seventh by a husband who had left home to live with another woman—whom he had also made pregnant. No financial reserves. A job that barely supported her family; and that job would be lost if she went through with the pregnancy and childbirth.

"What man of compassion and imagination could fail to be touched by the poor woman's plight? Dr. Samaritan is rich in both compassion and imagination. And courage. So he performed the simple operation the woman desired, and a family was saved from disaster." . . .

Mr. Sequitur, Margaret's attorney—a pudgy little man—mopped his florid face with a silk handkerchief and strolled back to his table. On cue,

\*Reprinted here by permission of the publishers, the Beacon Press, Boston. Copyright 1974.

his assistant lifted a box from the floor, a box big enough to hold an inflated basketball. Sequitur, placing his hand on the top, turned to the judge.

"If you will permit it, Your Honor, I have a little demonstration for the Court." He turned again to the box and very deliberately untied and opened it. He reached in and started to draw something out. A hush had fallen over the courtroom. All eyes were on the lawyer's hands. Sequitur, sensing the tension, thoughtfully removed his hands from the box and turned to the judge again.

"Before I go on with the demonstration, I must prepare the ground. You know that it is possible to transplant a fertilized egg from the womb of one woman to the womb of another. In this way it is sometimes possible to bring the blessings of motherhood to a woman who would otherwise be fruitless. This is a fine thing, but unfortunately it is difficult to get the fertilized egg in just the right condition for transplanting it into another womb.

"Sterility specialists have long recognized that what is really needed is a way of nourishing and maintaining a woman's ovaries in the laboratory, in 'tissue culture,' as they call it. This is easier said than done. Thousands of man-hours have gone into this work, without success.

"Today it is my great privilege to announce, for the first time in public, magnificent success in this humanitarian effort. The official announcement will appear in the *New England Journal of Medicine* next month. I am proud to say that it is scientists in our own Huxley University, led by the brilliant Dr. Bokanovsky, who have achieved this stunning success.

"Dr. Bokanovsky's group have found how to maintain a female ovary indefinitely in a culture apparatus in the laboratory. More: they have learned how to stimulate an ovary so that it will turn out eggs at a rate close to that at which a testicle turns out spermatozoa. Putting eggs and spermatozoa together they produce fertilized eggs ready for implanting in the waiting wombs of women yearning for motherhood. The Fertility Laboratory of Huxley University is now prepared to make every woman in the world happy with her very own baby. We may confidently expect the Nobel Prize to be awarded for this great accomplishment."

Sequitur paused and drank some water from a glass. Turning again to the bench, he continued.

"Dr. Bokanovsky, learning of this trial, has very generously lent me

some of his material. I have here in this flask"—Sequitur reached into
the box and pulled out a two-liter Erlenmeyer flask with a plastic cap on
it—"a suspension of living human eggs, all fertilized and ready to be
transplanted into expectant mothers."

The attorney sloshed the liquid around in the half-filled flask. The fluid
was milky and just slightly pink. Sequitur paced back and forth, thoughtfully jiggling the flask as he walked.

"How many fertilized eggs do you suppose there are in here? Dr.
Bokanovsky has carefully sampled this flask and made the calculations.
There are, he tells me, two times ten to the thirteenth fertilized eggs in
this little vessel. In numbers more familiar to most of us—certainly to
me—that's twenty trillion. That sounds like a lot. How many is it? What
can we compare this large number with?

"I think our best course is to compare it with the total number of people *who have ever lived* on this old planet of ours. Twenty years ago the
demographer Nathan Keyfitz calculated that this was 77 billion. With the
continued burgeoning of the population I am told that this number stands
today at 80 billion. That is, all the people who have ever lived, amount to
only 80 billion.

"According to the Twenty-eighth Amendment every fertilized egg is a
human being, in the full meaning of the law. *I have, then, in this flask,
twenty trillion human beings—two hundred and fifty times as many as
have ever lived before on earth.* Now—"

Sequitur removed the lid.

"Now—"

Quickly he inverted the flask and with a swinging motion sprayed the
contents in a semicircular swath on the floor. The audience gasped. The
judge, his mouth open, half rose to admonish the attorney, but Sequitur,
his voice loud and insistent, continued rapidly, precluding interruption.

"Bear with me! Bear with me! I know I have sullied the dignity of this
courtroom, but I will make amends. Bear with me! My argument is far
more serious than any minor disorder I may have created.

"A moment ago this flask had twenty trillion living human beings in it.
Now they are spread out all over this courtroom floor. They are still
alive. But they won't be for long. The most heroic efforts we could possibly mount would not save them now. They will die.

"And who killed them? *I* killed them. I, John Sequitur, killed them! In front of your very eyes, I have killed two hundred and fifty times as many people as have ever lived on earth. Adolf Hitler and Genghis Khan were pikers compared to me. I, John Sequitur, am the greatest murderer of all time.

"The law, it has been said, does not concern itself with trifles. My client snuffed out the life of *one* human embryo. The Twenty-eighth Amendment says that every woman's embryo is a human being from the moment of conception, and that my client is a murderer. I, my client's attorney, have just snuffed out the lives of twenty trillion human beings. So says the Twenty-eighth Amendment.

"Do not concern yourself with trifles, Your Honor. Release my client—and charge *me* with murder. Mass murder."

It takes imagination to see the truth. Do Right-to-Lifers have enough imagination?

We should never pass a law unless we are convinced that it will be good not just for today, but for many years to come. The environment in which laws must be judged is now dominated by technology. Technology, as everyone knows, changes at a rapid pace. And the pace accelerates.

But the law changes at a snail's pace. It always has. By the time we get an amendment to the Constitution passed and ratified, the technological environment may be so changed that the law will be no good—if, indeed, it ever was.

The attempt to predict what the future holds for us is called "technology assessment." One of its most powerful tools is science fiction. Science fiction arouses the imagination and helps it to see the truth. The probable truth, on which prudent men base their actions.

How probable is it that we shall some day culture human ovaries in the laboratory? Highly probable. Tissue culture—the growing of cells or groups of cells called tissues—is fiendishly complicated; but in principle all tissue-culture problems are soluble. Every tissue lives in an environment of nourishing fluid. No other tissue directly takes care of it—just the fluid produced by other tissues, and the fluid is not alive. We should be able to figure out what's in it, and furnish a similar fluid to tissues in a culture flask.

Tissue culture of human ovaries is probably "just around the corner."

We would be fools to pass a law that did not allow for this probable technological development. That is the message of the story of John Sequitur in tomorrow's courtroom.

Splattering twenty trillion living human embryos on a courtroom floor is a rather violent way to make a point. Sequitur could have made it another way. A way that might have been better from an intellectual point of view, though probably not as effective in a courtroom.

Let's turn the film back to the point just before the lawyer emptied the flask on the floor. Only this time he doesn't empty it. Instead. . . .

"Your Honor," Sequitur says, "since this court is bound to uphold the law there can be no question about its attitude toward the life of these twenty trillion little beings. The Twenty-eighth Amendment says that each and every one of them is a human being in the full sense of the law. The honorable court must, then, cherish the life of each and every one. To willfully kill even one would be murder. Even to allow one to die from neglect would be manslaughter.

"They don't look like human beings. But the Twenty-eighth Amendment says they are."

Sequitur walks toward the bench, saying as he approaches it: "Dr. Bokanovsky gave them to me—"

He stretches upward and puts the flask on the bench: "—and I give them to you."

He coughs.

"Bokanovsky is through with them. I'm through with them. Now what are you going to do with them, Your Honor?

"Their lives can be continued if each of them is placed in the welcoming womb of a healthy woman. How many of them can be taken care of this way? At the outside there are, in the world, one billion women of childbearing age who might conceivably—pardon the pun—act as havens for these little beings. So out of every twenty thousand fertilized eggs in this flask only one can be saved by placing it in some woman's womb. (Even that would be practically impossible, considering how widely scattered these women are over the globe. And what makes us think they would all welcome such a gift?)

"But granting that the practical problem could be solved, for every fertilized egg you saved, 19,999 would have to die.

"And neither you, nor I, nor Dr. Bokanovsky—nor anybody else—can do a thing about it."

Sequitur takes a drink of water before going on.

"The trouble is, Your Honor, the assumptions of the law are back end to. We are deceived by language. We speak of 'conceiving life' or 'creating life,' when we can do neither. The life of existing cells can merely be continued in new individuals, in new *loci*, as it were. Imprisoned in ancient presumptions, we think it is difficult to 'create' life, and easy to continue it.

"The truth is quite the reverse. The so-called creation of life is childishly simple, and indeed much of this creation is done by those who are little more than children in the level of their understanding. Any two fools of the opposite sex can procreate another child, another life, as we say. It is the continuance and nourishing of life that is tragically difficult. Fools can—and do—create more life than the wisest and most powerful men and women in the world can possibly take care of.

"You can't possibly save more than the tiniest fraction of those lives in the flask before you. The vast majority will soon die. Will *you* then be responsible for the trillions of deaths? Or will *I* who gave these fertilized eggs to you be responsible? Or will *Bokanovsky,* who created them (as we say), be the responsible party?

"If we feel a compulsion to find and label a crime, what is that crime?

"Does the crime reside in the early destruction of these surplus lives, not wanted by anyone?

"Or is it the creation of lives for which there is no place in the world that constitutes the true crime?

"Or is it an error to think that there *is* a crime? Maybe both the so-called creation of new lives and their destruction at an early stage are completely without moral significance?

"Maybe the mistake is in looking for a crime at this stage of the life cycle. God knows we have more than enough to do trying to patch up the broken and spoiled lives of millions of human beings in the years after birth. Why, in heaven's name, do we anguish over these little eggs and embryos?

"Is mere life so precious? Or should our abiding concern be for the quality of life?"

# PART TWO: RELIGION

# 7

## Failure Teaches

A basic dogma of modern applied psychology holds that we learn more (or better) from reward than from punishment. The belief springs from experiments in "operant conditioning" a la Skinner. At first glance the experiments seem to be decisive; "positive reinforcement" does seem to work better than negative. On such laboratory findings contemporary educational theorists base their philosophy that education should be founded solely on rewards.

A biologist has his doubts, based on field studies and the logic of evolution. A bluejay eats a monarch butterfly and becomes violently ill, regurgitating the meal. Thereafter he avoids monarchs. There's no gentle educator around to reward him; he's simply punished. Ancient bluejays incapable of learning from negative reinforcement were long ago eliminated as the ancestors of today's birds. Can it have been otherwise with man?

Few are the voices in today's world that have anything favorable to say for failure. One of the wisest of these is the economist Kenneth E. Boulding, who has put the matter rather neatly.[1]

I have revised some folk wisdom lately; one of my edited proverbs is "Nothing fails like success," because you do not learn anything from it. The only thing we ever learn from is failure. Success only confirms our superstitions.

For some strange reason which I do not understand at all a small subculture arose in Western Europe which legitimated failure. Science is the only subculture in which failure is legitimate.

The nineteenth century physicist and inventor Michael Faraday said that he was satisfied if his attempts to learn something or do something were successful one time in a thousand. No Skinnerian would dream of settling for such a frugal reward schedule, yet from no more generous a base have all the glories of science and technology been created. How fortunate it is that the education of scientists was never entrusted to the Columbia School of Education! (Can we even conceive what the course of biological evolution would have been had Mother Nature turned this problem over to the educationalists at the beginning of the Archeozoic? The mind boggles at the thought.)

The reformer, like any other technologist, must expect to fail most of the time. The "literature" does not correctly mirror the proportion of successes to failures, because for the most part no one is interested in reading about failures. (We have too much to read anyway.) But now and then we need to be exposed to the record of the all too numerous failures.

There follow two brief papers of mine that were outstanding failures, whatever their purpose. I don't suppose it was ever clear in my own mind what I intended to accomplish by publishing them. I wanted to get something off my chest, I guess. In that, I succeeded; but the silence that met their publication was chilling. As an exercise for the reader I pose this question: Why the silence?

The background of "Second Sermon" needs to be known. In 1956 the Catholic Institute for Social Ecclesiastical Research announced an international contest for an essay on "the population problem in underdeveloped areas," which was formulated as follows:

1. What social, economic and cultural means can be employed to ensure that during the development of the economically and technically underdeveloped areas the changes in the social structure, which will inevitably occur, will not result in religious and moral disintegration of the communities in question, but in the development within them of a

social structure satisfying the requirements of complete human well-being?

2. Assuming that the population increase in these areas will be so rapid as to cast grave doubts on the efficiency of the means suggested as a solution for 1. above, how can the population growth itself be influenced to the extent necessary to guarantee the effectiveness of these means?

The solutions proposed to the above problems must comply with the requirements of Catholic principles and at the same time must be effective from a positive scientific point of view.[2]

The last paragraph clearly describes a problem that is impossible of solution. Irritated by it, I decided I would enter the contest and show why this was so. In the scientific realm it is just as praiseworthy to demonstrate an impossibility as it is to solve a problem by finding a possibility. The Second Law of Thermodynamics which says (in effect), "It is impossible to invent a perpetual motion machine," is rightly regarded as one of the monumental discoveries in physics. Theology, pre-committed to certain conclusions, seems not to recognize the power of negative discoveries.

Nevertheless, I dashed off a "solution" to the problem posed, couched in a religious idiom. I had absolutely no illusions that it would be regarded as a serious candidate for the substantial monetary prize; I was just badgering the judges for fun. The judges were evidently more intelligent than the originators of the contest for they terminated the contest four years later without awarding the prize to anyone. Understandably, they did not make any public admission that the problem was insoluble within the limitations posed; instead they multiplied judicious-sounding words about the need for "team work" and "scientific co-operation on an international level" to solve this problem that was evidently too great to yield to "individual endeavours."

From which I suppose a cynic might deduce the following moral: if one man can't invent the impossible, hand the problem over to a committee—and they'll give birth to a budget.

Some time after the close of the contest I submitted my "solution" to Dwight Ingle's *Perspectives in Biology and Medicine,* one of the few respectable scientific journals that publishes off-beat writings like mine. He published my sermon, and the world rolled on, unperturbed.

# 8

# A Second Sermon on the Mount

*(1963)*

*Blessed are the meek, for they shall inherit the earth.*

Shall? They *have*. Look around you. How many heroes do you number among your neighbors? Or your colleagues? Few, you say; and are not surprised. How could it be otherwise, considering the way heroes are rewarded? Legend has it that the Spartan mother told her son: "Return with your shield or on it." Could there be a clearer prescription for genetic suicide? A hero throws both himself and his genes into the fray. Jealous, we all can spare the hero. But can we do without his genes? Where are the heroes of yesteryear? Where is Sparta now?

*Blessed are they that speak in beautitudes, for they shall be heard dumbly.*

What is a beatitude anyway? *"Blessed are. . . ."* What does that mean? Is it a statement of fact? A wish? A warning? A command? A prediction? Beatitudes, always ambiguous, are no proper part of scholarly

From *Perspectives in Biology and Medicine*, 6:366–371. Copyright © 1963.

writing. *Good,* you say. But note: that which a beatitude *means* may also be missing in our formal discourses. Loving rigor, we may throw out the baby with the bath. Ambiguous representations serve a purpose. They are a shield behind which the subconscious can carry on its work. The joke, the dream, the parable, the beatitude—all these defenses will be needed so long as there are problems we fear to face.

*Blessed are statistical tables, for they delay the day of our thinking.*

Run your eye down the rows of books on population published in the last ten years. Lose yourself in the thickets of tables of numbers. Is all this necessary? Is the population problem really so subtle? Are we unable to get along without this dissimulation of reality and the fatigue of prolixity that puts an end to genuine inquiry? Can we quench the human population explosion with a still greater explosion of books on population?

Wittgenstein once said: "A person caught in a philosophical confusion is like a man in a room who wants to get out but doesn't know how. He tries the window but it is too high. He tries the chimney but it is too narrow. And if he would only *turn around,* he would see that the door has been open all the time!"

Where is that door?

*Blessed are they that reproduce exorbitantly, for only they shall be.*

One is sometimes astounded at the stupidity of the ancients. Herodotus, certainly no fool, wrote: "The lioness, which is the mightiest and boldest of beasts, beareth one offspring once in her life; for as she beareth him, she casteth out her womb with her offspring. And the cause thereof is this, that when the whelp beginneth to stir himself in his mother's belly, then he teareth the womb with his claws, which are sharper than any other beast's; and as he groweth he pierceth it more and more with his scrabbling, until when the birth is near, no part remaineth sound."

It is incredible that the great historian did not perceive the instability of a reproductive system in which numbers are halved each generation. Yet there the quotation is with no hint of irony in it.

A reproductive system in which two produced exactly two in each generation would also lead to extinction, for there are always accidents. Only organisms that tend to increase each generation can survive. In a sense, it does not matter how little the increase is, so long as it is positive. In a sense, all potential growth curves are the same—it is just a matter of adjusting the scale. Every population growth curve points to infinity. This is the justification of the word "exorbitantly," which means "off the track." Bacteria, doubling in numbers every twenty minutes, reproduce exorbitantly; so do men, though their doubling takes a quarter of a century or more. Potentially exorbitant reproduction is a necessary quality of life, so no one is asking us for our approval. There being no other possibility, reproduction is beyond good and evil.

The problem is: how to stay on the track?

*Blessed are they that have enemies, for they shall endure.*

Consider the first "living" entity on earth, the Haldane-Oparin-Horowitz proto-organism. Once evolved, what was its most threatening peril? *That it should eat itself out of house and home.* Reproduction is positive feedback. Positive feedback is both necessary to life and suicidal in its tendency. The first great need of the first life was for an enemy, a predator, an agent of negative feedback, a density-dependent factor. Until its governor was found, the whole marvelous mechanism of the primitive self-reproducing entity was living under a sword of Damocles. Indeed, it is quite possible that life may have begun dozens of times, and extinguished itself all but one, that lucky last time when it found an enemy.

Periodically man forgets (or denies?) the need for enemies and seeks to protect the pets he loves by total elimination of their predators. So, in this century, did he imperil the deer of the Kaibab plateau by exterminating coyotes and mountain lions. As a result of his well-meaning stupidity the deer population exploded from 5,000 to some 100,000. Then, in two years' time, starvation brought the numbers down to 40,000. In another decade, the population had fallen to 10,000.

*Blessed are they that are plagued, for they shall know prosperity.*

Once *Homo sapiens* was, by his own cleverness, freed of the threat of large predators, what protections had he against unintentional suicide? For many centuries, he was blessed with the little predators, the disease germs. When there were crowds, then came crowd-diseases. Since disease germs attack living flesh only, and not man's works, every serious epidemic temporarily caused a favorable alteration in the ratio of men to capital goods, and was thus an unadmitted and inadmissible blessing to those who survived. Microbes were for long the most effective means of capital accumulation. Was it an accident that the beginning of the scientific revolution was contemporaneous with the most devastating plagues recorded in history?

*Blessed are they that have external enemies, for they shall know internal peace.*

With his predators slain, and his microbes on the run, what is there to keep man's life from becoming, in Hobbes's phrase, "a warre, as is of every man, against every man"? Nothing, except that some men should draw a circle within which fellowship prevails, sustained by threats from without.

Deprived of the external threats of predators and plagues, can man draw a circle that encompasses *all* men? Can man, trapped in a finite universe, tolerate exorbitant reproduction? Can man survive in One World?

*Blessed are they that are selfish, for they shall make joy possible.*

Malthus, in his most shocking passage, said:

> A man who is born into a world already possessed, if he cannot get subsistence from his parents on whom he has a just demand, and if the society do not want his labour, has no claim of *right* to the smallest portion of food, and, in fact, has no business to be where he is. At nature's mighty feast there is no vacant cover for him. She tells him to be gone, and will quickly execute her own orders, if he does not work upon the compassion of some of her guests. If these guests get up and make room for him, other intruders immediately appear demanding the same favour. The report of a provision for all that come, fills the hall with numerous claimants. The order and harmony of the feast is disturbed, the plenty that before reigned is changed into scarcity; and the happiness of the guests is destroyed

by the spectacle of misery and dependence in every part of the hall, and by the clamorous importunity of those, who are justly enraged at not finding the provision which they had been taught to expect. The guests learn too late their error, in counter-acting those strict orders to all intruders, issued by the great mistress of the feast, who, wishing that all guests should have plenty, and knowing she could not provide for unlimited numbers, humanely refused to admit fresh comers when her table was already full.

Not many men are as bull-headed as Malthus. Right or wrong—and he was often wrong—he clung to the children of his brain. But this delinquent passage was intolerable. He abandoned it after one printing.
But he never denied it.

*Blessed are they that deny the truth, for they shall get the lion's share.*

Competition is inescapable. A lie, Goffman tell us, is always found out—but it takes time. And in that time, a liar gains. If he lies by denying—in the psychological sense, that is, internally—his lying is more convincing, and he gains more time, thus reaping greater benefits. The world of action favors the truth-denier.

*Blessed are the powerful, for they shall gain in power.*

Ah! But what is power?

*Blessed are they that praise mercy, for they shall bury the merciful.*

The history of humanity is a progress of dialectic. Aesop's fox who lost his brush was found out; but real foxes are often not. The ideal of humanitarianism, always opposed, has grown ever more powerful. When humanitarianism is completely victorious, can quality long survive? "There but for the grace of God go I," says the victor as he shares his gains with the vanquished. Victory may even have a negative value. One-Upmanship is mightier than the sword.
And beyond One-Upmanship lies—what?

*Blessed are the meek that boast not, for they conceal the Game.*

What Stephen Potter said has been known for thousands of years. But he *said* it. That was his crime.

*Blessed are they that shun reason, for they shall prevail.*

Reason says, Desist. Ambition says, Breed. In competition with each other, which wins?

*Blessed are they that cling to the past, for the future shall be theirs.*

"It is unnatural," said Tertullian, "to act in plays, to paint the face, or to wear dyed cloth." Everyone knows, of course, that undyed cloth droppeth gently from the trees, ready to wear. Whatever comes down to us from ancient times is natural; that which hath been recently invented is unnatural.
*Sancta simplicitas!*

*Blessed are the women that are irregular, for their daughters shall inherit the earth.*

The inheritability of reproductive characteristics is amply proved to us by all God's creatures. Are not women God's creatures?
The rhythm method of birth control is, when used by women who have a rhythm, only two and a half times as bad as "artificial" methods, according to the studies of Tietze. But even if it were every bit as good, it would be self-defeating. For there would still be those arrhythmic women, about one woman in six, for whom the method is meaningless. Compelled by dogma to reject artificial methods, these women would soon outbreed the rhythmic ones. If there is even a tiny hereditary element in their irregularity (as there surely must be), natural selection would then ultimately produce a world populated only by irregular women.
Tidings of Darwin should be carried to Rome.

*Blessed are they that share with the improvident, for they shall know the peace of death.*

If we include freedom to breed as one of man's inalienable freedoms, and if we accept the obligation to share excess food with those who are starving, then how can any nation, class, or religious group that responsibly controls its numbers survive in competition with any nation, class, or religious group that refuses to act responsibly?

*Blessed are they that shun reason and praise mercy, for they shall bury those who are both reasonable and merciful.*

*Blessed are they that observe the taboos against speaking the truth, for they shall perish like sitting ducks.*

# 9

## Remarkable Reversal of Time
## at 41°52'N, 12°37'E

### (1968)

*Close scrutiny of recent events in the Vatican reveals that a remarkable scientific phenomenon, whose possibility has often been discussed by cosmologists, has actually occurred. It is now possible to predict with certainty the future course of events in the Church.*

Progress, growth and change in society present problems not so much because growth *per se* is painful as because of the stresses created by differential growth. Some parts grow faster than others. As near as we can estimate, scientific knowledge doubles about every 12 to 15 years. The computer capacity of the world is now said to be doubling every two years. But how fast is law changing? And what about the Church?

Not that anyone would maintain that the volume of legal statutes should double every 15 years, or that the church should do an aboutface every two (God is dead . . . No, he isn't . . . Yes, he is . . . No, he isn't . . . and so on). But neither is there anyone who seriously maintains that law and the church already have all the right answers.

Nowhere is resistance to change more evident than in the Roman Cath-

From *New Scientist*, 39(613):480–482. 128 Long Acre, London WC 2, England. Copyright © 1968.

olic church. When it censured Galileo in 1633, for all practical purposes it asserted that the Sun moves around the Earth. It did not budge from this position until 11 September 1822, when the cardinals of the Holy Inquisition agreed that "the printing and publication of works treating the motion of the Earth and the stability of the Sun . . . is permitted at Rome." An interval of 189 years. About par for the course.

In our day, contraception has replaced astronomy as the truth on which Rome gags. For a short while, during the reign of Pope John XXIII, it seemed as though the church might learn from the Galileo experience. But then John died and was succeeded by Paul. Within a year the Patriarch of Antioch was warning his colleagues: "I beg you, my brothers: let us avoid a new Galileo case. One is enough for the church."

Did Rome hear? With the publication of the encyclical *Humanae Vitae* on 29 July 1968 it became all too clear that Galileo has suffered in vain as far as his church was concerned. How could Paul ignore the lessons of history? Only the church mice know.

It's futile to be indignant. It is better—for our psychic health, if nothing else—to view the goings on in the Vatican as data, which we should study objectively, by scientific means. If more trouble is in store for the world, it can be faced better if it is foreseen.

A most striking characteristic of the Vatican is that time moves there at a different pace than it does in the rest of the world. The phenomena recorded in the Table below make this clear. After his elevation to the throne of Peter, Pope Paul VI took a year deciding to increase the size of the Birth Control Commission set up by his predecessor; during this period the population of the world increased by some 63 million people ("souls" in Rome), roughly equal to the present population of Nigeria. Sixteen more months passed before the Pope decided to attack contraception in public; during this period an increment equal to the population of both East and West Germany was added to the world's population.

And so on. Rome fiddled while the world bred. (D. H. Lawrence would have worded it differently.) After five years Pope Paul finally came up with his never-to-be-forgotten *Humanae Vitae*—"Of Human Life." Completely ignoring the recommendation of a large majority of the 60-man Papal Commission, Paul not only disapproved of "artificial" birth control—he even warned against the too-frequent use of the rhythm method (commonly called "Roman Roulette").

PAPAL PROGRESS MEASURED AGAINST WORLD POPULATION GROWTH

| Date | Event (or non-event) | World population increases by the equivalent of: |
|---|---|---|
| June 1963 | Giovanni Battista Montini becomes Pope Paul VI | |
| June 1964 | Pope increases Birth Control Commission to 60 members | Nigeria |
| October 1965 | At United Nations, in New York, Pope calls contraception "irrational" | East & West Germany |
| March 1966 | Pope creates commission of 16 bishops to review 60-man report | Philippines |
| June 1966 | 16 bishops submit report to Pope | The Congo |
| November 1966 | Pope says he needs more time to study matter; appoints 20-man commission | South Vietnam |
| April 1967 | Report of 60-man commission leaks to press; majority favours change | Poland |
| December 1967 | 20-man commission reports to Pope | Italy |
| 29 July 1968 | Pope issues *Humanae Vitae* (Flourish of trumpets; groans) | Turkey |

(Note: From the time of the Pope's ascension to the issuance of his encyclical the population of the world increased by 328 millions, equal to approximately six United Kingdoms.)

He did, however, speak out unambiguously in favour of chastity.

One of the amazing things about scientific investigation is how hard it is to see the obvious. Darwin, recalling the difficulty he had in seeing a "perfectly obvious" element of his theory of evolution, said: "It is astonishing to me, except on the principle of Columbus and his egg, how I could have overlooked it (for so long)." In a modest way, I have shared in this feeling. When I completed the Table, I stared at it for some time in wonder, viewing it at first as an example of the differential growth of two aspects of society—the sort of thing Sir Julian Huxley has studied under the rubric of "relative growth." Different parts of an animal body develop at different rates at different times; hence a two-month-old human embryo looks strikingly different from an adult. The head of a newborn child is about a fourth as long as the body, instead of a seventh (as in the adult). At any one period, the parts of the body grow at different rates.

Plainly, I said, this Table presents us with an example of differential growth rates in society. Population is growing at one rate; understanding in the church at another. Rates of growth themselves may change. The church eventually caught up with Galileo. We can confidently anticipate that in the future it will catch up with Gregory Pincus and John Rock. To predict the future we may have to calculate second derivatives; or even third derivatives. Or there may be discontinuities or singular points. Theoretical difficulties in predicting the future are great!

Not being a mathematician, I toyed with the idea of looking for a collaborator to attack this question: When will the church catch up with the rest of the world in matters of birth control? . . . Then suddenly, without warning, I recognized Columbus with his egg. Suddenly, I saw that I had been on the wrong track entirely. The answer to the question, "When will the Vatican catch up with the world?" is simply: *Never*. This is not a new Galileo case. It is something more awesome. The Pope is not moving slowly forward. He is not even standing still. *He is moving backward*. The encyclical *Humanae Vitae* is not an announcement that time must have a stop. Instead it is an assertion that Papal thinking has progressed backward to the position of the *Casti Conubii* of 1930—even perhaps a bit earlier, because Pope Pius XI at least said it's all right to play Roman Roulette whereas Paul insists on adding *but not very often*.

We are forced to conclude that a remarkable scientific phenomenon has appeared in the region of the Vatican—a reversal of time. Milne and other cosmologists long ago speculated about this possibility and how we would recognize it. Now, plainly, the unthinkable has happened: time reversal has been observed.

Curiously, it's a very local reversal in time—*very* local indeed, being centred in an elliptical area of about $14 \times 26$ cm, the force of it falling off exponentially with distance from the cerebrum of Giovanni Battista Montini, Pope Paul VI. Without doubt, my discovery is the most exciting development in cosmology since Copernicus.

The causes of the phenomenon are going to be difficult to discover. This will be the labour of ages. We should, however, be able to describe its formal properties now.

We can represent time in the world at large by the conventional symbol *t*, and time in the Vatican as *V*. We have two firm "fixes":

$$t_{1963} = V_{1963}$$
$$t_{1968} = V_{1930}$$

The first fix is a charitable one and can be justified methodologically as following the Law of Parsimony. The second fix is factual, and conservatively estimated.

In the most general terms,

$$V = f(-t) \tag{1}$$

i.e., Vatican time is some sort of negative function of world time. What kind of function? An exponential function? A power function? If so, what power? Here we are, for the moment, stopped. We need one more fix, one more point on our curve. Pope Paul will no doubt furnish us with another fix sooner or later; but in the meantime, can we make any educated guess of the analytical relationship between $t$ and $V$?

I think we can—if we take seriously the insights of the poet. Let us, in imagination, project ourselves forward to the year 2000 or beyond and imagine that we are interested in reading about the history of the Roman church in the twentieth century. Let us imagine that we have been referred to the definitive history of that institution, written by the Edward Gibbon of the twenty-first century. What is the title of this work? We can hardly predict the *exact* title; but, with the eye of the poet, we can confidently predict that somewhere in its title there occurs the word *Fall*. This poetic insight points the way to the resolution of our analytical difficulties.

What does the poetic word "Fall" suggest to a scientist? . . . The phrase "free fall" leaps to the mind. Let us, then, assume that Vatican time is falling freely away from world time, i.e., the relation between the two, as derived by the calculus, is:

$$V = -\tfrac{1}{2}\, at^2 \tag{2}$$

If we take 1963 as the origin of the coordinates, then when

$$t = + \cdot 5 \text{ (i.e., 1968)}, V = -33 \text{ (i.e., 1930)}.$$

$$-33 = -\tfrac{1}{2}a(5)^2$$

Solving for $a$:

$$a = (-33)(-\tfrac{2}{25})$$

which gives us the equation we seek:

$$V = -1.3t^2 \tag{3}$$

The means whereby we have derived this equation are admittedly somewhat unorthodox, involving as they do a transmigration from the mathematical realm to the poetic, and a subsequent migration back again. The procedure is, however, justifiable with complete rigour. Percy Bysshe Shelley said that "Poets are the unacknowledged legislators of the world." The business of legislatures is the making (or discovery) of laws. Laws may be either man-made statutes or man-discovered Natural Laws, which are the business of scientists. It follows that the discovery of scientific laws is the legitimate business of poets. Therefore the poetic induction of the idea of the Fall of Rome, and the mathematical deduction of its quantitative consequences, are completely justified. Since the logic is impeccably Thomistic we may, in all modesty, assert that the conclusion is infallible.

The acid test of a scientific theory is its ability to predict. If equation (3) is true, it should predict the future backward progression of the papal intelligence. Time will tell. We'll just have to wait and see.

One particular future intersection of world time and Vatican time is of more than ordinary interest. The future, whether it lies ahead (as it does for $t$) or behind (as it does for $V$), can never be predicted, but it can be invented—as Dennis Gabor has so penetratingly pointed out. Just recently, Franz Cardinal Koenig of Vienna has indicated that the church is seriously considering a retrial of Galileo. In Gaborian terms, the revitalized church is on the verge of (re)inventing Galileo. With this hint of the church's intensions we can devise a critical test for our theory.

The date of the first trial of Galileo, 1633, was at $V = -330$, if we take 1963 as the origin of the coordinates. What is the value of world time for this date?

$$V = -1.3t^2$$

$$-330 = -1.3t^2$$

$$t^2 = \frac{-330}{-1.3}$$

$$t^2 = 254$$

$$t = 15.9$$

Within the bounds of observational error we can say that $t = 16$. In the year 1979 (i.e., 1963 + 16) we can, if our theory is correct, expect to see the second trial of Galileo. In this year, the mortal body of Paul VI will be just 82-years-old—the very prime of life for one in his profession. The date inside the magisterial cerebrum will then be 1633. A vintage year.

And what will be the outcome of the Second Galileo trial? No one knows. But I would like to indicate where I think the balance of probabilities lies by first owning up to an ambition I have long nourished in my bosom.

Legend has it that Thales of Miletos, foreseeing a bountiful olive harvest, contracted in advance for all the oil presses of the region. When the predicted bounty materialized, Thales became a rich man from the subleasing of the presses. Thus did he demonstrate to a materialistic world that a man of science is quite capable of making money if he wants to.

I should like to follow in Thales' footsteps. I hereby announce that if any of my colleagues are so naive as to think that Galileo's second trial will result in his exoneration by the Church, I shall be more than happy to cover any bets they might care to make.

# 10

## *Learning to Say Nothing*

The "Remarkable Reversal of Time . . ." was written, of course, out of
annoyance with Pope Paul's retrograde encyclical, *Humanae Vitae*. It
was, I suppose, an attempt to guard against personal paranoia (an occupational disease of reformers) by making fun of things. The style was paro-
chial, the parish physics. Those whose education is restricted to the
humanities no doubt found the humor forced; but many scientists have
told me they enjoyed it. Following the publication of this *scherzo* in a
British journal a reader from Devon, H. W. Heckstall-Smith, entered into
the spirit of things and calculated that the Second Coming of Christ
would occur in 2002 A.D. In contrast, the Vicar of Keyingham (East
Yorkshire), the Reverend D. E. Ashforth, wrote to the editor: "I am sad-
dened to see you descend to the level of printing Professor G. Hardin's
scurrilous attack on the Pope." It had not occurred to me that I was being
scurrilous, so I consulted a dictionary and found that this adjective seems
to come from the Etruscan word *scurra*, a buffoon. Perhaps my piece was
buffoonlike. Anyway, I sent a copy of it to the Vatican where it evoked
the response appropriate to most statements made by buffoons: silence.

Looking backward now I am thankful that these two caprices evoked
no other reaction. Had they been taken seriously they would, I think,

only have harmed the cause for which I struggled, the importation of rationality into the realm of birth control and population control. If effective at all, my articles would have been counterproductive for a tactical reason: the writer was on the outside of an internecine battle that was progressing quite satisfactorily enough without his well-intentioned but misguided help.

During the late 50's and 60's a revolution got under way within the Roman Catholic Church, a revolution to modernize its intellectual and moral commitments. Devout members of the Church were criticizing it as strongly as Protestants had criticized it a decade earlier, as can be seen (for instance) in a collection of statements by Catholics published in 1964 under the title *Objections to Roman Catholicism.*

What I did not sufficiently appreciate was the counterproductiveness of interference in a family quarrel by someone outside the family. Such an attack, if noticed, is all too likely to unite the family in a common cause. Fortunately my attacks were not noticed, and the lay members of the Church continued the internal battle, producing, in a decade, an amount of change that was astonishing.

The moral (and it's as old as the hills): there are times when it's best to say nothing.

# 11

## *Vulnerability—the Strength of Science*

### *(1976)*

More than half a century has passed since the Scopes "monkey trial" took place in Dayton, Tennessee, and still science is beleaguered. Legislatures are urged to suppress at the source all attempts to point out the human implications of evolution and anthropology. Opposition to science brings together strange bedfellows: fundamentalists who worship the Bible (but don't understand it), political authoritarians who fear change, and youthful anarchists who think they want nothing but change. How long can science survive such attacks?

If science dies, its death (like all deaths) will be partly suicide. Science is a subtle art, and transmitting it from one generation to another is subject to entropic losses. It is easier to pass on the conclusions of science than it is the means by which those conclusions were reached. Critics of science charge scientists with dogmatism. In truth, there is some merit in the charge: the champions of science are sometimes needlessly inflexible. Scientists who volunteer to confront the opponents in public should first reread act III, scene 2 of *Julius Caesar*.

We can hardly be in a less favorable position than Mark Antony at the

From *The American Biology Teacher*, 38(8):465. Copyright 1976.

beginning of the scene. In an act of skillful one-upmanship, Brutus graciously gives Antony leave to speak. And how does Antony respond? Not as Brutus expected, by an argumentative defense of the dead. Instead, like a judo master yielding in order to overcome, Mark Antony begins by saying "I come to bury Caesar, not to praise him," thus depriving a hostile audience of its psychological resistances.

The science that our opponents oppose is (they say) dogmatic science. If that is so, surely we can join hands with them in burying this kind of science.

*To win you must be willing to lose:* this is the central principle of the art of disputation. Our chances of persuading others are greatest when we convince the audience that we are willing to lose if our arguments are without merit.

Adopting this stance is good tactics, of course; but it is much more. All scientific conclusions are tentative: it is only recently that we fully realized how tentative. For this recognition, the philospher Karl Popper, more than anyone else, is responsible. If by the word "prove" we mean *certainly* prove, in a deterministic sense, then we must admit that we never prove anything in science. We can merely disprove—sometimes. What is left is science. To have any science at all we must generate falsifiable statements and have nothing to do with statements that are not falsifiable. Science is inherently vulnerable. It is proudly so.

By contrast, the antiscientific mind dares not risk refutation; it builds its world-systems out of nonfalsifiable statements. In the past some antiscientists have explained the properties of living things by postulating a "vital spirit" as cause; others have explained the phenomena of adaptation by an "entelechy." The concepts were so defined that they were immune to falsification by observations. They were not science.

When a critic of science triumphantly asserts that evolution has never been *proved* we should promptly and cheerfully agree with him. We should point out that the theory of evolution is implicitly based on a large collection of falsifiable statements. In its historical aspects evolution could be falsified by (for example) finding the bones of a bird in undisturbed Devonian strata. On the experimental side, it could be falsified by showing that a many-generation exposure of mosquitoes to DDT makes the insects more, rather than less, sensitive to the poison.

But where in the creationist theory are the falsifiable statements? No doubt there are some: but notice what this implies. As rapidly as falsifiable statements were identified they would be tested against reality. Those that failed to pass the test would, we presume, be rejected by the creationists (who understandably would not want to be caught out with demonstrably false beliefs). But the falsifiable statements that survived rigorous testing would become part of the body of science and so could not be used for making a *distinction* between the creationist and the scientific views of the origin of species.

So what would be left as the distinctive component of creationist theory? Only this: a collection of nonfalsifiable statements. And that is not science.

*The distinction between science and nonscience is one not of fact but of method.* Scientists welcome vulnerability. Others may reject it; if they do, what they produce is not science, and we should say so. Science has no quarrel with nonscience: there is simply no communication between the two worlds. Perhaps nonscience should be included in public education; that is for the public to decide. But it should not, out of a perverse sense of fairness, be taught in classes labeled "science."

It is a paradox of human existence that intellectual approaches claiming the greatest certainty have produced fewer practical benefits and less secure understanding than has science, which freely admits the inescapable uncertainty of its conclusions. We must not only admit this: we must proclaim it from the housetops. At the same time we should point to the immense fruitfulness of science. Science shares with judo a justified faith in controlled vulnerability. No one has expressed the wonder of this juxtaposition of vulnerability and power better than the mathematician Clarence R. Wylie, Jr., in his poem "Paradox," a sonnet that can, in my humble but no doubt biased opinion, stand up with the best of Shakespeare and Wordsworth:

> Not truth, nor certainty. These I foreswore
> In my novitiate, as young men called
> To holy orders must abjure the world.
> "If . . . , then . . . ," this only I assert;
> And my successes are but pretty chains
> Linking twin doubts, for it is vain to ask
> If what I postulate be justified,
> Or what I prove possess the stamp of fact.

Yet bridges stand, and men no longer crawl
In two dimensions. And such triumphs stem
In no small measure from the power this game,
Played with the thrice-attenuated shades
Of things, has over their originals.
How frail the wand, but how profound the spell!

# PART THREE: TECHNOLOGY

# 12

## The Semantics of "Space"

### (1966)

The space effort is founded on irony: the most sophisticated scientific-technological effort ever made is repeatedly supported by a total rejection of rationality. Asked why we should try to get to the moon, President Kennedy quoted the words used by George Mallory when he was asked why he wanted to climb Mount Everest: "Because it is there." [1]

As an explanation, this is a perfect panchreston—an explain-all that fits all cases equally well. [2] Is there anything in the world that is not at some "there"? Obviously not. Since Mallory's phrase explains all cases, it explains none.

Lloyd V. Berkner, former Chairman of the Space Science Board of the National Academy of Sciences, has a simple explanation of our behavior: "Man prizes the idea of escape from the earth as the highest symbol of progress." [3] Who is this *man* Berkner speaks of? Me? I deny it. You? I doubt it. Is it the unemployed, the unemployable, the impoverished, the hunger-stricken, or the resentful victim of race-discrimination? Has Berkner asked these people? But perhaps we should ignore them on the grounds that they are not interested in progress.

From *ETC.*, 23:167–171. Copyright © 1966.

There is a lovely Freudian slip in Berkner's statement: the word *escape*. It suggests that the space effort is a fantastic form of escapism. Escape from the necessity of solving earthly problems. And who is the *man* who prizes this escape? The speaker, of course. But we are not required to imitate him.

"All of us," said George Eliot, "get our thoughts entangled in metaphors, and act fatally on the strength of them."[4] Consider these lovely verbal spider webs:

"Outer space is fast becoming the heart and soul of advanced military science."[5]

"The moon, because of its low gravity and lack of atmosphere, is a 'Panama Canal' to the riches of the deep space 'Pacific' beyond."[6]

"The creative forces of modern science and technology, through which man is beginning to realize some of his finest powers of reason and constructive ability, are now moving like the breakup of an Arctic river in the spring. . . . The changes have accelerated, so that today we seem about to witness a major loosening of the ice jam of our intellectual past."[7]

What ice jam? Evidently the ice jam created by poor Newton, Faraday, Gauss, Darwin, Mendel, Hopkins, Einstein, von Neumann, and Gödel. Bunglers all.

The path to space is strewn with Class III truths[8]—truths that cease to be truths upon being verbalized. "All Cretans are liars, and I am a Cretan" is a Class III truth. So also are all statements about the "unthinkable."

Speaking of research into space, Frederick Seitz, President of the National Academy of Sciences, said: "It is unthinkable that our society, particularly Western society, can ignore this challenge."[9]

But, my dear Dr. Seitz, you have just thought the unthinkable. . . . Shall we dance?

> The tendency to expand the realm of human knowledge and power without question is deeply fundamental in human nature. Any infringement or abandonment of this primal urge would cut deep into the roots of man's very being.

Therefore, since survival is the issue, man has no choice but to keep on expanding his fund of knowledge and command of his environment. Freedom of will is not involved here. Man's very nature will not permit him to truncate or mutilate a process of development already a hundred thousand years in progress.

Man's unfolding would be aborted only by some mortal disease of the spirit. But among the majority of human beings, and especially among the young, there is no sign of this.

It can be said without fear of contradiction that in obedience to the very laws of his existence, man will reach out as a matter of course to know, and establish dominion over, the realm of space, as he has done over earth.

Always we human beings have tried to know what could be known. And it would be unnatural and unworthy of the human race, even barbarous, if suddenly we should balk at unraveling the most enticing of all nature's mysteries when opportunity offers through space science.[10]

The strategy of this argument of Eugen Sänger's is interesting. In some states the highway patrol officer is compelled by law to write the license number of the offending vehicle on a numbered ticket *before* he speaks to the driver. Since the officer must account for all his tickets, he is now helpless to tear up the ticket. He *must* hand it in (though he may check a lesser offense). "I would if I could—but I can't." From impotence, invulnerability.

The secret ballot similarly converts weakness into strength. "I would glady sell you my vote for fifty dollars—but I'm powerless to prove that I won't doublecross you. So sorry."

*"Man has no choice* but to keep on expanding his fund of knowledge and command of his environment," says Sänger. "Man's very nature . . . in obedience to the very laws of his existence. . . ."

*"Man has no choice . . . ."* If I unconsciously assume that this is a Class I truth, a scientific truth, then it will be a Class II truth, a self-fulfilling postulate, because I believe it. But if I see through the strategic ruse and identify the assertion of impotence as a would-be Class II truth, then it becomes a Class III truth by the operation of Freudian negation.

"We never discover a 'No' in the unconscious," said Freud.[11] The moment we say we have no choice, we acknowledge that we have. Thus is the unthinkable thought.

"The road to the stars," says Arthur C. Clarke, "has been discovered none too soon. Civilization cannot exist without new frontiers; it needs them both physically and spiritually. The physical need is obvious—new lands, new resources, new materials. The spiritual need is less apparent, but in the long run it is more important. We do not live by bread alone; we need adventure, variety, novelty, romance."[12]

Brave words, these. *Adventure . . . variety . . . novelty . . . romance. . . .* Six pages later we find: "Weightlessness will open up novel and hitherto unexpected realms of erotica."

For that, we lay out five billion dollars a year?

"Science," says Dennis Gabor, "has never quite given man what he desired, not even applied science. Man dreamt of wings; science gave him an easy chair which flies through the air. Man wanted to see things invisible and afar (ask any psychoanalyst what he wanted to see most); he got television and can look inside a studio"[13]—and see cigarette ads.

Wanting space is the strangest desire of all. How can I *possess* space? I am either *here . . .* or *there.* If I am *here,* why should I want *there?* Is it worth twenty billion dollars? Two hundred billion? (Please don't quote Mallory—not again. Not for two hundred billion.)

Wanting space, we get—what?

Can we get anything we happen to want? Can we traverse the light-years between stars? *Yes,* says Clarke: "Many conservative scientists, appalled by these cosmic gulfs, have denied that they can ever be crossed. Some people never learn; those who sixty years ago scoffed at the possibility of flight, and ten (even five!) years ago laughed at the idea of travel to the planets, are now quite sure that the stars will always be beyond our reach. And again they are wrong, for they have failed to grasp the great lesson of our age—that if something is possible in theory, and no fundamental scientific laws oppose its realization, then sooner or later it will be achieved."[14]

The form of the argument is interesting. Fred Gruenberger has referred to it as the *Fulton non sequitur:* "The true crackpot can frequently be spotted on this test alone. He proceeds with an argument like this: 'They laughed at Fulton. He was right. They're laughing at me. *Therefore,* I must be an equal genius." [15]

The sad fact is that the laughter does not prove I'm *not* Fulton, either. There is nothing in the logical form of the argument to reveal who I am.

But: *would you like to bet?*

# 13

## *Interstellar Migration and the Population Problem*

### *(1959)*

Anyone who discusses population problems with lay audiences is, sooner or later, confronted with questions of this sort: "But why worry about overpopulation? Won't we soon be able to send our surplus population to other planets?" It is not only the audience that adopts this point of view; sometimes the lecturer does, as appears from an Associated Press dispatch of 6 June 1958. Monsignor Irving A. DeBlanc, director of the National Catholic Welfare Conference's Family Life Bureau is reported as favoring such mass migration, "deploring an often expressed idea that birth control is the only answer to problems created by a fast-growing world population."

Neither physicists nor professional demographers have, so far as I know, recommended extra-terrestrial migration as a solution to the population problem, but the idea appears to be gaining ground among the laity even without scientific support. The psychological reasons for embracing this idea are two. On the one hand, some Roman Catholics welcome it because it appears to offer an escape from the dilemma created by the Church's stand against "artificial" methods of birth control. On the other

From *Journal of Heredity*, 50:68–70. 1959.

hand, citizens of all churches worship the new religion called Progress, of which Jules Verne is the prophet. In this religion all things are possible (except acceptance of the impossible). Who is to set limits to Science (with a capital *S*)? Yesterday, the telephone and the radio; today television and ICBM's; and tomorrow,—Space!—which will solve all our earthly problems, of course.

This is heady stuff. Strictly speaking, since it springs from an essentially religious feeling and is non-rational it cannot be answered by a rational argument. Nevertheless, for the sake of those bystanders whose minds are still open to a rational analysis it is worthwhile reviewing the facts and principles involved in the proposal to solve the population problem by interplanetary travel.

## The Cost of Space Travel

It now seems possible that, before the century is out, manned landings may be made on Venus or Mars, with the establishment of temporary quarters thereon. But all evidence points to the unsuitability of these, or any other planets of our sun, as abodes for *Homo sapiens*. We must, therefore, look beyond the solar system, to other stars for possible planets for colonization.

The nearest star is Alpha Centauri, which is 4.3 light-years away. How long would it take us to get there? The rockets that we are now planning to send to the moon will have a maximum velocity in the neighborhood of 10 kilometers per second, or about 19,000 miles per hour. This may sound fast. But a body traveling at such a speed towards Alpha Centauri (which is $4.07 \times 10^{13}$ kilometers distant) would require 129,000 years to reach its destination. Surely no one believes that a fleet of spaceships with so long a transit time would solve our explosive population problem. The question is, then, what is the probability of improvements in space travel that would significantly cut down the time required to make such an interstellar journey? In trying to answer this question I have relied on an analysis by L. R. Shepherd,[1] to which the interested reader is referred for technical details.

Shepherd presumes a technology in the release and utilization of nuclear energy that may take several centuries to achieve. To give the worshippers of Progress the maximum advantage we will assume that such an advance technology is available *now,* and see how long it would take to travel to the nearest star. Using fantastically optimistic assumptions, Shepherd calculates that it might be possible to make the transit in a mere 350 years. The average speed of the trip would be about 7,000,000 m.p.h., though the maximum speed would be somewhat more, since 50 years would be required for acceleration at the beginning of the trip and another 50 years for deceleration at the end. (In passing, it should be noted that acceleration is more of a limiting factor than is velocity.)

To evaluate interstellar migration as a population control measure we must examine its economics. Here the unknowns are obviously great, but from data assembled by A. V. Cleaver[2] it appears that the foreseeable cost of a rocket ship could hardly be as little as $50 a pound, assuming economies of mass production and allowing nothing for research and development costs. How many pounds of ship would be required per man? Since we have no data on such a spaceship, let us borrow from our knowledge of atomic submarines, which are perhaps not too dissimilar. A spaceship designed to be self-maintaining for 350 years could hardly be less complicated or less bulky than an underwater craft capable of operating away from its depots for only a month or two. According to a news release[3] the submarine *Seawolf* weighs 3,000 tons and carries 100 men, a burden of 60,000 lbs. per man. A spaceship of a similar design, at $50 a pound, would cost $3,000,000 per man travelling in it. Would this be a reasonable cost for solving the population problem? Those who propose such a solution presume, or even recommend, that we do not alter our present reproductive habits. What would it cost to keep the population of the United States fixed at its present level by shipping off the surplus in spaceships?

According to a recent estimate of the U. S. Bureau of the Census[4] our population is increasing by about 3,000,000 people per year. To ship this increase off to other planets would, on the above conservative assumptions, cost about 9,000 billion dollars per year. The Gross National Product is now nearly 450 billion dollars per year. In other words, to solve our national population problem by this means we would, then, have to spend 20 times as much as our entire income on this purpose alone, allowing nothing for any other use, not even for food. It would surely be unrealistic to suppose that we shall do this in the near future.

Another aspect of the population problem is worth commenting on. Many philanthropically minded citizens feel that it is an obligation of the United States to solve the population problems of the entire world, believing that we should use the riches produced by our technology to make up for the deficiencies in luck or foresight of other peoples. Let's examine the economics of so doing. According to a recent estimate[5] the population of the world is increasing at a rate of 123,000 per day. To remove one day's increment by the postulated spaceship would cost about 369 billion dollars. In other words, we Americans, by cutting our standard of living down to 18 percent of its present level, could in *one year's time* set aside enough capital to finance the exportation of *one day's increase* in the population of the entire world. Such a philanthropic desire to share the wealth may be judged noble in intent, but hardly in effect.

In passing, it should be noted that we have so far made no mention of certain assumptions that are of critical importance in the whole picture. We have assumed that our nearest star has planets; that at least one of these planets is suitable for human habitation; that this suitable planet is uninhabited—or, if inhabited, that the humanoids thereon will gracefully commit suicide when they find we need their planet for our *Lebensraum*. (The tender feelings that would make impossible the control of reproduction on earth would presumably not interfere with the destruction of life on other planets.) Should Alpha Centauri have no planet available for migratory earthlings, our expedition would presumably set out for an even more distant star, perhaps eventually becoming a latterday interstellar Flying Dutchman.

## Paradoxes of Space Emigration

Cogent as the economic analysis of the problem is, it does not touch on issues that are of even greater importance. Consider the human situation on board this astronautical Mayflower. For 350 years the population would have to live under conditions of complete sociological stasis, the like of which has never been known before. No births would be permitted, except to replace the dead (whose substance would, of course, have to be returned to the common stores). Marriages would certainly have to be controlled, as would all other social interactions, and with an iron hand. In the spaceship, Progress would be unendurable. The social organization would have to persist unchanged for 10 generations' time, otherwise there would be the risk that some of the descendants of the original crew might wish to change the plans. It would be as though the spaceship had to set sail, so to speak, under Captain John Smith and arrive at its goal under President Eisenhower, without the slightest change in ideas or ideals. Can we who have so recently seen how fragile and mutable a flower Education is suppose that we could set up so stable a system of indoctrination? Paradoxically, only a people who worship Progress would propose to launch such a craft, but such worshippers would be the worst possible passengers for it.

Those who seriously propose interstellar migration as a solution to overpopulation do so because they are unwilling to accept the necessity of consciously controlling population numbers by means already at hand. They are unwilling to live, or to admit living, in a closed universe. Yet— and here is the second paradox—that is precisely the sort of universe the interstellar migrants would be confined to, for some 10 generations. Since the present annual rate of growth of the world's population is 1.7 percent,[6] by the time the first ship arrived at its destination, the whole fleet of spaceships en route would enclose a total population six times as large as that still present on the earth. That is, in attempting to escape the necessities of living in a closed universe, we would confine to the closed universes of spaceships a population six times as great as that of the earth.

Moreover, there would be a differential element in the emigration from the mother planet. The proposal to emigrate is made by those who, for religious or other reasons, are unwilling to curb the reproductive proclivities of mankind. But not for such as these is the kingdom of a spaceship. They must stay behind while the ship is manned by those whose temperament creates no need for emigration. The reproductively prudent would be exiled from a world made unbearably crowded by the imprudent— who would stay home to perpetuate the problem into the next generation. Whether the difference between the two groups is basically biological, or merely sociological, would not matter. In either case, natural selection would enter in. The end result of this selective emigration would be to create an earth peopled only by men and women unwilling to control their breeding, and unwilling, therefore, to make use of the very means they propose to escape the consequences.

The proposal to eliminate overpopulation by resort to interstellar migration is thus seen to yield not a rational solution at all. The proposal is favored only by men who have more faith in gadgetry than they do in rationality. Should men of this temper prevail, and should the gadgetry prove equal to the quantitative demands put upon it, the result would nevertheless be the ultimate production of a world in which the only remaining controls of population would be the "misery and vice" foreseen by Malthus 161 years ago.

# 14

## *A Rapout of O'Neill's Dream*

### *(1976)*

[In the mid-1970's Gerald O'Neill, a physics professor at Princeton, came up with a scheme for solving the population problem by creating giant space platforms to "hang" between the earth and the moon, held there by the balanced gravitational attractions. His scheme was presented before Congressional committees and described in numerous popular articles. A good description can be found in the *CoEvolution Quarterly*, No. 8, Winter 1975. The editor of the journal solicited critical comments by many people, which were published in No. 9, Spring 1976. The following essay is from that issue.]

Sure and it's an intoxicating vision Gerard O'Neill has given us, the dream of creating a shiny new world all of our own out toward the moon. How nice it would be to escape earth's population problems! But we had better be wary of intoxication, even by 100 Proof Technology. The trip may not be worth the hangover.

The image fails. This hangover would come before the trip—which probably would never take place. Let me explain why.

I'm not going to spend any time on the technical details, though I think Brother O'Neill has overlooked a few things. But he's done a pretty good job. An exciting job. Let's not carp at trivia.

On the economic side I think his vision fails. We must always measure proposals like his against Hitch's Rule, which says that a new enterprise always costs from two to twenty times as much as the most careful official estimate. The more exotic the technology, the greater the cost overruns. O'Neill's space colonies are so exotic that the cost will surely go beyond Hitch's Rule.

So what? We're rich, aren't we? Yes, but not infinitely rich. For awhile, the cost of mammoth public works can be met by normal (though painful) adjustments in the economic system. But at a certain level, corrective feedbacks fail and the system goes into the destructive positive feedback mode. Uncontrollable inflation takes over; prices and taxes spiral upward out of reach. Attempts to evade the flopover point of the economic system introduce new evils.

History has something to tell us. In the 16th century the Papacy became intoxicated by the dream of building a monumental new Saint Peter's in Rome. Hitch's Rule soon ran the cost out of sight, and the Church had to finance the project by the sale of "indulgences"—advance forgiveness of sins yet to be committed. Parish priests pushed indulgences with all the subtlety of second-hand car salesmen on Saturday night television. Resentment of the hard sell led to the Reformation, and the Church never recovered its temporal power.

O'Neill says his space program will cost hundreds of billions of dollars. Applying Hitch's Rule we can be sure it will cost thousands of billions. Would such a venture push the economic system past the flopover point? Would O'Neill's space stations be civilization's Saint Peter's?

But there is a more serious criticism to be made. Let us, for the sake of argument, grant all of Professor O'Neill's technological and economic assumptions. The space station has now been completed. It is ready for occupancy. Question: Who is going to be permitted to move in?

Because of our powerful (though recently developed) tradition of integrating minority groups it is obvious that the complement of the spaceship would, if it were U.S. controlled, have to include blacks, whites, Puerto Ricans, Chicanos, Indians from Wounded Knee, Wallaceites, American Legionnaires, Weathermen and members of the Symbionese Liberation Army. If the emigrants were drawn from the whole world they would have to include Moslems, Hindus, Irish from both Belfast and Dublin, Greeks, Turks, Israeli, Arabs, Lebanese and Palestinians.

Some of the groups just mentioned are races, some are religions, some are political groups. It doesn't matter. Generically we can call them all *tribes,* where a tribe is defined as a group whose members pursue one code of ethics in their in-group relationships, and another code for their out-group.

A libration point spaceship is a precision instrument, far more delicate in its construction and far more vulnerable to sabotage than is our massive earth. How could such a fragile craft withstand the buffeting of warring tribes?

Paradoxically, the creators of such a spaceship would be psychologically least suited to be its permanent inhabitants. The Professor O'Neills of the world might make brief visits and inspection tours, but they could not tolerate the sort of life that permanent residents would have to pursue there. People of great originality and independence of spirit would be intolerable in the spaceship community, particularly if they belonged to different tribes.

For a libration point colony to survive it would have to have only one tribe on it. (This is a necessary but not sufficient condition, for even an initially uniform tribe may differentiate in time.) This means that the political system of the spaceship must include progress-stopping features from the first day people go on board. This means totalitarianism.

What group would be most suitable for this most recent Brave New World? Probably a religious group. There must be unity of thought and the acceptance of discipline. But the colonists couldn't be a bunch of Unitarians or Quakers, for these people regard the individual conscience as the best guide to action. Space colony existence would require something more like the Hutterites or the Mormons for its inhabitants. Scientists and college professors would, as residents, be disastrous.

The peopling of a spaceship creates an ironic problem for a society like ours. We worship "integration" and consent to forced diversification via "affirmative action." But integration could not be risked on this delicate vessel, for fear of sabotage and terrorism. Only "purification" would do.

How could we possibly sell a purification program to our people? If residence on a libration point colony was regarded as a plus, then every tribe would demand the right to live there. If it was regarded as a minus, no tribe would consent to be made the sacrificial goat. It seems unlikely that precisely one tribe would view residence as a plus, and all others see it as a minus. Yet that is what it would take to make a selective residence system work.

Let's go back to fundamentals. What was the motivation for this space colony proposal anyway? It was just this: to solve earth's population problems. But there is another way to do this: institute political controls of population here, setting and enforcing limits to the size of families. Technologically, this would be easy; politically, we haven't the foggiest notion how to do it. (We all are appalled by the thought of "a policeman under every bed.")

The principal attraction of the space colony proposal is that it apparently permits us to escape the necessity of political control. But, as we have just seen, this is only an apparent escape. In fact, because of the super-vulnerability of the spaceship to sabotage by tribal action, the most rigid political control would have to be instituted from the outset in the selection of the inhabitants and in their governance thereafter. So the whole project fails by reason of a pair of paradoxes. (1) The people who can conceive of this clever solution cannot be part of it. (2) The reasons for seeking the solution—refusal to accept political control—require that the solution be rejected.

What has just been carried out is an exercise in futurology. Every discipline has its distinctive techniques. We have just uncovered what is—or should be—a basic technique of futurology. Let me spell out the details.

In Euclidean geometry there is a technique called the *Reductio ad Absurdum* proof. A question is settled once and for all if it can be shown that the necessary assumptions lead to a logical absurdity (as that A both is, and is not, equal to B at the same time). A *Reductio ad Absurdum* proof is of overriding power; it puts an end to further investigation. (The only exception: one can look for errors in the proof itself.)

In futurology we have just seen the workings of a *Reductio ad Paradoxum*—let's call it RAP for short. If the very means of "solving" a problem thwarts the reason for using those means, then the "solution" is no solution. RAP overrides all other approaches—fancy technology, computer readouts and whatnot. O'Neill's colonies run right up against a political *rapout*. There is no need to look further into problems of technical feasibility once we understand the political rapout.

Will this explication of the rapout put an end to the dream of libration point colonies? Most unlikely. Near the end of the 20th century we still have the Flat Earthers with us. From now on we will no doubt have the Librationists too. O'Neill may have given birth to a new religion.

People don't like to have their dream-balloons punctured. The rapout here explained was first presented (not quite so explicitly) in a paper I published in the *Journal of Heredity* fifteen years before O'Neill's proposal. In my 1959 paper I criticized an earlier escapist proposal that was rather similar to O'Neill's. The way my paper was noticed was significant. My cost estimate, a minimum of three million dollars per emigrant from the earth, was frequently quoted. But the *Reductio ad Paradoxum* analysis was (so far as I know) never mentioned. Yet any cost estimate is only tentative, whereas a rapout is final and decisive.

Why should the least decisive result be cited while the most decisive one is ignored? I suspect it is because of our rather decent underlying love of "fair play." A decisive argument stops the game; so we pretend we never heard it, thus permitting the argument—now pointless—to go on. Our behavior does credit to our hearts, but not to our minds. If embarking on a hopelessly escapist program leads to the downfall of a civilization, a mere sense of fair play will be a poor excuse for having closed our eyes to the practical implications of a rapout.

# 15

## *The Insanity of the SST*

### *(1970)*

[The proposal to develop a commercial supersonic transport plane (an SST) seems to be impervious to logic and experience. From the beginning it has been attacked with a vigor far beyond that accorded any other major innovation save nuclear energy. Americans were urged to support the SST to keep other nations from getting a head start in the technology of the future. As it turned out Russia, and then France and England jointly, did beat us, but their priority turned out to be a head start to failure. The Russian SST, after a few years of flying, seems to be grounded permanently; the Concorde is kept aloft only by continued infusions of money by the French and British governments, which panic at the thought of losing face—and thus lose face.

One might suppose that such experiences would move those minds that are unable to understand systematic analysis, but they do not. Of course there are immense profits to be gained by a few people if an SST is funded by the American government: the Boeing company in the state of Washington will be the principal beneficiary. The prospect of gain produced immense pressure to permit landings of the Concorde in the United

From *The Bulletin of the Atomic Scientists*, 26(1):17–20. Copyright © 1970.

States in order to get people used to SSTs. During the last days of President Ford's administration the Secretary of Transportation, William Coleman, approved landings of the Concorde at the Washington Dulles airport for a trial period of sixteen months. This delayed the final decision until the next administration, which proved to be Carter's. The new president had a reputation for being more concerned than his predecessor about the environment—his concern could hardly have been less!—but his first choice for Coleman's successor raised doubts. As "Pot Shots", a syndicated newspaper feature put it: "Proposed Transportation Secretary Brock Adams is from the great state of Boeing. If you thought the last secretary favored the SST, you ain't seen nothin'."

One of the remarkable features of the SST controversy is the way in which the proponents refuse to discuss fundamental economic matters. Their arguments employ only a truncated economics in which only gains (such as the wages of workers) are mentioned, never losses. Mostly the promoters just wave the flag of (presumed) national honor, repeating monotonously, "You can't stop Progress."

I attempted to break the taboo in an article entitled "To Trouble a Star: the Cost of Intervention in Nature." What follows is the last half of this piece, with minor changes and corrections. The economic argument developed here has not been refuted or even responded to: evidently economics is a tabooed subject in the business community when its practical conclusions are inconvenient.]

I think one of the few predictions that we can confidently make as we move into the 1970s is that economic analysis is going to become ecologized; or perhaps we should say ecology will engulf economics. Whether ecologists will become economists or vice versa is of only secondary importance. What is important is that the more inclusive science will encompass the less inclusive, which has proved too narrow a base for carrying out cost-benefit analyses.

It is interesting that the roots of the words "ecology" and "economics" are similar. The first part of the two words comes from the Greek *oikos,* meaning house or home. Both studies have something to do with a house or household. *Logos* means words or discourse and by tradition is used to indicate any field of study. So ecology is the study of households—or perhaps, in modern terminology, we should say of orderly or organized systems. The second part of the word "economics" comes from the Greek *nomos*, which means law or custom. Economics might be defined as the study of the *customary* arrangements of a system.

It would be indefensible to claim that the etymological difference between the two words sprang from a profound perception of the distinction between the two fields. Nevertheless, by accident as it were, the names are unusually apt. Economics, as it has been practiced by most economists since the time of Adam Smith, has had as its purlieu the customary arrangements of systems. The systems in question have been the subsystems of individual business enterprises. Those who paid the piper called the tune. With some exceptions, economists have assumed that "whatever is, is right," to quote William Graham Sumner, who was quoting Alexander Pope. Ecology, neither so fortunate nor so unfortunate as to have patrons, has taken a larger view. The ecologist studies all inputs and outputs, regardless of who pays for them or who benefits by them. In the past, the ecological eye has been focused only on nonhuman economic situations. The focus is now changing as ecology engulfs economics.

Logic dictates this engulfment, but logic alone does not determine history. Power relationships also must be favorable. I think the power relationships now favor a change. In the past, economics was to a large extent the handmaiden of business. The vast majority of economists were either employed directly by businesses, or had jobs in university departments of economics that were unusually sensitive to business interests. In recent decades, the steady increase in the number of economists employed by governmental and quasi-governmental agencies points toward the day when the tunes played by economists will be different. A different sector of society is paying the piper. Whether this means that economists will enjoy greater intellectual independence is not clear and may well be doubted. However, the shift in the balance of power should favor the development of a broadly ecological view among economists and that will be a social gain.

## The Case of the SST

But even as the thinking begins to become ecologized in one sector, old patterns of nonecological thinking continue in others. I can cite no more striking example of aboriginal economic analysis projected into the

future than that now supporting the SST, the supersonic transport airplane. One might suppose that an innovation that will cost some $5
billion would be rigorously justified by an exhaustive economic analysis.
What are the facts?

The first and most significant fact is that no business concern has ever
proposed to finance the SST. The government will pay at least 90 percent of the cost. As far as the prime contractor is concerned, this is like
writing "Santa Claus" on the assets side of the ledger book—very nice,
but not economics.

Since we, the people, are financing the SST, presumably we are doing
so because we have carried out a cost-benefit analysis ahead of time and
have found that the balance is favorable? Not so. *No one has ever carried
out a cost-benefit analysis for the SST.* Still our legislators propose to
spend $5 billion of our money in ignorance of economic realities.

Yet the elements of a cost-benefit analysis are easy to lay out. The cost
of the SST will be far more than the cost of the special alloys and engineering skills required to make it. The true cost of the operation of the
SST must also include the cost of building giant new airports far from
major cities, the cost of new transportation subsystems to take passengers
from cities to distant airports, the cost of the deterioration of the environment for wide areas around new airports and so on.

No economist has drawn up a balance sheet showing all these costs.
Only the design and manufacture of the plane itself is counted as an essential cost. All other costs are conveniently labelled "external costs," or
"externalities." New airports, new ground transportation, and the decay
of communities of homes are all part of the "externalities" of the SST
program. They are seldom mentioned, even under this invidious name,
by the proponents of the supersonic plane.

It will be useful to pause to examine the role of language in controversy. Language serves many functions, and of these, two are most
important: description and coercion. The descriptive function of language
is generally frank and open, but the coercive function is usually hidden
under a disguise of putative descriptiveness. When a pesticide sprayer
speaks of the "side effects" of his actions, he is making use of the coercive function of language. But effects are effects. In calling certain effects "side-effects," the apologist is implying that they are secondary,
that they don't really count, that you shouldn't be concerned about them.

He is trying to coerce your attention in other directions. "Side-effects" is a bit of word magic by which the user seeks to control the world, or people's perception of the world.

Similarly, the economist who refers to the destruction of home environments and to the need for added airports and ground transport as "externalities" in the SST program is seeking to coerce the public's attention away from an open, honest accounting of all the costs. "Externalities" is not description; it is word magic.

Perhaps the worst of the "external" costs of the SST, and the most difficult to deal with, is sonic boom. The seriousness with which it is viewed depends on one's age, perhaps one's sex, the noisiness of the environment in other respects, previous conditioning, temperamental characteristics and perhaps even one's political predilections. Inside a building the effect is generally much worse than it is outside; a room may vibrate like a musical instrument. The aural experience is like being inside a drum beaten on by an idiot.

"Well, that's the price of progress for you," says the cheerful apologist. O.K.: What precisely *is* the price? What does a cost-benefit analysis tell us about the SST?

The only benefit in sight is saving time. (Don't tell us that it will employ people; the same can be said for peddling heroin.) The current model of the American SST is planned for a capacity of just under 240 passengers. Whisked coast-to-coast, they will save two hours each at the most optimistic estimate. So 480 man-hours will be saved. What are they worth? Let's assume that everyone who is so eager to save this time is an important executive, making an average salary of $60,000 a year. Such people probably work at least 60 hours a week 50 weeks a year, or 3,000 hours a year. Their time is, then, worth $20 an hour. The time saved by a planeload of such people is worth $20 × 480, or $9,600 for each load. This is the benefit.

**Figuring the Cost**

What is the cost? The cost is borne not by the passengers, but by people on the ground. Occasionally plaster is cracked or even windows broken; the prehistoric cliff dwellings at Mesa Verde National Park, in

Colorado, may be damaged; a surgeon performing a delicate eye operation may be startled and botch his work; invalids troubled with insomnia may become more troubled. But let's ignore all that. Let's think only of the ordinary citizens who don't like sitting inside a drum beaten by an idiot; let's ask exactly how much diseconomy they must suffer to wipe out the economy of $9,600 enjoyed by the people on the plane. Where is the break-even point?

It has been estimated that a typical flight from the west coast to the east coast of the United States would produce a traveling cone-shaped boom that woud disturb 20 million people. Dividing $9,600 by this number we obtain 0.48 mils. That is, if the discomfort of each person receiving a boom has a negative value of one-half mil or more, the aggregate value of the transcontinental supersonic flight is negative. And remember, this calculation ignores the more spectacular damages and assumes that all the passengers earn $60,000 a year. The diseconomy of the flight is even more striking if some of the passengers are society women flying from one coast to the other to attend a garden party, or officials in the Federal Aviation Agency going out to give lectures on the national importance of the SST.

As one who has been often boomed by military supersonic planes—which are not so large or as obnoxious as the commercial plane will be—let me say that I would regard half a mil per boom as inadequate compensation. I think most people who do not get all dewy-eyed when hearing the word "progress" would agree with me. Why, then, must we put up with such a behemoth? The reason, I think, is simple: The decision-making processes have only the loosest of couplings to the social control mechanisms that we hint at by the word "responsibility."

"A decision is responsible," the philosopher Charles Frankel says, "when the man or group that makes it has to answer for it to those who are directly or indirectly affected by it."

Putting the most charitable possible construction on the decision-making in the SST affair, we might say that the decision to have such a facility is made by the 240 high-salaried passengers who will ride the plane from coast to coast. But they don't have to pay the cost. The cost is paid by the 20 million people on the ground who suffer each time some 200 passengers save two hours. The decision to produce and fly the SST is, in the deepest sense, an irresponsible decision.

In passing, let it be noted that a responsible decision in the SST matter would be easily reached if all airline executives, all 45,000 employees of the FAA and all 535 members of Congress were compelled to live in the path of SST sonic booms, thus making them answer for their decisions, as Frankel recommends.

Economics employs *partial* analysis to reach its decisions. This defect is not essential to the subject of economics, but it is traditional. Because of the increasing pressure of population and because of our greater knowledge of the consequences of our actions, economics is being rapidly altered away from its classical mold in the direction of ecology. The public interest in every proposal will in the future weigh more and more heavily in reaching decisions on the expenditure of public moneys. Cost-benefit analyses must be carried out within an intellectual framework that comes closer to incorporating the total system. The myth of "externalities" must be abandoned. Economics must become ecologized.

### Will Progress End?

When ecology engulfs economics, many of the dreams of imaginative engineers will be deliberately aborted because cost-benefit analysis will indicate an aggregate value that is negative. Many a dam will go unbuilt. The SST and many other technical marvels will never be realized or will be subsequently abandoned. Does this mean that all material "progress" will come to an end? Does it mean that we will be so inhibited by complete ecological-economic analysis that we can never again take a new technological step?

I think not. "We can never do one thing," and we can (in principle) never carry out an absolutely complete analysis, but it is nonetheless possible to institute changes safely. Two intellectual tools make this possible. The first is model-building, as mathematicians understand the term. With an intellectual model, one works out the feedback consequences of alterations in the system in an immaterial realm where the "costs" can be borne without pain. The second tool is dynamic programming, that is, the use of an adaptive logical system that can correct the model (or its real life analog) rapidly, before runaway feedback processes take control. Every order-of-magnitude improvement in the state of the art of computers brings with it a corresponding improvement in the efficacy of model-building and dynamic-programing. Such improvements in turn increase our confidence in our ability to foresee the consequences of interventions in ecological systems, and our willingness to undertake innovations.

The engulfing of economics by ecology thus will reintroduce responsibility into the political system, though at the risk of putting an end to all change. Fortunately, however, the powers of modern computers give man the capability of dealing with almost incredibly complex systems and thus regaining confidence in his ability to alter the systems in which he lives in a creative and responsible way.

[Since this article was published two additional elements have come into the picture. First, there is now evidence that the exhaust gases of SSTs may contribute significantly to the removal of stratospheric ozone, thus increasing the penetration of ultraviolet light to lower levels, with unpredictable effects on the climate. The danger is not clear, but it is enough to worry about. Secondly, since the so-called oil crisis of 1973, the cost per passenger mile for all planes has gone up significantly. Both of these factors have made the cost-benefit ratio less favorable to the SST. Looking to the future, one cannot even imagine a development that will improve the total economics of this albatross, but it is easy to see many things that could make it worse.]

# 16

## Earthquake: Prediction Worse than Nature?

### (1967)

[Nothing that I have written has been rejected as much as the following article. The central idea was first put forward in a Letter to the Editor of *Science* magazine; it was rejected. I then expanded it into an essay which, in various metamorphoses, was rejected by *Saturday Review*, *New York Times Magazine*, *Atlantic Monthly*, *Saturday Evening Post*, *National Review*, *Scientist & Citizen*, and *Ramparts*. These magazines cover a wide spectrum on the political axis, but they evidently share a common fear.

The article was finally accepted by the *Bulletin of the Atomic Scientists*, but when they delayed publication several times, my by this time not-so-latent paranoia led me to withdraw the manuscript and submit it to *Per/Se*, whose editor, Robin White, accepted it. This literary quarterly is now defunct. I like to think that there is no cause and effect relationship here.]

In the closing months of 1965 the Office of Science and Technology proposed that the Congress should allocate some $137 million for earthquake research. The aim of this work would be to increase our knowledge of the causes of earthquakes, in the belief that his knowledge would en-

From *Pop Research and the Seismic Market*. Copyright 1967 by PER/SE, 2(3):19–24.

able us to predict the time, location, and severity of future quakes. The proposal was lost somewhere in the committee maze on Capitol Hill. With the recent cutback in support of scientific work as a result of the demands of war, this particular project will probably not be funded until the international situation improves. But that day may come, and when it does it would (I maintain) be most unfortunate if the Congress were to support this kind of earthquake research. At best, if the research were unsuccessful, $137 million would be wasted. If, however, the research should end in a "successful" conclusion, it would set in motion an uncontrollable chain of events which would cause great anxiety in the United States, entailing monetary losses measured in the billions of dollars. If such consequences are predictable, how can we justify the research?

I am not unaware of the perils of prediction. "Only fools and children prophesy," goes the old saying. In the realm of technology there is a wealth of cautionary examples. In the early days of airplane, Octave Chanute had this to say about the probable future of aircraft: "The question occurs as to what is to be the probable use to man of these new modes of transit. We can already answer that they will have no commercial value for the regular transportation of freight or passengers, as the useful loads will be too small and the trips too uncertain and irregular . . . Apparently the chief use of flying machines will be in sport. Their advantages will be their cheapness, as the cost need not exceed 5,000 dollars; also the superioritry of their speed, which is now 40 m.p.h. and presently will be increased to 50 m.p.h. or more. Moreover, they are small and cheaply housed." Even H. G. Wells, superb prophet that he was, underestimated the potentialities of the airplane in 1901: "I doubt very much whether flying will be a practical proposition, or will have important effects on human existence. I therefore consider it most unlikely that aeronautics will ever be able to exercise a decisive influence on travel. Man is not an albatross, but a biped."

We are used to laughing at prophecies which err on the conservative side. We conveniently forget the equally abundant prophecies that err in the opposite direction. For example, in the *Scientific American* for July, 1899, there was an amusing discussion of the probable effects of the motor car, once mass production lowered its price: "The improvement in city conditions by the general adoption of the motor car can hardly be overestimated. Streets clean, dustless and odorless, with light rubber-tired vehicles moving swiftly and noiselessly over their smooth expanse, would eliminate a greater part of the nervousness, distraction, and strain of modern metropolitan life.'' Every driver should have this passage engraved on a card, placed in front of the steering wheel where he may contemplate it as he sits motionless, caught in the five o'clock rush, engulfed in petroleum smog.

Returning to the airplane, we find that errors on the safe side of overoptimism were made there also. In 1883, one Hermann Ganswindt said: "I am convinced that within a few years every household will have one or more flying machines." This prediction, in spite of its chronic nonfulfillment, ran like a Wagnerian leitmotif through the science fiction of the 1920's and 30's. Today, more than half a century after Kitty Hawk, we are farther than ever from the goal of two planes in every garage; indeed, this dream of Progress has been quietly renounced. What has happened? In a word, overpopulation. As the engineer Dennis Gabor has pointed out, "Overpopulation has blocked a fine avenue for adventure before it was ever open."

Overcome by the fantastic development of science during the last two centuries, we protect ourselves against the embarrassment of errors by assuming that the future will always be better than our most carefully made predictions. But it can also be worse. The explosion in technology has produced not only a wealth of desirable consequences, which are amply advertised, but also rather too many undesirable ones, the importance of which we try to minimize by calling them "side effects." Among these are traffic jams, airport accidents, sonic booms, smog, polluted waters, loss of wilderness for spiritual renewal, and exposure to detergent- and insecticide-laden foods. As population increases the relative importance of the so-called side effects increases.

There is no automatic formula for predicting the consequences of developments in knowledge and technology. However, some useful guidelines can be laid out. Faced with poor predictions made in the past we must agree with biophysicist John Platt that "the errors in these forecasts were due not to a lack of imagination, but to a lack of analysis. They are not to be cured by making the prophecies wilder . . . What we need is more realism, not less."

Following Platt's advice, what can we predict about the possible consequences of a successful termination of a program of earthquake research? The exact meaning of "successful" is, of course, uncertain. Let us be conservative and suppose that we ultimately attain an earthquake-predicting ability comparable to that which we now have in meteorology. The weather, and our reactions to it, can in fact be used as a model of the seismological problem.

Our ability to predict weather, limited though it be, is a positive good; and it is clear that an increase in this ability would be even better. When planning a picnic, both disappointment and economic loss are minimized if we can predict a coming rainstorm, even when we can do so with a lead-time of only a day or two. Obviously, the longer the range of our successful weather predictions, the more valuable they are. Prediction of mild meteorological events like rainstorms permits us to avoid most of their bad effects.

With more heroic events like hurricanes the situation is somewhat different. Everyone who has lived through a hurricane comes out of it with a healthy respect for the incredible power of natural forces and a chastened view of the limits of man's ability to withstand these forces. So nearly irresistible are nature's mightier meteorological manifestations that it might even be questioned whether the savings made possible by an advance warning system are worth the cost. However, it would probably be bootless to ask for an honest cost accounting because of the psychological satisfactions derived from battening down the hatches just before a hurricane, futile though such measures often prove to be. Psychological satisfactions like these are not to be lightly dismissed even though they cannot be measured in dollars and cents.

Let us grant that hurricane warnings are worthwhile. Would earthquake warnings be similarly valuable? At first glance, they might seem so, and this is probably why the Office of Science and Technology has proposed to spend over $100 million in an attempt to develop such warnings. However, there are certain significant differences between the two natural catastrophies that need to be pointed out. To begin with, what is the nature of a hurricane warning? It takes various forms at different communicational levels, but in its most scientific form it runs something like this: "With a probability of 0.8 your area will be struck by winds of hurricane velocity within the next 48 hours." Can we expect earthquake warnings to be similarly precise?

The prophet's position is risky, but let me suggest that it is highly probable that the best earthquake warnings we could ever hope to achieve would take a different form: "With probability of 0.6 your area will be subjected to an earthquake with intensity registering between 5 and 6 on the Richter scale sometime within the next 6 months." If this prevision is correct, earthquake warnings will differ significantly from hurricane warnings in their effects on society.

First of all, it is quite likely that we could expect to have a much longer warning of an earthquake than of a hurricane. The meteorological events leading up to a hurricane are, in any scientifically understandable sense, extremely short-lived. So complex are the movements of the atmosphere that it is operationally meaningless to speak of a hurricane a month before the big blow begins. However, in every earthquake zone of the world, earthquakes exist in some operationally potential sense for months and even years before a big shake occurs. Anyone who lives in Santa Barbara, as I do, knows that sooner or later—probably in his own lifetime—another big shake is going to occur. The presumptive result of successful earthquake research would be a lowering of the warning time from a vague "lifetime" to a relatively precise few months.

The relation between "lead-time" and reliability would be quite different for earthquake warnings. For hurricanes, the relationship is inverse: the longer the lead-time, the less reliable the warning. The probability of a hurricane six months away is very low. Human beings are incurable optimists with respect to small risks, so daily life in a hurricane belt goes on in a daily way, little influenced by the knowledge that a hurricane is always possible. People build houses, plant trees, and take business risks on the working assumption that the relatively improbable event will not happen—*to me*. Lending agencies must shade their rates to take account of hurricanes, but their actions have little psychological effect on home owners.

Just before the hurricane there is an abrupt change in psychology. Suddenly, the formerly remote possibility becomes almost certain; and the certain will happen soon. What are the psychological results of this foreknowledge? Men rise to the occasion and, in a flurry of activity, take precautionary measures. Accompanying the understandable fear of suffering and dread of loss there exists a more puzzling feeling of exhilaration and pleasurable excitement, at least among the more youthful of the community. The definiteness of the danger and the shortness of the lead-time arouse men to their greatest heights of cooperative exertion. It would be presumptious to try to evaluate the total psychological and sociological effects of a hurricane, but certainly such a catastrophe is not without its admirable side effects.

On the basis of all we know about earthquakes, it is almost certain that in an earthquake warning system, lead-time and reliability would be *directly* related. With a long lead-time, say six months, we might be able to predict with a high degree of reliability. With shorter and shorter lead-times the probability of the predicted event would become less and less. How would this statistical relationship affect the lives of people who had the "benefit" of an earthquake warning system?

There isn't much one can do to prepare for an earthquake. Houses can be constructed according to a soundly conceived building code—but this should always be done in an earthquake zone anyway. You don't need a warning system to tell you to do this. If you knew at the last minute that an earthquake was coming you could take the china off the shelves and pack it in excelsior. But this would make sense only if there was a high probability that the quake would take place soon. With a low probability for an imminent earthquake, little evasive action will be taken. If you pack your china away today because an earthquake will probably occur sometime in the next six months, what do you eat off of in the meantime? The china is only symbolic of a whole class of arrangements that are necessary for normal, sane, everyday living. Unreliable early earthquake warnings would be a veritable sword of Damocles hanging over the heads of the citizenry.

What would be the psychological effects of such a threat? Perhaps we can find the answer in some interesting experiments performed with monkeys by Joseph V. Brady. Two monkeys were placed in a situation in which a punishing shock of electricity could be avoided by pressing a button in response to a premonitory stimulus. Both monkeys could perceive the warning, but only one monkey had access to the button. After many repetitions of the experience, one of the monkeys developed ulcers—the monkey who had access to the button. In traditional literary terms, we can say that the monkey to whom the electrical shock was merely a random, irresponsible manifestation of an uncontrollable "Fate" enjoyed better psychological health than the monkey that had gained a measure of control of fate. With this control the monkey had taken on an increased load of responsibility.

We who live in earthquake zones feel little anxiety about the future earthquakes that will come at completely unforeseeable times; Freudian denial arms us against their psychological threat. The development of an ability to predict a quake months away with considerable reliability would tend to remove seismic phenomena from the category of fate. Being able to predict an earthquake, we would feel that we should do something about it; but our relative impotence would generate anxiety. If the reliability of our predictions decreased with decrease in lead-time, we would become even more anxious.

Think what would happen to real estate values on the day some federal bureau suddenly announced: "There is a high probability of a severe earthquake in your town within the next six months." Who would buy a house at such a time? Who would invest in a local business (say a quality glassware store!) at that time? But there would always be people who had to sell. Some of the sellers would be men who had taken jobs elsewhere, perhaps for reasons unconnected with the impending earthquake. Other sales would be required to settle estates. Whatever the causes, the existence of a surplus of sellers would produce a catastrophic drop in real estate values. Panic selling might even extend to the shares of locally-based business concerns.

What would be the human response to the capability of making earthquake predictions? It is not difficult to predict. It would not take many experiences of this sort to produce a mobilization of various interested parties to suppress the predictions. Realtors, business men, bankers, insurance agents—indeed, almost all people with a vested interest in the locality—would band together to put pressure on the federal government. At first they might merely try to get all such reports put on a "classified" basis, not to be released until after the earthquake was over. This stratagem would not work for long, however. Official Washington is a notoriously leaky informational sieve. Someone who had a friend in the to-be-shaken area would almost surely leak the forecast—in confidence, of course.

Even in the unlikely event of no violation of security, harm would still be created by the suppressed findings. Entrepreneurs who now hawk tips on the stock market would branch out into the seismic market. The fact that they had no real pipeline into the federal agency would not matter. The success of rumor-mongers is not noticeably dependent on the reliability of their output. The game of speculation is a "zero-sum game"—that is, a game in which technically there is no net change in value because one man's loss is another man's gain. But this does not mean that the game of speculation is unaffected by the public interest. Secondary consequences of the game, namely its tendency to promote public chaos, are reason enough to suppress it. There would be only one way to stop the game of speculation in earthquake rumors: we would have to destroy the facility for making predictions. This would have to be done in a very public manner, by some sort of a latter-day auto-da-fé; only so could the trafficking in rumors be stopped. Thus we would bring to an end the technological facility we had spent hundreds of millions of dollars developing—after it had done billions of dollars worth of damage.

In making these predictions it will be noted that I have made use of almost no technical knowledge—merely horse-sense. It is disturbing to note that the document prepared for the Office of Science and Technology by the Ad Hoc Panel on Earthquake Prediction shows not the slightest recognition of the psychological and social matrix in which the proposed prediction facility would be imbedded. The Panel consisted of fourteen men from such prestigious scientific institutions as Caltech, University of California, Princeton and M.I.T. The Panel's report covers 134 pages, and goes into great detail. It discusses at length the importance of fluid pore pressure, phase transformation, shear melting, creep fracture, brittle fracture, landslides, land subsidence, soil liquifacation, tsunami damage and fault tectonics. Detailed estimates of the cost of various types of study are given. In the end, the authors honestly say that "they are not unmindful of the possibility that no practical method of specific prediction may be made"; but nowhere do they indicate that they have the slightest inkling of the psychological and sociological dangers of the scientific advance they hope for. Their analysis is a beautiful example of the pathology of specialism—the tendency of a technician to use his particular tools, and only his tools, to solve the world's problems. In their bland indifference to the total meaning of earthquakes these geophysicists remind us of the apocryphal surgeon who "solved" the problem of the weeping patient by extirpating her tear glands. Faced with the threat of earthquakes our geophysicists propose to establish a prediction system that will prolong the period of foreboding.

There is yet one more aspect of the proposed system of earthquake prediction that should be exposed—and again, it is an aspect the experts failed to see. The dangers of a prediction facility are conditioned by the economic system of the country that employs it. The dangers are greatest for a "free economy," such as we have (or purport to have) in the United States. A free, capitalistic economy can be thrown into disorder by storms of rumors. A controlled economy, like that of Soviet Russia, is much less vulnerable. The marketplace of houses cannot fluctuate wildly if there is no market. In a controlled economy, knowledge of an impending catastrophe may still have serious effects, but it will not set in motion runaway processes that produce ruinous secondary consequences.

We can put this another way. We can view earthquake-predicting ability as a political weapon and ask ourselves, who would be harmed most by the "gift" of this weapon? Plainly, the United States would be harmed far more than Russia.

I cite this fact with some trepidation. It is just the sort of fact that the far-rightists in our country like to point to as evidence of an intellectual conspiracy to undermine the country. This interpretation is, I am convinced, nonsense. The political danger of earthquake research arises in my opinion not because scientists are communist conspirators but because they are merely specialists who seldom look farther ahead than their shoelaces. Their intentions are good—if that's any consolation.

In vulgar language, we need an earthquake-predicting facility like we need a hole in the head. We should not support such research; but can we prevent it? At first glance, preventing it might seem impossible. It is an article of faith among scientists that the "secrets" of Nature cannot be kept. Scientists have gone a long way toward converting the rest of the world to this faith. At the conclusion of World War II the scientific community mounted a tremendous educational campaign to convince congressmen that the secrets we had wrested from the center of the atom could be pried loose again, and in less time, by our enemies. The lesson has been well learned. Congressmen now agree with scientists.

It is therefore impossible to prevent our learning how to predict earthquakes? Not necessarily. Economic considerations indicate a real possibility of controlling the development of this sort of science. Two important questions can be identified: (a) How much will attaining the knowledge cost? (b) Who will pay for it?

If the research costs no more than a few thousand dollars we would have to assume that it could not be stopped. But the estimated price tag is $137 million, which is not peanuts. Furthermore, as former Undersecretary of Defense Charles Hitch pointed out, the actual cost of any really new equipment or facility generally turns out to be from two to twenty times as great as the first careful estimate. We should not be surprised if the cost of this seismic research were to exceed a billion dollars.

The expensiveness of this research gives us hope that it can be prevented. Private enterprise could hardly finance it. The money to be made speculating in stocks and real estate in an earthquake area would not justify gambling a billion dollars to develop a private enterprise prediction facility. Only the government can support a project of this magnitude, and it is in the corridors of government that the validity of the proposal must be questioned. When there is renewed pressure to spend hundreds of millions of dollars to learn how to predict earthquakes let us hope that some influential voice will be raised to ask, "Why?"

[I find myself unable to resist adding a footnote ten years later. In the mid-1970's a team of social scientists at the University of Colorado, operating with a $500,000 grant from the National Science Foundation, reached essentially the same conclusions. Of course their work was more detailed: for half a million dollars one can afford a bit of detail. A crucial question is this: does it take a large expenditure of money to change the public's mind about a matter for which simple logic, operating with common knowledge, should be sufficient?]

# 17

# Is Civilization Ready for Nuclear Power?

## (1976)

For more than two decades we have struggled with the question, "Is atomic energy safe?" Every year the proponents say it is. Then doubters point to a near-disaster, the possibility of which had not been foreseen. Following this, safeguards against that particular accident are engineered into the system and the proponents say, "See? It's safe now!" and the dance goes on. The dialectic sounds like a broken record.

The Rasmussen report, which cost two million dollars, should have put an end to the bickering. Two million dollars is a lot of money. Some of the best technological minds were brought to bear on the problem, and they cranked out an exhaustive and subtle analysis. Their conclusion, simply put, is that your chance of being killed by a nuclear accident is less than the chance that you will be killed by lightning. That should satisfy any person of good common sense. Did it?

It did not. For good reasons. In 1957, after several years of unsuccessfully trying to get private industry to tool up for atomic energy, Congress passed the Price-Anderson Act. Industrialists had been reluctant to enter this new field because they were worried about their liability in case of

Originally published under the title *"The Fallibility Factor"* in Skeptic No. 14. © 1976 Skeptic Magazine, Inc. All rights reserved.

massive accidents. Insurance companies wouldn't insure them, and they weren't about to insure themselves. So Congress stepped in.

By the terms of Price-Anderson, government and the private sector combined to insure against the cost of a single accident up to a maximum of $560 million. It is noteworthy that private industry underwrote $60 million of this, while the government's share was $500 million. The private share later rose to $95 million but we are still reminded of the celebrated recipe for "50 Percent Rabbit Pie": one horse to one rabbit.

More remarkable is the fact that beyond $560 million there is no insurance at all and—by the terms of the Price-Anderson Act—*there is no legal liability.* Yet at the same time this act was passed there was already in existence an Atomic Energy Commission study, the so-called Brookhaven report, which concluded that a believable accident could cause $7 billion in property damage—12.5 times the liability limit of Price-Anderson—in addition to the loss of 3,400 people killed and 43,000 injured.

What happened between 1957 and 1975 when the final Rasmussen report was released? Several things. First: atomic energy plants in being, and on the drawing boards, grew much bigger. Second: another AEC study was carried out, but its existence was denied until 1973, and the findings released only after a Freedom of Information suit was filed. The suppression led to some justifiable suspicions, and it was no doubt to allay these that the Rasmussen study was funded. Now that that has been completed is the issue settled?

**Put Your Money Where Your Mouth Is**

I submit that it is not. If it is really true that the danger of nuclear accidents is less than the danger from lightning then private insurers, always interested in making money, should leap at the chance of writing nuclear accident insurance. After all, they write lightning insurance, and make a packet out of it.

But in December of 1975, 18 years after the original congressional act—and *after* the release of the Rasmussen report—Congress renewed the Price-Anderson Act on the same basis.

The Rasmussen report is filled with accounts of sophisticated statistical techniques (e.g., "fault trees") by which analysts seek to allow for every conceivable contingency. Very impressive. But more impressive still is the wisdom of the folk saying, *"Put your money where your mouth is."*

The atomic energy establishment, with multiple manifestations of sincerity, tells us, "It's perfectly safe." But its deeds do not match its words. If the energy industry does not show by its acts that it believes its own press releases, why should anyone else?

What is behind the refusal of the nuclear energy industry to insure itself? Since its spokesmen are less than candid in discussing the matter we must find our way through the thicket of facts and principles on our own. Fortunately the most significant facts do not depend on sophisticated analytical techniques.

Our first problem is to escape the mental corner the nuclear establishment would like to paint us into. Most of the two million dollars the Rasmussen committee spent was focused on the safety of reactors. But reactors are only a small part of the problem. We can grant, for the sake of argument, that the committee's views on reactor safety are sound. The report still leaves untouched some very important areas.

**The Waste-Disposal Problem**

For one thing, there is the matter of the safe disposal of atomic wastes. The worst of these is plutonium-239, which has a half-life of 24,300 years, by which we mean that the intensity of the radioactivity of a chunk of it diminishes by only 50 percent in 24,300 years. How does one safely store such lethally dangerous material for long periods of time?

Simply, say the proponents of nuclear power. We first form it into rods, and then place the rods in sturdy steel cylinders. Now "sturdy steel cylinders" sound very reassuring—until we remember that the radioactive wastes put into tanks at Hanford, Washington, during the last two decades were stored in "sturdy steel" tanks—which after a few years' time started leaking like sieves. The fact is that under irradiation *all* materials change their nature. The world of radioactivity is a world of continuous inexorable change. Fuels change, containers change, reactors change. No materials are constant or reliable, except for short periods of time. The danger, and the change-causing effectiveness, of radioactive substances goes on essentially forever, as human beings ordinarily reckon time.

Suppose the pharaohs had built nuclear energy plants. They might have elected to store the resulting radioactive wastes inside the pyramids they built. Not a bad solution, considering how well the pyramids have lasted. But plutonium-239 stored in the oldest of them—some 4,600 years ago— would today still exhibit 88 percent of its initial radioactivity.

How much would the radioactivity have to be reduced to be "safe"? It depends on how much material we have to begin with. If the pharaohs had stored quite a lot of plutonium in the pyramids the radioactivity might have to get down to the one percent level to be "safe." If so, their initial deposits would still have more than 150,000 years to go.

Who would watch over it for so long a period of time? The civilization of old Egypt lasted less than 2,000 years, according to the historian Arnold Toynbee. Will ours last any longer? So far, it has lasted about 1,300 years. But 150,000 years. . . ?

Of course, we hope to find a more enduring storage place than some old pyramid. We *hope.* . . . ERDA (the Energy Research and Development Administration), the successor to the AEC, still hasn't given the seal of approval to any storage scheme. (At one time we thought the salt mines of Kansas would be safe, but they turned out to be sieves.) The proponents of nuclear power are certain that a suitable permanent storage site will be found. But is their assurance sufficient in so vital a matter?

We are plunging ahead on atomic energy in the hope that the storage problem will be solved. Is this prudent? What would we say if a man jumped off the World Trade Building with a bag of hardware in the hope that he would figure out a way to build a parachute on the way down?

**The People Problem**

The neglect of the waste storage problem is not the only deficiency in the Rasmussen report. Much more serious is the way it fails to take account of the human factor. This failure springs from rhetoric that is peculiar to science, the rhetoric of the depersonalized passive voice.

In exhibiting the structure of a manufacturing system scientists like to use "flow diagrams," sets of little boxes with words inside, connected by arrows to show what goes where and what turns into what. The elements of a flow diagram for atomic energy production might (in abbreviated form) read like this:

radioactive ores mined ————→radioactive ores
transported————→radioactive ores processed————→radioactive
concentrates transported————→radioactive reactor elements
formed————→radioactive reactor elements
transported————→radioactive reactor elements
installed————→reactors operated and monitored————→reactors
periodically disassembled————→spent radioactive elements
shipped to processing plant

At this point, the chain doubles back on itself as the spent elements are converted to radioactive concentrates which enter the system again, while some unusable radioactive wastes go into a spur line that leads to the waste storage problem discussed earlier.

Remember, the Rasmussen report focused almost entirely on the problem of operating and monitoring reactors. The rest of the elements in the above flow list—which is much compressed—went almost unnoticed.

More dangerous still is the frame of mind fostered by the passive voice which gives no indication of the active agents—*people*—who cause and supervise the acts mentioned in the flow diagram. The elements of the diagram really should read as follows:

PEOPLE mine radioactive ores————→PEOPLE transport
radioactive ores————→PEOPLE process radioactive
ores————→PEOPLE transport radioactive concentrates ————→
PEOPLE fashion radioactive reactor elements————→PEOPLE
transport radioactive reactor elements————→PEOPLE install
radioactive reactor elements————→PEOPLE operate and
monitor reactors————→PEOPLE periodically disassemble
reactors ————→PEOPLE ship spent radioactive reactor elements to
processing plant . . .

By failing to mention the people involved at multitudinous points in the chain of actions, technologists may mislead the unwary (including themselves) to suppose that everything happens in a wholly impersonal system, the way acts of nature happen.

People are the quintessential element in all technology. ("Technology" comes from the Greek *tekne,* skill or art, which is—by definition—the skill and art of human beings.) Once we recognize the inescapable human nexus of all technology our attitude toward the reliability problem is fundamentally changed. It is no longer enough to ask how reliable are inanimate materials or integrated circuits; we must also ask, How reliable are human beings? Are they reliable enough to entrust with the care of the incredibly explosive and incredibly long-lived poisons generated by atomic energy systems?

People are unreliable in two ways: inadvertently, and deliberately. People cause genuine accidents; they also engage in deliberate sabotage and terrorism.


## Accidents

Let us take up the accident problem first. The NASA program was the most rigorous, safety-oriented endeavor humankind has ever embarked on. Yet despite all precautions accidents did occur. On the Gemini 6 flight a dust cover was left off. Cost: $900,000. (But the protocols indicated this had been checked.) Apollo 13 nearly failed in space because of improper voltages used in testing on the ground. Superb improvisation brought the crew back alive, but it was a near thing. (Again protocols failed to warn of the procedural error.)

Still, the safety record was not bad for so large an effort. But it is doubtful if such meticulous monitoring will ever again be done: it is fiendishly expensive, and there's no such thing as "100 percent inspection." The whole atomic energy system, including as it does hundreds of thousands of people, cannot possibly be as reliable. Furthermore, we contemplate continuing it forever, whereas the NASA program was pretty much a one-time thing. It is easier to be alert and careful for a short time.

People install, inspect and monitor machines. How reliable can people be? There is no simple, single answer. Boredom introduces a variable factor. In proportion as we make the human input into a procedure simple we thereby increase its reliability—for a while. But as people repeat simple operations year after year, without an accident, they become bored and careless. And disbelieving of the possibility of an accident. There is a sort of reciprocal relationship between the frequency of (past) accidents and the probability of (future) accidents. The smaller the first value the larger the second. This reciprocity sets some sort of undefined limit to human reliability. A long and distinguished safety record sets the stage for a serious accident at an unforeseen time.

Boredom has a second deleterious effect: the more boring a job is the more difficult it is to hire intelligent, alert caretakers. Competent overseers will, in time, be replaced by incompetent.

If someone in overall charge of an energy system dared, he might actually cause mini-accidents to happen from time to time. Perhaps a few people might be killed and a few million dollars in damage be done. Properly engineered, such accidents could, by minimizing boredom, save lives and minimize damage in the long run. But it would be much too Machiavellian to embark on such a program so we might as well forget it.

## Sabotage and Terrorism

The really intractable problem in atomic energy is the problem of sabotage and terrorism. Radioactive materials can be hijacked or embezzled from many points in the system, which is far more complex than our diagram indicates. Criminals may do this within a nation. A legitimate government also can behave criminally (from an international point of view): thus India embezzled radioactive material for a bomb from the system furnished her by Canada solely for peaceful purposes.

It takes so very little material to do a great deal of damage. The "critical mass"—the quantity that is capable of exploding if it is brought all together in one chunk—of plutonium-239 is only slightly larger than a golf ball in diameter.

Given a critical mass can amateurs assemble an explosive device? *No* says the atomic energy establishment. *Yes* says Theodore B. Taylor, who has designed more different atomic bombs than anyone else. Lacking experience and access to the most advanced technology an amateur may not devise a very good bomb, but even a "fizzle" is more destructive than anything possible before the Second World War. The prudent man believes Ted Taylor rather than the establishment, which has a vested interest in allaying our fears.

Sabotage is nothing new, of course. What is new is the magnitude of the possible damage it can do. Those who comfort themselves with the pious belief that there's nothing new under the sun should focus their attention on what has happened to what is technically called the "utility function" of terroristic action. (This utility—damage—is, of course, a negative quantity.)

The expected damage is the probability of an act of sabotage multiplied by the (conditional) damage caused by a successful act. In the last 35 years the conditional damage has risen by at least six orders of magnitude; that is, it is at least a million times greater now. The maximum possible bomb before Hiroshima was measured in tons (of TNT); now it is measured in millions of tons. As for the poisonous effects of the radioactive elements released, these vary; but plutonium-239 is at least as poisonous as botulinus toxin and it lasts for tens of thousands of years. Botulinus toxin released into the environment is destroyed in a few days by microbial action.

For a negative utility to remain constant over time, if the conditional damage rises by $x$ orders of magnitude the probability of sabotage must fall by the same number $x$. The conditional damage has increased a million-fold; has the probability of sabotage and terrorism *decreased* a million-fold since 1940?

I think not. In fact, I think there are a number of reasons for holding that sabotage and terrorism are more serious now than before the Second World War, and that they will grow still more serious.

For one thing there is population. The multiple pressures of different populations on each other, in a world in which the frontier as an absorbing barrier has disappeared, exacerbates both international and intranational conflicts.

Then there is tribalism. When the United Nations was founded in 1945 many of us fondly hoped it marked the beginning of the decline of nationalism. Alas! It did not. Every decade a few more nations split, and there have been no fusions. Within many nations more and more groups demand greater privileges, in the pursuit of which they are perfectly willing to employ terrorism.

On the intellectual side, the passion for justice increases the danger of terrorism. A cold-blooded rationalist is easier to control by threats than is a passionate idealist who fights for what he perceives to be justice.

Let's put the matter this way: How would you like it if there were a complete atomic energy system now operating in the vicinity of Belfast? or Beirut?

This is not to say that Belfast and Beirut are intrinsically disorderly communities. But they are at the moment. With the passage of time the site of greatest disorder moves from one area to another, in a way not predictable long in advance. Perhaps the United States has enough civil order to safely rely on atomic energy now—*perhaps*. (The area we now call Ireland may have looked safe enough in 1600; so also with Lebanon.) But what about three, four, or five centuries from now? We must remember that the danger from radioactive materials increases as we generate more and more residual radioactivity with every kilowatt of electricity. The potential amount of damage is hardly reduced by the slow rate of radioactive decay.

The atomic energy establishment hopes to double the size of its operations every ten years. This means doubling the amount of radioactive residues every ten years. But it takes 24,300 years for each year's residue of plutonium-239 to lose half its activity.

What is to be done? Since it is human nature that is the most seriously unreliable element in the atomic energy system we naturally think of controlling that. But what does that mean, concretely? It means we must establish and maintain an elaborate surveillance system affecting millions of workers in mining, processing, transporting, machining, inspecting, monitoring, and auditing radioactive materials. And the surveillers must themselves be surveilled: an infinite regress.

In the monetary area we still have not learned how to bring the embezzlement rate anywhere near zero. Yet, with respect to radioactive materials, that is what we must be able to do. Before we can do that we should call for a new Rasmussen study, this time one made by men who do not suffer from the naiveté shown by those who are merely capable scientists and engineers.

It may seem strange to call scientists naive, but there is good reason for doing so. Philip Morrison has commented on how frequently his fellow physicists have been taken in by fraudulent extrasensory perception demonstrations, by Uri Geller and the like. Morrison has an explanation for their naiveté. Einstein, he points out, once said that "The Lord God is subtle, but he is not malicious." The kinds of puzzles physicists try to unravel are of the utmost intellectual difficulty. Very few human beings are equal to this task. It is probably absolutely necessary, in this difficult work, that the scientist believe in the trustworthiness of nature. A physicist who thought that the laws of nature frivolously changed from time to time would probably be unable to bring the full force of his intellect to bear on his problems. Trust in nature (or nature's God) is probably essential to success.

Trust can become a habit. Unfortunately in human affairs, in some situations, trust is not the best policy. When someone tells you he can bend spoons by thought processes, communicate at a distance by non-physical means, or foretell the future accurately, your attitude toward him had better be laced with the skepticism with which you view the accomplishments of stage magicians. As Morrison says, "Not Einstein, but Machiavelli and W. C. Fields must be your guides then." Unlike nature and nature's God, human beings can be malicious, so maliciousness is one of the variables to be plugged into any analysis of the possible outcomes of a human-based system.

## A Blue-Ribbon Committee

In terms of a human-based nuclear energy system no analysis of its safety carried out by mere scientists and engineers will be convincing. These bright men and women are, for good and sufficient reason, too naive to evaluate the dangers realistically. What we need is a new Rasmussen committee which, in addition to scientists and engineers, includes people from these categories: competent prestidigitators, convicted terrorists, convicted hijackers, convicted embezzlers, convicted bankrobbers, convicted con artists, and convicted computer thieves. Oh yes: and a few certified paranoids. With a committee like that we might begin to make a little progress on the reliability problem. Such people would understand the power of malice.

Actually, impressive as such a committee would be, it would still not be the best conceivable committee. The most valuable criminals would not be convicted ones, but the criminals who are so successful in their professions that they have never been convicted. Better still, they should be unindicted. But it is operationally difficult to identify those truly successful criminals, and so we would have to settle for the second best, the convicted ones. Their records of conviction would be the equivalent of the union card or the Ph.D. degree—an assurance of training if not of the highest competence.

## Grave Implications

With the most competent malicious men still outside the system we could expect sabotage and terrorism to continue, though at a lower level of effectiveness. But so fearful are the dangerous dimensions of "the peaceful atom"—oh, noble whitewash!—that the toll of sabotage and terrorism (together with some simple accidents) might be such that we would come to regret the decision to make ourselves dependent on atomic energy. Desperately seeking security, we would no doubt accept more and more controls in civil life until finally we would slip into the kind of political system that can only be called totalitarian. This is not certain, but it is a real enough possibility so that we should pause before going further down the nuclear road.

Why have we started down this uncertain road? Hans Bethe has expressed the "conventional wisdom" as well as any. He says: "This country needs power to keep its economy going. Too little power means unemployment and recession, if not worse."

What Bethe is saying is that an industrial society needs energy ("power"). But no one has ever denied this. He says that too little energy will produce unemployment and recession. Would the Chinese agree? Their per capita energy budget is only a fraction of ours—perhaps a twentieth—but, by all accounts, everyone is employed (perhaps too thoroughly so). And the Chinese would have difficulty discerning a meaning in our word "recession." So the "too" in the phrase "too little" has no objective meaning.

Obviously "too little" energy has meaning only with respect to some implied social, political, and economic system. Change the system appropriately and "too little" can become "quite enough" or even "too much."

For his cryptic last phrase "if not worse" I deduce that Hans Bethe is saying that a totalitarian system like China's would be worse than unemployment and recession. He may be right, he may be wrong; I will not argue the point. The significant thing I think is this: Bethe—and a host of other defenders of atomic energy—are saying that our type of society cannot survive *without* atomic energy. What they do not think to ask is: "Can our civilization survive *with* atomic energy?"

One of the great guiding principles of ecology is this: *We can never do merely one thing.* Those who hope to keep our type of society intact and

essentially unchanged while introducing so bizarre and dangerous a technology as atomic energy are flying in the face of ecological wisdom.
Non-atomic energy will prove too little only if population and/or per
capita use of energy grows indefinitely. To stop either (or both) of these
from growing—or possibly even to lessen one or the other—will require
that we relinquish some of the freedoms we have enjoyed for a short two
centuries. The atomic apologist says that is unthinkable and so we must
have atomic energy.

But, if the analysis here given is substantially correct, we can enjoy the
benefits of atomic energy only if we change to the very sort of political
system we reject in embracing the atom, a system in which not only the
actions but to a large extent even the thoughts of its members are controlled by the state. If I were living in China I would likely argue for
atomic energy rather than against it, since the danger of sabotage is much
less there. (Actually, of course, if I were an ordinary Chinese citizen I
wouldn't argue one way or another, because the question would not exist
at my political level.)

So here is the paradox we face: *A society that cannot survive without
atomic energy cannot survive with it*. The questions crying for answers
are not scientific or technological; they are social, economic and political.
The essential problem we must solve is the problem of living within an
energy budget. Technology will not enable us to escape this problem.

# 18

## Pejorism: the Middle Way

### (1976)

How should we face the future? After nearly two centuries of optimism fostered by the Idea of Progress—interrupted only partially by *The Education of Henry Adams* (1906) and Spengler's *The Decline of the West* (1926–1928)—our euphoric mood was at last broken by ecologists and others who became convinced that ecology was the key to understanding the human condition. Reluctantly at first, then with increasing willingness, the general public has come to see merit in the views expressed in William Vogt's *Road to Survival* (1948), Rachel Carson's *Silent Spring* (1962), the Paddocks' *Famine 1975!* (1967), Paul Ehrlich's *The Population Bomb* (1968), the Club of Rome's *The Limits to Growth* (1972), and Robert L. Heilbroner's *An Inquiry into the Human Prospect* (1974).

Success breeds opposition. These influential books quickly evoked denunciations of their authors as "merchants of doom." The critics, the "technological optimists," assert that technology and good intentions can solve all human problems. There is much to be said on their side: optimism can be immensely productive of good. It stirs the soul to seek the impossible—which sometimes proves possible. In the right way it draws

From the *North American Review*, 261(2):9–14. Copyright © Garrett Hardin, 1976.

on the creative power of the self-fulfilling prophecy; and it sets the body's juices to flowing deliciously.

Why then promote anything but optimism? Obviously because we think that sometimes there is an unwanted future that cannot be willed away. We can regard the total future as being made up of many little realities, components of the whole unknown. For two centuries we have been selectively drawing out of the total the pleasant realities, bringing them into being by optimism and technology. What is left is a population in which the unpleasant realities compose an ever larger proportion. As the years pass the optimistic attitude will pay off less often, the pessimistic more often. Given a different pay-off a change in public attitude must follow, however reluctantly. As Malthus said: "Like the commodities in a market those virtues will be produced in the greatest quantity for which there is the greatest demand." Our desire for pleasant realities may be undiminished, but the demand for counterproductive optimism diminishes daily.

Before we can make significant progress in seeing what virtues are called for in the future I think we must jettison the traditional optimism-pessimism dichotomy. Each of the contrasting terms emphasizes a *state*, the optimum in one case, the pessimum in the other. The implied question they are a response to is this: "What *is* (or will be) the future?" But we need to shift from concern with states to a concern with processes. We need to ask not "What *is* the future?" but "What is the tendency of future-making processes?" With this change in attitude we are enabled to discover a new dichotomy, one that bears a family resemblance to the old but which can lead to a different emotional adjustment.

The first half of the new dichotomy is called "meliorism," from the Latin word *meliorare,* to make or become better. A melioristic process is one that tends to improve matters. No better example of such can be cited than the one described exactly two centuries ago by Adam Smith in *The Wealth of Nations*. In a market in which an enterpriser is free to make whatever goods he wants to and to sell them in free competition with other enterprisers for whatever price he can get, Smith wrote:

> Every individual . . . neither intends to promote the public inter-
> est, nor knows how much he is promoting it. By preferring the sup-
> port of domestic to that of foreign industry, he intends only his own

security; and by directing that industry in such a manner as its produce may be of the greatest value, he intends only his own gain, and he is in this, as in many other cases, led by an invisible hand to promote an end which was not part of his intention.

Since the process of free competition automatically (according to Smith) works out for the best there is no need for—in fact, there is a positive danger in—government regulation. The best policy is one of laissez faire—"Do your own thing": Adam Smith's "invisible hand" will see to it that all comes out well.

This is no place to inquire into the substantive merits of Smith's position. Suffice it to say that in the two centuries since he stated it we have found more and more instances in which real economics is governed not so much by a benign "invisible hand" as it is by what Herman Daly calls the "invisible foot"—which kicks us when we are not looking. Wisely, no nation in the world lives by pure Smithian principles.

Nonetheless, the melioristic approach exemplified by the laissez faire doctrine has largely shaped the political institutions of our industrial world. With each manufacturer making whatever product he can sell, hawking his wares blatantly and jettisoning his waste products wherever no one is looking, it has been assumed that all would turn out for the best. The most serious doubts of this view have been put forward by the ecologists who have pointed out that "we can never do merely one thing," from which it is deduced that the burden of proof (of non-harm) should fall on him who proposes to change things, to make an innovation in our way of exploiting nature. In other words, "Guilty until proven innocent" should be the principle by which every innovation is judged. This is a most un-melioristic view, and has led to such regulatory agencies as the Pure Food and Drug Administration and the Environmental Protection Agency; and to such revolutionary roadblocks to "progress" as mandatory environmental impact studies which must be carried out before an innovation is begun. We assume the worst rather than the best. It is no wonder that passions are aroused by the ecology movement: it flies in the face of the two hundred year old melioristic religion called "Progress."

The fact that there are anti-melioristic processes (as well as melioristic ones) should be reflected in our language. It is not. The Latin verb *meliorare* is matched by an antonym, *pejorare,* meaning to make or become worse; but the parallel English derivatives we expect to find in the dictionary, "pejorism" and "pejoristic," are not there. One suspects that the bias springs from the well-known unconscious denial of unpleasant facts to which Sigmund Freud called our attention.

Be that as it may, I propose to create these new English words, and I recommend that we take them seriously. I will first try to show the sort of situation in which the word pejorism is useful. Secondly I will run through a brief catalog of pejoristic statements already accepted as having merit. . . .

For a classic statement of a pejoristic principle let us examine Gresham's Law: *Bad money drives out good.* As with so many profound and simple truths it has a muddled genealogy. It is named after a 17th century banker, Sir Thomas Gresham, but it was not stated simply until the 19th century; the essence of it, however, was promulgated by Copernicus in the 16th century, and before him by Oresme in the 14th. And no doubt practical men have "known" it at an unconscious level for thousands of years.

Gresham's Law describes a process, one that is inescapably pejoristic. Let us see how this process works. We suppose that two kinds of coins are circulating in a marketplace that is governed by laissez faire, genuine coins and counterfeits. With no compulsion, what happens? Let us suppose that, wanting to buy something, I find I have one genuine and one counterfeit coin in my pocket: which do I use? Obviously, the counterfeit coin (if I can get away with it). This conclusion is based on the simple assumption that self interest governs most, if not all, of each person's actions.

Theorists of a certain tender-hearted stamp bristle at this assumption. "What about conscience? What about a feeling of obligation to others?" they ask. Should we not seek to inculcate in everyone a sense of responsibility that will put an end to the operation of Gresham's Law?

To this well-meaning proposal the pejorist has a simple and decisive response: *it won't work.* His argument is divided into two parts. In the first place, the gentle plan of fostering and depending on conscience sets an impossibly high standard of perfection: *literally everyone* must be ruled by conscience. If even one person in the community follows a lower standard that person prospers at the expense of the others. A laissez faire market system ruled by conscience alone rewards for a lack of conscience. The rule is counterproductive.

The second stage in the dissolution of a conscience-ruled system takes place because of envy. As the "good guys" see the "bad guys" prosper their envy is energized and one after another good guys become bad guys. Not necessarily all of them: there may be some incorruptible saints. But most people aren't saints.

So a laissez faire money system automatically tends to become worse. "Bad money drives out good" is a pejoristic statement. The proof of it rests on two assumptions so simple as to be indubitable: (1) that not everyone is perfect; and (2) that envy is not rare. However small we assume the "initial" supply of bad guys to be, they win out in the long run. Reversing a cliché, we find we are faced with the power of an "overwhelming minority." The system is unstable.

Part of the process of growing up is coming to realize the limits of conscience. For some the recognition is a harrowing experience. The 19th century poet Gerard Manley Hopkins expressed this anguish well:

> Thou are indeed just, Lord, if I contend
> With thee; but, sir, so what I plead is just.
> Why do sinners' ways prosper? and why must
> Disappointment all I endeavour end?
>     Wert thou my enemy, O thou my friend,
> How wouldst thou worse, I wonder, than thou dost
> Defeat, thwart me? Oh, the sots and thralls of lust
> Do in spare hours more thrive than I that spend,
> Sir, life upon thy cause . . .

In the 20th century the baseball player Leo Durocher acidly expressed the matter more briefly: *Nice guys finish last.*

Once we really understand the mechanism of a pejoristic process, pessimism becomes irrelevant. Should we be pessimistic because of the law of gravity or the principle of natural selection? Why weep because stones fall and genes mutate? We must take the world as it is and make the best of it.

The practical response to the overwhelming power of Gresham's Law is to alter the conditions in which it is true. Laissez faire has to be replaced by coercion—*mutual* coercion because we agree to coerce each other. *Pass on a counterfeit coin and you go to jail*—this must be the rule if we are to have a stable monetary system—which we must if what we call civilization is to persist. The freedom of everyone else threatens my freedom; I therefore agree to legislation that restricts the freedom of everyone *including myself*. So must each of us reason. "Mutual coercion mutually agreed upon" is the only workable basis for a democratic society, and the majority must rule.

With the detailed discussion of the particular pejorism we call Gresham's Law completed we are now ready for a rapid survey of the most important pejoristic statements made to date.

1. From the foundations of ethics: *Not to act is to act*. Faced with uncertainty we would like to "do nothing" until the scene clarifies; but this is not possible, for the world rolls on. You can't escape a quandary by sitting on it.

2. From the foundations of ecology: *We can never do one thing;* and *We can never do nothing*. The second statement is, of course, a rewording of the ethical principle given above; the first asserts the interconnectedness of the world.

3. From the foundations of economics: *There's no such thing as a free lunch.* (If there were, economics would disappear.)

4. From thermodynamics, three laws:

> *We can't win.*
> *We are sure to lose.*
> *We can't get out of the game.*

This set of laws is more than pejoristic, it is tragic. The essence of tragedy is that there is no escape from it. We can escape from the asserted consequences of Gresham's Law by changing the universe of rules in which we act. From the laws of thermodynamics there is no escape; there is no other universe.

5. From the foundations of probability: A *"fair game" is one in which the person with the smaller stake loses.* Or, as the Bible puts it: "To them that hath shall be given." A special case: in honest gambling customers always lose to the "house" because the "house" has the

greater stake (and the odds are shaded to take care of overhead and profit). In other words, "You can't win."

6. From the foundations of eugenics: *We get what we select for.*

7. From the foundations of psychology: *We get the behavior we reward for.*

8. From political science: *People get the government they deserve.*

(There is obviously a common element in the last three pejorisms, and that element is *selection,* a principle that far transcends biology, the science in which it has been made most explicit.)

9. Carson's Pesticide Princple: *Every pesticide selects for its own failure.*

10. *C. G. Darwin's Population Law: Every method of voluntary population control selects for its own failure.* As Darwin put the matter, voluntary population control selects for "philoprogenitive people," parents who would rather have children than riches, and so make (voluntary) population control impossible. The leaders of Zero Population Growth, Inc., still don't understand this. For the present, it is perhaps best that they do not.

11. Davis' Law: *If a population control policy is acceptable to the liberal temper, it won't work.* Only laissez faire population control is at present "acceptable," but this, in a world of varying standards of the quality of life, produces a Gresham's Law of Demography: *Low standards drive out high.* Vegetarians drive out meat-eaters—sanctimoniously, in our time.

12. Gregg's Law of Food and Population: *You can't cure a cancer by feeding it.* Believers in the Benign Demographic Transition hold that you can—on the flimsiest of evidence.

13. Parkinson's Law: *Work expands to fill the time available to it.*

14. Peter's Principle: *Every employee in a hierarchy tends to rise to the level of his incompetence.*

15. Murphy's Basic Law: *In a complex system, if anything can go wrong, it will.*

16. Murphy's Zipper Law: *When things go wrong somewhere they quickly go wrong everywhere.*

17. Fontaine's Law: *We believe no evil till the evil's done.* To those who plan for the future this statement by the 17th century fable maker may seem pejoristic enough, but on the basis of Sigmund Freud's dis-

covery of the power of psychological denial we can make a still more
disconcerting statement:

18. The Fontaine-Freud Law: *We believe no evil till the evil's done—*
*IF THEN*. Tigranes, the King of Armenia in the 1st century B.C., set
the fashion when he struck off the head of the man who brought him
news of the approach of a formidable enemy. Political leaders have
been following his example ever since.


With this collection of pejorisms before us we are prepared to note
some of their general properties. First, be it noted, a proper pejorism is
brief. This is not so much a statement of fact as it is a statement of professional standards. The person who gives pejoristic form to a fundamental insight is trying to influence policy. You don't have much influence if
you talk too much.

Contrast, for instance, Durocher's Law ("Nice guys finish last") with
a statement from the *Leviathan* in which Thomas Hobbes is trying to say
the same thing: "But if other men will not lay down their right as well as
he, then there is no reason for anyone to divest himself of his, for that
were to expose himself to prey, which no man is bound to, rather than to
dispose himself to peace." After struggling with that mind-muddler for a
while one certainly sees no reason to rename Durocher's Law "Hobbes'
Law." Priority must yield to clarity.

It might be wondered how it happens that intelligent men can state
things so unclearly as Hobbes (for he was not the last of this line).
Perhaps the commonest explanation is simply this: scholarship can be a
form of stuttering. Psychoanalysts have shown us that a root cause of
stuttering is ambivalence in the patient: he wants to talk but fears the criticism of a significant figure in his life. Stuttering is a way of saying and
not-saying at the same time. Scholars are constantly talking to significant
figures: their superiors, their peers, and the general public. I give two examples of the sort of stuttering-called-scholarship that this produces.

Statement by a leading enologist in *Scientific American* for 1964: "The
ideal climate for wine grapes is one that is warm but not too warm, cool
but not too cool."

Statement made by a demographer discussing the Benign Demographic
Transition in *Science* for 1975: "There is no reason to think that a *high*

level of development will prove to be any less sufficient or any more necessary for the establishment of the preconditions for fertility reduction; indeed, there is already good evidence that fertility declines have occurred in areas of both high and low development.''

Karl Popper has taught us that the other proper statements of science are falsifiable statements. To say that ''A either is, or is not, equal to B'' is to say essentially nothing. The two examples just quoted are splendid, but by no means unique, examples of non-Popperian stuttering.

Pejorisms don't stutter. Indeed, the principal criticism that may be leveled against them arises precisely because of their perhaps too great clarity. The happily phrased pejorism lacks qualifications. From a narrow point of view this may be a demerit: Murphy's Laws and Parkinson's Law surely are not *always* true: then why give them in so extreme and unqualified a form?

The motive for doing so lies in the psychological denial that stands ever ready to suppress the knowledge of danger that finds expression only in obscure or qualified statements. Parkinson's Law is not a universal truth like Newton's Law of Universal Gravitation; rather it is a universal admonition, an *aide-mémoire* to guard against denial. To judge a pejorism by the standards of Newton's Law, and therefore to deny it, is to open the door to more profound psychological denial and hence to disaster.

Of course some pejoristic statements *are* universally true, e.g., the laws of thermodynamics, which express tragic truths. For such we choose the pejoristic form to make sure that people do not forget what we say. If the absolutely true and the merely admonitory forms of pejorisms are not always distinguished from each other by labelling it is just as well: both encourage prudence, a virtue that will be ever more in demand in the markets of the future.

How neglected a virtue prudence has been in the recent past is well illustrated by the following quotation from an investment adviser's market letter of 16 July 1971: ''Taken as a whole, the petroleum industry can plan on nothing but persistent, year-to-year growth for as far down the road as one cares to look. This simple fact has been nearly obscured by the political, social, and ecological storms that regularly clobber the industry.'' Two years later OPEC lowered the boom on oil. The key operational words in the adviser's statement are, of course, ''as far down the

road *as one cares to look.''* One could hardly ask for a franker confession
of entrapment by psychological denial.

Although a few of the classic pejorisms are cast in the form of an affirmative statement, as a group they share a strong, even an aggressive,
negativity. This is no accident. In the unconscious, as Freud first recognized, there is no negation. To free the creative powers it is necessary to
wrench the mind loose from automatic affirmation. Negation, impossible
at the unconscious level, is unpleasant at the conscious. Negation is a
goad to thought. Even if a pejoristic statement is not wholly true it can be
useful in irritating the auditor to seek its disproof—a virtue not possessed
by a flabby affirmative equivalent. Compare, for instance, the tonic stimulus of the pejoristic form of the laws of thermodynamics given above
with, say, the statement that "The efficiency of a real machine is less
than one hundred percent"; or the ecologist's "We can never do merely
one thing" with its flabbier affirmative equivalent, "Everything in the
universe is connected to everything else."

Until forced to do otherwise the conscious mind tends to play along
with the unconscious; it rejects the sort of negative, limit-setting insights
that characterize pejoristic thinking. It is often easiest to gain a hearing
for this kind of insight by wrapping it in humor. Note how many of the
classic pejorisms were introduced in a humorous way: Murphy's Laws
(Who was Murphy? No one knows), Parkinson's Laws (only one was
mentioned here), Peter's Principle and a host of implicit axioms by Stephen Potter, whom I have not discussed. Humor is a door through which
repressed truths may enter consciousness. But the success of the entrance
is ambiguous: humor must often suffer Cassandra's fate. Cassandra possessed the gift of seeing and telling the truth for which she paid this price:
no one believed her. So it often is with humor, and the humorist is something of a court jester. Viewed objectively, the humorous work of C.
Northcote Parkinson is a major contribution to the theory of organizations, but it is generally dismissed as "merely" a joke. (Is there such a
thing as "merely a joke?" Psychoanalysts say not.)

For those who are ready for it, the discipline of deliberately searching
for pejorisms is an invaluable way of neutralizing some of the repressive
powers of the unconscious. The personal advantage of being keenly
aware of the "personal equation" in investigative work shows up clearly
in a passage in Charles Darwin's *Autobiography:*

I had . . . during many years followed a golden rule, namely, that whenever a published fact, a new observation or thought came across me, which was opposed to my general results, to make a memorandum of it without fail and at once; for I had found by experience that such facts and thoughts were far more apt to escape from the memory than favorable ones.

In the same way it helps to deliberately and routinely seek to discover the impotences of our lives and express them pejoristically. In those situations in which an escape from apparent impotence is possible we will discover it sooner if we are stimulated to do so by a brief and clear pejorism. (Are there escapes from Gregg's and Davis' Laws? If there are, explicitly stating them will hasten the work of finding the escapes.)

On the other hand when there is no escape we had better know it early, for there is nothing to be gained by banging our heads against the wall. Tragic limits are the deepest kind of necessity and (as Hegel said) freedom—psychological freedom, that is—comes from the recognition of necessity.

# 19

## *Will Xerox Kill Gutenberg?*

### *(1977)*

*Dead: one small commercial service that made life easier for lazy students.* In this news report there is nothing that obviously should worry scientists and scholars; yet trouble can first appear as "a cloud no bigger than a man's hand."

For 40 years a student-founded business near the Berkeley campus of the University of California supplied "Fybate Lecture Notes" to students who were unwilling or unable to take adequate notes. Graduate students earned money working for Fybate. Many professors cooperated by correcting the final draft. The enterprise filled a need, it gave employment, and it satisfied the customers. Why did the system collapse?

Xerography was the culprit. Fybate Notes were copyrighted, but students copied them and thus evaded paying their share of production costs and profits. The word "profits" has a bad press in our day; many students find virtue in preventing them. So the goose has been killed: there will be no more Fybate originals to copy. One can argue that the change is educationally for the better; but will the fate of Fybate next overtake books and journals?

From *Science*, 198:883. Copyright © 1977 by the American Association for the Advancement of Science.

When modern copiers were new, copies cost 10 cents or more per sheet, and few scientific books cost more than 3 cents per page. It was then silly to copy a book still in print. Now the economics are reversed. The cost of the 43 "Books Received" listed in *Science* for 28 October 1977 averages out at 7.1 cents per page. The most expensive item, *Transient Waves in Visco-Elastic Media,* costs 17.6 cents per page. Copying costs only 3 cents a sheet, and sometimes two book pages can fit on a single sheet, halving the cost. A really expensive book may be copyable for one-tenth its purchase price.

Unauthorized copying of copyrighted material is theft, but who among us can claim more than Hamlet, who said, "I am myself indifferent honest"? The higher book prices go, the less we hesitate to infringe copyrights. We face a textbook example of the destructive force of positive feedback. Original publication, with its expensive editorial and typographic costs, is markedly subject to economies of scale. In contrast, the cost of xerographing individual copies is nearly constant. Every increase in the economic advantage of xerography encourages more copying and less buying of books; this increases the price of future books published, encouraging more copying, which raises the price further. Are you willing to pay 17.6 cents per page for a book? How about 50 cents? Or a dollar? Publishers are caught in a vicious spiral.

Those who understand the danger best—authors and publishers— may hesitate to speak, knowing their arguments will be labeled "self-serving"—as indeed they are. But if the author were to give up his royalty the price per page would drop only to about 6.4 cents; and if the publisher followed suit, the price might fall as low as 5.7 cents. This would still be almost twice the price of xerography. The dynamics of the positive feedback system would be unaltered. How much longer can scholarly books and journals be published?

Must the gift of Gutenberg be nullified by the new technology? Or can we devise an institutional defense against the imminent bibliocide? The floor is open to suggestions.

# PART FOUR: COMPETITION

# 20

## Competition, a Tabooed Idea
## in Sociology

Few people outside the academic community have any conception of the abyss that separates biologists and sociologists within a university. By temperament, training, and the unexamined assumptions of their professions they differ, I think, more than either group differs from most people outside Academia. They don't often fight: they simply ignore one another. No doubt most members of each group think the others fools; but they usually observe the amenities of "professional courtesy"—a euphemism for taboo?— and say nothing in public. They seldom come to grips with the intellectual issues that separate them. This is a pity because there is real need for interdisciplinary work in the overlapping areas.

The contrast between the two disciplines appears nowhere sharper than in the treatment of competition. To the biologist, this topic is central to all discussion of group phenomena. The literature of evolution, ecology, and ethology is saturated with discussions of competition. Sociology being (as biologists see it) but a special sub-field of ethology (animal behavior) one would expect it too to be much concerned with competition. Is it?

I made a rough and ready investigation of the matter by going to the library and examining the first twenty textbooks of sociology I laid my hands on. The only conscious selection made was in terms of recency: only books published 1960 or later were looked at. In each I noted the total number of pages, exclusive of appendices and index; and the number of pages indexed under the entry "competition."

The books averaged 476 pages in length, and of this 2.15 pages, on the average, were indexed under "competition"—0.45 percent, or 1 page out of every 221. Seven of the twenty books had *no* pages indexed under "competition." Is it too much to say that for this 35 percent of the sociologist-authors competition is under a complete thought-taboo?

Of course there are errors in this rough approach. On the one hand, an author may discuss the phenomenon without using the name of competition. Balancing this, I can report that my method of measuring coverage often produced an overestimation. Sometimes the author literally wrote but a single deprecatory sentence about competition; in such cases I counted the coverage as one page, since that was the way it was indicated in the index.

To a biologist, the attitude of sociologists towards competition is nothing short of astounding. Omitting competition from a study of group processes is like leaving gravity out of a treatise on space travel. To those unlearned in classical physics gravity may seem to be a denial of flying, but the equations for flying include the factor of gravity. Similarly, to those unlearned in social physics, competition may appear to be a denial of cooperation; but here too the equations for the latter must surely include a recognition of the former.

A survey of twelve leading ecology texts[1] showed that out of 718 pages devoted to interspecific interactions only 5 percent dealt with mutualistic relations, while 45 percent were given over to predator-prey interactions and 50 percent to competition. Comparing this with the above survey of sociology texts I think we may deduce that biologists pay a hundred times more attention to competition than do sociologists. What accounts for the sociologists' reluctance to deal with a process that is surely inescapable in societies living in a finite world? This is a worthwhile subject for subtle and extensive investigation. In the absence of such I here make only a few comments, beginning with a quotation from one of the most recent textbooks in elementary sociology:

> Faith in progress has played an important part in American society generally; faith in education has been an essential ingredient of this

larger faith. The virtues enjoined by the latter have been, among
others, individual ambition and competitiveness. The American educational system is based on these virtues and in turn fosters them,
beginning with nursery school and going on through college. The
games that American children play are very largely competitive,
indeed are training devices for competition. Essential to this is the
win/lose formula. In every game, in the end, somebody wins and
somebody loses; the aim, of course, is to be a winner. It is only very
young children who sometimes wish, wistfully, that "everyone
should win"; they soon learn that this is "impossible"—in American society, that is, for there are other societies in which children actually play games in which "everyone wins."

The educational system not only fosters competition but (except in
some sports) *individual* competition. Each individual competes with
all others. The academic sin of "cheating" brings this feature out
very clearly. To give help to a weaker peer in an examination is
defined and morally reproved as "cheating" in American education;
in another society (and, indeed, sometimes in the sub-society of the
peer group even in America) the same act may be defined as an
expression of "friendship," and morally approved or even required
as such. A further refinement of this particular definition of the situation is the so-called "honor system," still operating in many schools
and colleges. Here, the individual is not only not supposed to
"cheat" but to keep an eye on all others to make sure that *they*
don't—and to report them to the proper authorities in case they do.
All of this expresses a morality both competitive and individualistic,
and by the same token discouraging of such solidarity between individuals that would impede successful achievement in the system by
each of them. [2]

In evaluating the repugnance for competition shown in this passage it
will help to borrow some terms from game theory in mathematics. A
*zero-sum game* is one in which the losses of one person are exactly coun-
terbalanced by the gains of others, the sum of the signed numbers being
zero. The game of matching pennies can stand as an example: if I lose six
cents my opponent gains six cents, and the sum of gains and losses is
zero. A *non-zero-sum game* is one in which the sum of gains and losses is
not zero. Such games come in two varieties: *benign and malign*. Russian

roulette is an example of the latter: if one of two players blows his head off his loss is surely greater than any putative gain of the other, who witnesses his loss; and the sum is negative.

For a benign non-zero-sum game we might consider the game of scientific research with its sharing of information. Although there are competitive, zero-sum aspects to this game, still the sharing of the results of research through open publication usually benefits everyone. Sharing produces hardly any losses, and a multitude of gains; the sum is positive.

Given "our 'druthers" we would choose non-zero-sum games—benign ones, that is—over zero-sum games and malign non-zero-sum games. But: "If wishes were horses, beggars would ride." Is it within our power to create a world in which all games are benign non-zero-sum ones? I judge that many sociologists think so; aware of the creative power of words (and silence) they seem engaged in trying to will out of existence all zero-sum games by means of the repressive force of taboo. We can grant that their motives are noble: but will they succeed?

The passage from the sociology text quoted previously is in a section entitled, "Am I *Bad* if I Flunk?" We may praise the author for the humanity of his intentions, for he clearly hopes to diminish the suffering that accompanies labeled failure. But we go far astray if we think that academic-type examinations are merely part of a zero-sum game that society puts into play for facetious or sadistic reasons. When the supply of proven ability is markedly less than the demand, a rational society must judge among applicants, for the good of all members of society, regardless of the harm judging may do to those weighed in the balance and found wanting.

Should we, for fear of hurting the losers' feelings, allow anyone who wants to, to practice brain surgery? Or choose the winners by lot? Would either system of selection produce a net gain for society?

A sociologist whose actions were consistent with the passage quoted would refuse to countenance a competitive system that denied anyone the right to become a brain surgeon. Such a sociologist would also defend those who cheated in medical school examinations on the grounds that they thereby exhibited a commendable spirit of "solidarity" which only an immoral society would condemn.

In fact, no sociologist, so far as I know, pursues the train of anticompetitive thought to its logical conclusions. No doubt a subconscious recognition of the ridiculousness of such conclusions accounts for the scamping given to the entire topic of competition in the pages of introductory sociology texts. Academic productivity is throttled by hidden thought-taboos.

In the preface to this book I postulated as one of the four forms of taboo the taboo against thought, which follows as an ultimate consequence of word-taboos. Since the only evidence we can deal with is couched in words, the postulate of a thought-taboo looks very much like a "waterproof hypothesis," a hypothesis that can be neither proved nor disproved, and which is therefore no proper part of science. (The hypothesis of solipsism is such.) But I think the case for thought-taboos is not quite that bad. I offer in evidence of this assertion the story told in Chapter 22.

The most remarkable part of this story is the flagrant error made by a biologist in asserting the exact opposite of one of the conclusions of the "competitive exclusion principle." The author of the error has done much good scientific work. For him, at his level of competence, to commit so elemental an error in population theory is comparable to a high-school graduate's asserting publicly that two plus two equals five. I think the only reasonable way to account for errors as flagrant as these is by postulating that thinking processes can be interfered with by repression—that there are, in fact, thought-taboos.

Whether all thought-taboos can be avoided I don't know: I am unable to see my way through the theory. But I do feel sure that more thought-taboos must be eliminated from the field of sociology if we are to make progress in setting human existence on a rational and dignified foundation.

# 21

# The Cybernetics of Competition

*(1963)*

Science fiction depends heavily on the postulation of Martians, who are invariably assumed to be more advanced intellectually than we. The psychological reason for this assumption seems clear: the whole apocalyptic myth of the men from Mars fulfils needs that were earlier satisfied by the idea of an imminent Kingdom of Heaven. To the objective eye of an anthropologist, our fictional Martians are manifestly gods, and science fiction is a kind of theology.

The odd thing is that before another human lifetime has passed, we may have a chance to see what Martians are really like (if they exist). And if we do, will it be gods that we are finding, or something less than human? I predict the latter, on the grounds that we have not yet heard from them, as we should have if their technology were really more advanced than ours. If they exist and if they trail us in knowledge, we will then be faced with an interesting complex of problems. Should we educate them? Can we educate them? How?

In the past, in dealing with the backward peoples of the earth (a similar problem), we have taken the easy path and have given them the answers

From *Perspectives in Biology and Medicine*, 7:58–84. Copyright © 1963.

ready-made. But suppose for once we decide to give our backward brethren, not the answers, but the *questions*—and let them work out their own answers? Suppose we expose the men from Mars to all the complexities of our technological situation and let them figure out the explanations? Watching them, we should learn a great deal about epistemology!

This *Gedankenexperiment* is introduced for nontrivial reasons. The point I wish to make is this: Martians faced with the riddle of our technology would have a far harder time than we did in creating the underpinning of physical theory, even if they are as intelligent as we. Faced with airplanes, how could they arrive at a theory of gravitation? Listening to the radio, would it occur to them that the intensity of electromagnetic radiation obeyed an inverse-square law? In the presence of an atomic explosion, how could they conceive of a conservation law? They might, of course. After all, we found the laws of nature. But in our search we were fortunate in this respect: most of the time invention was only a very little bit ahead of theory; often it was even behind. We were able to discover theory because the world was simple. A theory-poor Martian confronted with our invention-rich world would have a much harder time discovering theory than we did. He might fail utterly.

Picture if you will a convention of Martians, reading scientific papers to each other, papers concerned with the theory of the Earth. One of them proposes a universal law of gravitation. Pandemonium breaks loose. In the absence of all knowledge about combustion, Newton's three laws of motion, electricity, magnetism, superconductivity, radio-activity, and all the rest, it would be all too easy for the Martian auditors to cite evidence upon evidence to refute the idea of universal gravitation. Only a total complex of theory ("model") can be tested against a factual complex. If the elements of a theoretical construct are tested one by one against the complex world, they will, one by one, be "disproved." Probably our visitors from Mars could arrive at a workable theory only if we earthlings agreed to play "Twenty Questions" with them—to give them a nod of approval whenever they stumbled across a fruitful element of theory. (They would, of course, have to have faith in us; for how could they know that we were not merely playing tricks on them?)

The relation of our hypothetical Martians vis-à-vis the physical world is, I submit, our relation to the social world we have created. Over a period of thousands of years, out of necessity and our unconscious, we have elaborated fantastically complex mechanisms of social interaction, inventions so subtle and pervasive that much of the time we cannot even *see* them, much less explain them. In trying to discover or invent social theory we are in the position of the Martians of our thought-experiment. We have too many facts and not enough theory. Data-rich and theory-poor—that is the social world. And there is no one to play "Twenty Questions" with us.

## I. The Nature of Theory

Popular writing commonly pictures the great scientist as an extremely critical person. There is much truth in this, but the contrary is also partly, and significantly, true. I know a chemist who frequently says to his graduate students, "Don't let a fact stand in the way of a good hypothesis." This is certainly dangerous advice, but inasmuch as the speaker has won a Nobel Prize for his revolutionary chemical theories, we must assume that he knows something of the requirements for creativity. A good scientist should be a good critic part of the time; but he cannot be a good critic all of the time, not if he hopes to discover new and surprising truths. Different occupations require different temperaments. In mentally reviewing a large roster of successful scientists, I am struck with the fact that it includes no men who were ever lawyers. I can recall scientists who in their early years were artists, musicians, actors, machinists, carpenters, businessmen, and even wearers of the cloth—but no lawyers. From the past, Advocate Fermat is the nearest to an exception I can think of—but he became a mathematician, not a scientist.

A good critic must be tough-minded, to use William James's term. Good lawyers are like other good critics. The successful developer of scientific theory, on the other hand, must be *tough-motivated*. A scientific theory, in its early stages at least, is incapable of explaining all the data it is confronted with. This fact may be illustrated by a joke that was standard in engineering circles for several generations: "The bumble bee doesn't have large enough wings to fly, but fortunately the bee doesn't know this, and so he flies anyway." This was a way of acknowledging that the theory of aerodynamics was inadequate to explain the facts. But engineers did not abandon their theory. Instead they retained it (because of its many successes) in the hope—indeed, in the *faith*—that it would one day be enlarged in such a way as to make possible an explanation of the flight of the bumble bee. How scientists decide which theories to have faith in, and which not, is a problem of great subtlety, which has been courageously attacked by Polanyi [1].

In the development of social theory we must follow the path that has proven successful in the natural sciences: we must be critical but not too critical. We must be willing to *entertain* partial theories while we see whether they are capable of fruitful enlargement. In the early stages we must expect to be confronted with markedly different theoretical models. What is offered here is one biologist's conception of the foundations of social and economic theory. "What presumption!" social scientists may say. Admitted; but biology, as Warren Weaver has put it, is "the science of organized complexity"—and what is the social scene if not one of organized complexity? Some of the principles worked out in one field should be at least part of the theoretical structure of the other. Particularly relevant are the principles of *cybernetics,* the science of communication and control within organized systems. Let us see what some of these are, as they have been developed in the natural sciences, and how they may apply to the social sciences.

## II. Positive Feedback

Money put out at compound interest and the unimpeded reproduction of any species of living organism are both examples of systems with positive feedback. Mathematically they are most conveniently represented by equations of the form

$$y = Ce^{bt} \tag{1}$$

where $C$ represents the initial amount (of money or organisms), $y$ is the number or amount after time $t$, $e$ is the base of natural logarithms (2.71828 . . .), and $b$ is a measure of the rate of increase—the greater the rate, the greater is $b$. (For example, if there is no increase at all, $b = 0$; when the rate of increase is 10 per cent, $b = .0953$.)

The exponential function just given may be graphed as shown in Figure 1. Notice that the curve rises ever more steeply with the passage of

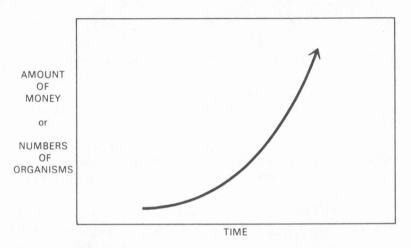

AMOUNT
OF
MONEY

or

NUMBERS
OF
ORGANISMS

TIME

FIGURE 1.

time. Money which is initially interest becomes principal-money, earning more interest-money. Children become parents and produce more children. Hence the use of the term "feedback." The output (part of it, at least) feeds back as input. When the exponent $b$ is positive, we speak of positive feedback. To persist indefinitely, a species must be capable of positive feedback reproduction. To attract investment, a borrower must offer the same possibility for the sums invested.

The exponential equation can be represented by a family of curves, one curve for each value of $b$. But we can generalize the graph shown and say that if we imagine a flexible abscissa—the time axis—one curve stands for all positive exponential functions. With elephants, the scale would read in decades; with bacteria, in minutes, Similarly, with money at compound interest, we have only to stretch or contract the scale on the abscissa to make one curve fit all rates of interest.

In all cases, we should note this: the curve of unimpeded positive feedback "approaches infinity" with the passage of time. This is true no matter how slow the rate of reproduction, no matter how low the rate of interest. *But ours is a finite world.* Therefore it is clear that positive feedback is not tolerable as a permanent state of affairs. It can be tolerated only for short periods of time. In biology no species can indefinitely increase in keeping with its potential, or soon all the world would be nothing but salmon, elephants, men, or whatever. In economics no sum of interest can be allowed to earn compound interest except for very short periods of time. Suppose, for example, that the thirty pieces of silver which Judas earned by betraying Jesus had been put out at 3 per cent interest. If we assume these pieces of silver were dollars, the savings account would today amount to a bit more than $2 \times 10^{26}$ dollars, or about 70 million billion dollars for every man, woman, and child on the face of the earth. Since the real economic wealth of the world is certainly much less than that amount, it would be quite impossible for Judas' heirs (all of us, I presume) to close out the account. The balance in the bankbook would be largely fictional.

A modern William Paley [2] contemplating bank failures, embezzlements, business collapses, runaway inflation, and revolutions might well argue that these catastrophes are examples of "Design in Nature," for by their presence the impossible consequences of perpetual positive feedback are avoided. A professional economist would be more likely to suggest that we could achieve the same end by falling interest rates, which could fall to zero if need be. Historically, however, this more pleasant possibility has seldom, if ever, developed. Failures, inflation, and revolution have been the historically important counteractants to positive feedback.

In contemplating the implications of the exponential growth function, we see also a fundamental criticism of all forms of "Growthmanship" (to use William H. Peterson's term). Plainly the idea of continuous national growth is a dangerous myth. Recent public debate as to whether our economy should grow at a rate of one or two or three percent annually deals with a question which is, in the time scale of human history, of only evanescent interest. Continuous economic growth of the order of magnitude hoped for is possible only for a short period of time—a few centuries at most. If a political and economic unit can achieve enduring stability—and we don't know that it can—it can only be with *zero* percent growth. Not a bit more. Not if growth is measured in material terms, with statistics that are corrected for the effects of inflation. (If growth is in nonmaterial terms, that is another, and a far more interesting, question, which will be neglected here.)

## III. Negative Feedback

If a system that includes positive feedback is to possess stability, it must also include "negative feedback." The meaning of this term can be made clear by an example from engineering.

The temperature of a room is kept constant by the combined operation of a furnace and a thermostat. The result is a cybernetic system which can be represented by a type of diagram previously introduced [3]. As indicated in Figure 2, when the temperature rises, a bimetallic strip in the thermostat is distorted, thus breaking an electric contact, thus turning off the furnace, and so lowering the temperature. On the other hand, a lowering of the temperature leads to a re-establishment of the electric contact, thus starting the furnace, thus raising the temperature. The temperature of the room will thus fluctuate about the "set point" of the thermostat—and this is what we mean when we say "the temperature is held constant." The variations do not exceed certain limits.

Now for an example from biology. In any natural setting, the population size of a given species is relatively constant for long periods of time—usually thousands, or even millions, of years. How this constancy is maintained is shown in Figure 3. If the population should increase above the "natural" population size—which we may call the "set point" of the population—various kinds of negative feedback will be brought

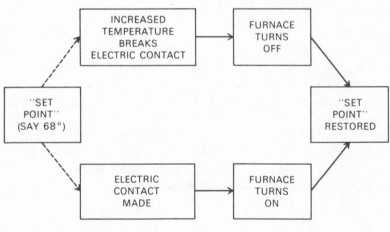

FIGURE 2.

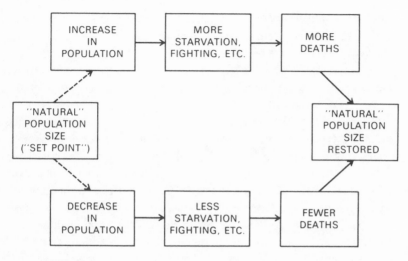

FIGURE 3.

into play. Shortage of food may lead to starvation. Fighting may lead to deaths or to interference with breeding. And so on. The result of all this will be more deaths, and perhaps fewer births, and the population will fall. The consequence of a decrease in population can be read from the diagram. Again we have a cybernetic scheme that produces fluctuations about a "set point." What determines the "set point" is not so easy to tell. That is, our knowledge of the interactions of the natural controls of population size is usually insufficient to enable us to *predict* what the "carrying capacity" of the land will be. We have to go into the field and measure it; we determine it *ex post facto*. Nevertheless, we retain this model and interpret our inability to make an *a priori* determination of the set point as indicating a deficiency in our knowledge rather than a defect in the model.

The cybernetic model can be carried over into economics, as shown in Figure 4, which depicts the control of price in the Ricardian economic scheme. The well-known course of events can be read from the figure. Again we see that negative feedback produces stability about a "set point," which Ricardo called the "natural price." The model would be more realistic if it were constructed in terms of *profit* rather than price, but for historical continuity we retain the classic Ricardian element *price*. As with the biological example previously used, the meaning of "natu-

ral'' can, in general, only be determined *ex post facto*. The word ''natural'' is here (as elsewhere) a verbal cloak for ignorance. Nevertheless, it
or an equivalent word is needed to remind us of the state of affairs. There
is mystery here. It was this mystery together with the unpremeditated
consequences of the economic cybernetic system that led Adam Smith to
speak of an ''Invisible Hand.''

An effective cybernetic system produces stability, i.e., fluctuations
within limits, and this we esteem. A system that produces a stable temperature, or a stable population, or a stable price, seems to us somehow
*right*. When we examine any cybernetic system we discover that it is
more or less wasteful. The thermostated room wastes heat; the natural
population wastes lives; the economic system produces price wars and
business bankruptcies. We may refine the controls and minimize the
losses (of heat, or of money, for example), but a close examination of the
system convinces us that there must always be some losses, waste in
some sense. This is so because the controls that serve to produce equilib-
ria are themselves so many modes of loss. Accounting procedures, insurance programs, police forces, sweat glands, electric fans, predation,
crowd diseases, delicate thermostats—all these are forms of waste. We
do not regret them, for the negative feedback produced by each of these

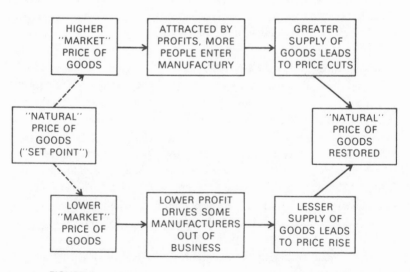

FIGURE 4.

elements acts as a check to some kind of uncontrolled and ruinous positive feedback. But each negative feedback device has its price, and we
cannot get rid of one form of loss without incurring another. In a deep
sense we see that some waste is inevitable and natural, and we recognize
as immature the man who compulsively tries to do away with all waste.
We recognize as pathological the goal of a waste-free world. This recognition is an important element in that complex of temperament that we
label "conservative." Insofar as we think deeply, we all, of necessity,
partake of this temperament to some extent.

But because the mature person acknowledges the inevitability of some
waste, it does not follow that he must be reconciled to any amount and
kind of waste. In the first excitement of discovering the beauties of economic cybernetics, David Ricardo quite naturally made such an error. In
speaking of the cybernetic system that stabilizes the population of laborers, Ricardo [4] wrote: "When the market price of labour is below its
natural price, the condition of the labourers is most wretched: then poverty deprives them of those comforts which custom renders absolute
necessaries. It is only after their privations have reduced their number, or
the demand for labour has increased, that the market price of labour will
rise to its natural price. . . ."

Attention should be called to the use of the word "natural" in this
question. It would be antihistorical to expect Ricardo to speak of the "set
point of labor" inasmuch as the term "set point" was not used for
another century; but that is not the only criticism that can be made of the
word "natural." Looking at the problem through the eyes of Stephen
Potter [5], what do we see? Plainly, that an advocate is likely to use the
word "natural" in order to insinuate approval of the "natural" thing into
the mind of his auditor. By so doing, the advocate frees himself of the
necessity of developing a defensible argument for the "natural" thing—
for who can disapprove of that which is "natural"?

This attack on the use of the word "natural" is more than a mere Pot-
terian counterploy, as is clearly shown by the following defense given by
Ricardo [6].

Labour, like all other things which are purchased and sold, and
which may be increased or diminished in quantity, has its natural
and its market price. The natural price of labour is that price which

is necessary to enable the labourers, one with another, to subsist and perpetuate their race, without either increase or diminution.

These then are the laws by which wages are regulated, and by which the happiness of far the greatest part of every community is governed. Like all other contracts, wages should be left to the fair and free competition of the market, and should never be controlled by the interference of the legislature.

This passage leaves no question in our mind that Ricardo identified the momentary state of things in his own time as "natural" and that all attempts to modify it further by new legislation were "unnatural" and hence improper in some deep sense. With rare exceptions, most of us post-Ricardians have been unwilling to accept this view. Ricardo, at least on paper, accepted both. But—perhaps because of a delicate consideration of the feelings of others?—he used a most elegant euphemism for the facts. "It is only after their privations have reduced their number," he wrote; and insisted that "wages should be left to the fair and free competition of the market." The market must be free, that we may enjoy the blessings of cybernetic stability. Most of us now think that Ricardo's price is too high. We are willing to make use of "unnatural" controls of the price of labor even if it means losing some of our freedom. The history of the labor movement since Ricardo's time may be regarded as one long struggle to substitute other forms of waste for the "natural" form which Ricardo, who was not a laborer, was willing to accept.


## IV. The Competitive Exclusion Principle

Perhaps more important than the humane argument just given against the Ricardian model is a theoretical argument which indicates that the cybernetic system he described is fundamentally unstable. Before we can discuss this matter we need to introduce a biological principle known by various names but recently [3] called the "competitive exclusion principle." The historical origin [7] of this principle is complex; no one man can be given credit for it. In the last decade it has become increasingly clear that it is a basic axiom of biological theory; and it will be my argument here that it is basic also to sociological and economic theory. But first, let us develop the principle in an exclusively biological context.

Consider a situation in which two mobile species, X and Z, live in the same habitat and also live in the same "ecological niche," i.e., live exactly the same type of life. Species X multiplies according to this equation:

$$x = Ke^{ft}, \tag{2}$$

where $x$ is the number of individuals of species X at time $t$; $e$ is the base of natural logarithims: $K$ is a constant standing for the number of $x$ at $t = 0$; and $f$ is a constant determined by the "reproductive potential" of the species.

Species Z multiplies according to this equation:

$$z = Le^{gt}, \tag{3}$$

in which the constants have the same meaning as before (though, in the general case, with different values).

Suppose these two species are placed in the same universe to compete with each other. What will happen? Let us represent the ratio of the number of the two species, $x/z$, by a new variable, $y$. Then:

$$y = \frac{Ke^{ft}}{Le^{gt}} \tag{4}$$

Since $K$ and $L$ are both constants, they can be replaced by another constant, say $C$; and making use of a well-known law of exponents, we can write:

$$y = Ce^{ft-gt} = Ce^{(f-g)t}. \tag{5}$$

But $f$ and $g$ are also constants, and can be replaced by another constant, say $b$, which gives us:

$$y = Ce^{bt}. \tag{6}$$

which is, of course, our old friend equation 1 again, the equation of exponential growth. The constant $b$ will be positive if species X is competitively superior, negative if it is species Z that multiplies faster.

What does this mean in words? This: in a finite universe—and the or-

ganisms of our world know no other—where the total number of organisms of both kinds cannot exceed a certain number, a universe in which
a fraction of one living organism is not possible, one species will necessarily replace the other species completely if the two species are "complete competitors," i.e., live the same kind of life.

Only if $b = 0$, i.e., if the multiplication rates of the two species are *precisely* equal, will the two species be able to coexist. Precise, mathematical equality is clearly so unlikely that we can ignore this possibility completely. Instead we assert that the *coexistence of species cannot find its
explanation in their competitive equality*. This truth has profound practical implications.

## V. Have We Proved Too Much?

It is characteristic of incomplete theory that it "proves too much,"
i.e., it leads to predictions which are contrary to fact. This is what we
find on our first assessment of the competitive exclusion principle. If we
begin with the assumption that every species competes with all other
species, we are forced to the conclusion that one species—the best of
them all—should extinguish all other species. But there are at least a
million species in existence today. The variety seems to be fairly stable.
How come?

There are many answers to this question. I will discuss here only some
of the answers, choosing those that will prove suggestive when we later
take up problems of the application of the exclusion principle to human
affairs. The following factors may, in one situation or another, account
for the coexistence of species.

*Geographic isolation.*—Before man came along and mixed things up,
the herbivores of Australia (e.g., kangaroos) did not compete with European herbivores (rabbits). Now Australians, desirous of retaining some of
the aboriginal fauna, are trying desperately to prevent the working out of
the exclusion principle.

*Ecological isolation.*—English sparrows introduced into New England
excluded the native bluebirds from the cities. But in very rural environments bluebirds have, apparently, some competitive advantage over the
sparrows, and there they survive today.

*Ecological succession.*—It is not only true that environments select organisms; in addition, organisms make new selective environments. The conditions produced by a winning species may put an end to its own success. Grape juice favors yeast cells more than all others; but as the cells grow they produce alcohol which limits their growth and ultimately results in new predominant species, the vinegar bacteria. In the growth of forests, pine trees are often only an intermediate stage, a "subclimax," being succeeded by the climax plants, the hardwood trees, which outcompete the pines in growing up from seeds in the shade of the pine tree.

*Lack of mobility.*—The universal application of the exclusion principle to plants is still a controversial issue, which cannot be resolved here. It may be that the lack of mobility, combined with certain advantages to being first on the spot, modify the outcome significantly. Although this explanation is questionable, it is a fact of observation that a pure stand of one kind of plant hardly ever occurs.

*Interbreeding.*—If two competing populations are closely enough related genetically that they can interbreed, one group does not replace the other, they simply merge. This does not end competition: it merely changes its locus. The different genes of the formerly distinct groups now compete with each other, under the same rule of competitive exclusion.

*Mutation.*—Continuing with the example just given, one gene never quite eliminates another because the process of mutation is constantly producing new genes. The gene for hemophilia, for example, is a very disadvantageous gene; but even if hemophiliacs never had children (which is almost true), there would always be some hemophiliacs in the population because about three eggs in every 100,000 produced by completely normal women will be mutants that develop into hemophilic sons.

## VI. The Cybernetics of Monopoly

We are now ready to take a second look at the Ricardian thesis. The model implicit in his writings may not unfairly be stated as follows. We conceive of a single product manufactured by a number of entrepreneurs, each of whom must, for simplicity in theory construction, be imagined to be engaged in the manufacture of this product only. Under these conditions the Ricardian cybernetic scheme diagrammed in Figure 4 will prevail—but only for awhile. History indicates that the number of entrepreneurs is subject to a long-term secular trend toward reduction. In the early days there were many scores of manufacturers of automobiles in the U.S.; today there are less than a dozen. Ball-point pens, transistors—every new product—have followed the same evolution. The history of the oil industry (to name only one) indicates that under conditions of perfect laissez faire, competition has a natural tendency to steadily decrease the number of competitors until only one is left. In industries with heavy overhead this tendency is a consequence of the economy of size. But even without this size effect, a simple extension of the competitive exclusion principle into economics shows that a reduction in the number of competitors will take place as the more efficient entrepreneurs squeeze out the less efficient, until ultimately only one is left. If this were not so, we would have to conclude that the free enterprise system has no tendency to produce the lowest possible price; or, to put it differently, that it has no tendency to produce the maximum efficiency. Either conclusion would deny the claims to virtue put forward by the defenders of the free enterprise system.

If a monopoly is produced, what then? Here is a question which Ricardo did not face. At first glance one might say that the monopoly price should be stable, because if it were to rise, new entrepreneurs would be attracted to the field and would lower the price. But this is a naïve view. We know that it is more difficult to start a business than to continue one, and consequently a monopolist can maintain a price considerably above the "natural price." Furthermore, a realistic model must include much more than we have indicated so far. We must consider the whole complex of phenomena that we include under the word "power." *Social power is a process with positive feedback.* By innumerable stratagems a monopolist will try to manipulate the machinery of society in such a way as to ward off all threats to re-establish negative feedback and a "natural" cybernetic equilibrium. And, as history shows, the monopolist in one field will seek to extend his power into others, without limit.

What has just been said about business monopolies applies equally to labor monopolies, *mutatis mutandis*. Insofar as they meet with no opposition, there is little doubt that labor monopolies seek to produce an ever higher price for labor. At the same time, they protest the appearance of business monopolies. Contrariwise, unopposed businessmen seek to promote a free market in labor while restricting it in their own field (by "Fair Trade" laws, for instance). It is not cynicism but simple honesty that forces us to acknowledge that Louis Veuillot (1813–1883) was right when he said: "When I am the weaker, I ask you for liberty because that is your principle; but when I am the stronger I take liberty away from you because that is my principle." In other words, such verbal devices as "principles," "liberty," and "fairness" can be used as competitive weapons. Each purely competitive agent, were he completely honest and frank, would say, "I demand a free market—but only for others." It is, in fact, a natural part of *my* competitive spirit to seek to remove from *my* field the natural competition on which the validity of the Ricardian scheme rests.

Such an analysis, which is based on the observed behavior of competing groups, may seem depressing. Rather than dwell on the possible emotional consequences of the facts, let us see what we can do about arranging the world to our satisfaction. Let us try to enlarge the model of our theory. To do this we acknowledge that we are *not only* unconscious "purely competitive agents," but that we are also capable of being conscious. We can predict the results of our own actions, as well as the results of the actions of those opposed to us. We acknowledge that *words are actions,* actions designed to influence others. Because we can see that others resort to high-flown rhetoric when they want to influence us, we become suspicious of our own arguments. We operate under the basic and parsimonious rule of the Theory of Games [8], which says that we must impute to others intelligence equal to our own. Under these conditions we seek the *boundary conditions* within which the rule of laissez faire can produce stability.

## VII. The Limits of Laissez Faire

Laissez faire has a strong emotional appeal; it seems somehow right. Yet we have seen that, in the limit, the rule fails because of the positive feedback of power. Can we *rationalize* the rule of laissez faire by harmonizing it with boundary conditions?

I suggest that there is, in biology, a useful model already at hand [9]. Consider the cybernetic system that controls the temperature of the human body, a system that is enough like that shown in Figure 2 so that it need not be diagrammed here. This system works admirably. So well does it work that, for the most part, we can safely adopt a laissez faire attitude toward our body temperature.

The system works without conscious control or planning. But only within limits. If the environmental stress is too great, temperature control fails. At the upper limit, too great a heat input raises the body temperature to the point where the physiological thermostat no longer functions. Then higher temperature produces greater metabolism, which produces more heat, which produces higher temperature, which—and there it is, positive feedback, leading to death, to destruction of the whole system. Similarly with abnormally low temperatures. The working of the system is shown in Figure 5. There is a middle region in which a laissez faire attitude toward control of the environment works perfectly; we call this middle region the *homeostatic plateau*. (The word "homeostatic" was coined by W. B. Cannon to indicate constancy-maintained-by-negative-feedback.) Beyond the homeostatic plateau, at either extreme, lie positive feedback and destruction. Plainly, our object in life must be to keep ourselves on the homeostatic plateau. And insofar as it is within our power to affect the design of a system, we would wish to extend the plateau as far as possible.

Is this not the model for all cybernetic systems, sociological and economic as well as biological, the model on which ethics must be based? The desire to maintain *absolute* constancy in any system must be recognized as deeply pathological. Engineering theory indicates that excessive restraints can produce instability. In psychiatry also, the desire for complete certainty is recognized as a most destructive compulsion. And in the history of nations, attempts to control rigidly all economic variables have uniformly led to chaos. The psychologically healthy human recognizes that fluctuations are unavoidable, that waste is normal, and that one should institute only such explicit controls as are needed to keep the social system on the homeostatic plateau. On this plateau—but not beyond it—freedom produces stability.

We can do this only if we explicitly give up certain superficially plausible objectives which are incompatible with stability. In the realm of economics, the most dangerous will-o'-the-wisp is the word "efficiency."

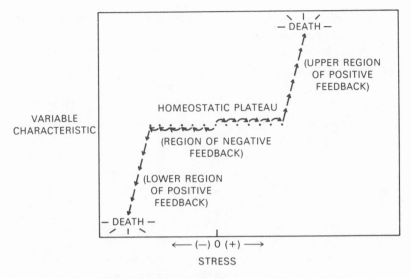

FIGURE 5.

Consider the classical Ricardian economic system. If we decide that all waste is bad and that we must maximize efficiency, then we will stand admiringly by and watch the competitive exclusion principle work its way to its conclusion, leaving only one surviving entrepreneur, the most efficient. And then? Then we find that we have a tiger by the tail, that we have allowed the positive feedback of power to go so far that we may be unable to regain anything that deserves the name of freedom. It is suicidal to seek complete efficiency. The Greek Solon said, "Nothing in excess," to which we must add, *not even efficiency*. Whatever it is that we want to maximize, it cannot be efficiency. We can remain free only if we accept some waste.

How are we to keep a social system on its homeostatic plateau? By laws? Not in any simple way, for the effect of an action depends on the state of the system at the time it is applied—a fact which is, I believe, not systematically recognized in the theory of law. An act which is harmless when the system is well within its homeostatic boundaries may be quite destructive when the system is already stressed near one of its limits. *To promote the goal of stability, a law must take cognizance not only of the act but also of the state of the system at the time the act is performed.* In his effort to obtain the maximum individual freedom, it is to be expected, of course, that "economic man" will try to defend his actions in terms of some tradition-hallowed "absolute" principles that take no cognizance of the state of the system. Absolutists of all sorts may, in fact, be defined as men who reject *systematic* thinking.

Consider this question: Should a man be allowed to make money, and keep it? In the history of Western capitalism our first approximation to an answer was an unqualified *Yes*. But as we became aware that money is one means of achieving the positive feedback of power, we looked around for curbs. One of these is the graduated income tax, which most men would now defend as a reasonable brake to the positive feedback of economic power. Yet it can easily be attacked as being "unfair," and in fact has been so attacked many times. As late as 1954 (according to a press report) the industrialist Fred Maytag II, speaking to a meeting of the National Association of Manufacturers on the subject of discriminatory taxes, issued this clarion call for action: "The hour is late, but not too late. There is no excuse for our hesitating any longer. With all the strength of equity and logic on our side, and with the urgent need for taking the tax shackles off economic progress, initiative is ours if we have the courage to take it."

One cannot but have a certain sympathy for the speaker. He is right when he says that the existing tax structure is contrary to "equity." But if discussion is to be carried on in terms of such abstractions, Mr. Maytag would find his opponents introducing the word "justice" and saying that this is more precious than equity. Rather than use such verbal bludgeons, we should think operationally in terms of the homeostatic plateau. We should think in terms of systems rather than individual acts. That this sort of thinking presents difficulties for the law is admitted; but it is clear also that we have made some progress in the solution of these difficulties, e.g., in the graduated income tax. It is clear also that our systematic thinking has not produced perfect solutions to our problems (e.g., it is still possible to become a millionaire via the capital gains route).

Indeed, the recognition of the relevance of the whole system in judging the desirability of an individual act can be traced back to antiquity. One of the greatest of the technical social inventions of ancient Athens was that of *ostracism*, which was invented by Cleisthenes. We are told [10]:

Once a year the popular Assembly deliberated on whether any citizen should be required to go into exile for ten years on the grounds that his presence in Athens was a threat to the constitution. If the Assembly voted to hold an ostracism, a second vote was taken. Then, if six thousand citizens wrote the same name on an *ostrakon,* or potsherd, the man named must leave Athens for ten years. But he did not lose his citizenship, his goods were not confiscated, he did not even suffer disgrace. In fact, it was only the man of great ability who was likely to be ostracized, yet the possibility of ostracism was a constant deterrent to overweening political ambition.

In other words, ostracism was a device aimed at stopping the positive feedback of power, a tool designed to maintain the political system on a homeostatic plateau. Recognition of the dangers of this positive feedback must surely be almost universal among practical men and produces the most diverse strategems, many of which would seem quite paradoxical to one who was ignorant of the positive feedback of power (as adolescents in our society often are). For instance, we are told [11] that "in the early history of the Church, bishops had to take solemn oaths at the time of their ordination. The first oath was that they would discharge the duties of that office faithfully in the sight of God and man. The second oath was called the oath of 'Nolo episcopari'—'I don't want to be a bishop.' . . ." Those who frequent the university campuses of our own time will surely have noted that one of the best ways to achieve a deanship is to insist that one doesn't want to be dean (but not too loudly!). Competition and the desire to limit power produce strange strategies.

## VIII. The Persistence of Variety

An important part of the unfinished work of theoretical biology revolves around the question of variety: how are we to account for the variety of the living world? The competitive exclusion principle points always toward simplification; yet the world remains amazingly, delightfully complex.

The same problem exists in economics. Why do there continue to be so many competing units? The economist's problem is, I suspect, even further from solution than the biologist's, but we can briefly list some of the social factors, which resemble those mentioned earlier in the biological discussion.

*Geographic isolation.*—A less efficient company may be able to coexist with a more efficient one if it is at a considerable distance and if transportation charges are heavy, as they are, for instance, in the coal and steel industry. (It is interesting to note that major steelmakers of the United States two generations ago tried to negate this factor by enforcing the "Pittsburgh-plus" system of pricing.)

*Product differentiation.*—In biology, ecological differentiation is the necessary condition for coexistence; in economics, product differentation [12] plays the same role. Patents, copyrights, and mere advertising gimmicks enable entrepreneurs partially to escape pure competition.

*Mergers* prevent extinction in economics in the same sense that interbreeding prevents extinction in biology.

In the social realm we have in addition various peculiarly human characteristics that contribute to the persistence of variety. Curiosity, envy, dislike of boredom, yearning for destruction are a few of the factors which work against the efficiency of the market and hence tend to perpetuate variety. We are a long way from understanding the economic system. It is, however, transparently clear that any satisfactory over-all theory of economics must include a large measure of psychology in it. The *Homo economicus* of classical theory has been useful as a first approximation only.

## IX. The Idea of a System

One of the most important ideas in modern science is the idea of a *system;* and it is almost impossible to define. There are a number of good essays available on this subject [13]. Here we will try to define by example.

Our first example is a caricature from the nineteenth century—the idea of a system that connects the welfare of England with the existence of old maids. The argument is simple: old maids keep cats, cats eat rats, rats destroy bumblebee nests, bumblebees fertilize red clover, and red clover is needed for horses, which are the backbone of English character training. Ergo the strength of England depends on a bountiful supply of old maids. Now that is a caricature, but it gets across the idea that the many cybernetic systems of nature are connected in complex ways. So complex are they that we can seldom predict exactly what will happen when we introduce a new element into a system. By way of illustration, consider the following examples from three different fields of biology.

*Ecology.*—Charles Elton [14] tells the following history.

Some keen gardener, intent upon making Hawaii even more beautiful than before, introduced a plant called *Lantana camara,* which in its native home of Mexico causes no trouble to anybody. Meanwhile, some one else had also improved the amenities of the place by introducing turtle-doves from China, which, unlike any of the native birds, fed eagerly upon the berries of *Lantana.* The combined effects of the vegetative powers of the plant and the spreading of seeds by the turtle-doves were to make the *Lantana* multiply exceedingly and become a serious pest on the grazing country. Indian mynah birds were also introduced, and they too fed upon *Lantana* berries. After a few years the birds of both species had increased enormously in numbers. But there is another side to the story. Formerly the grasslands and young sugarcane plantations had been ravaged yearly by vast numbers of army-worm caterpillars, but the mynahs also fed upon these caterpillars and succeeded to a large extent in keeping them in check, so that the outbreaks became less severe. About this time certain insects were introduced in order to try and check the spread of *Lantana* and several of them (in particular a species of Agromyzid fly) did actually destroy so much seed that the *Lantana* began to decrease. As a result of this, the mynahs also began to decrease in numbers to such an extent that there began to occur again severe outbreaks of army-worm caterpillars. It was then found that when the *Lantana* had been removed in many places, other introduced shrubs came in, some of which are even more difficult to eradicate than the original *Lantana.*

From this example (and scores of comparable ones are known) it is easy to see why it is so difficult to secure the permission of the U.S. Department of Agriculture to import any species of plant or animal. However, though we are very conservative about the introduction of biotic elements into our ecological systems, we show the most juvenile irresponsibility in our attitude toward new chemicals. To get rid of insects, we spray promiscuously with such potent poisons as Malathion. As a result, we kill not only millions of insects, but also thousands of birds. Because birds are a great natural negative feedback for insect populations, using insecticides often causes a secondary *increase* in the numbers of insects later. We may refer to this as a "flareback"—thus verbally acknowledging our failure to think in terms of systems. We are only now beginning to see the magnitude of the problems we have created for ourselves by *unsystematic* thinking, for which belated insight we are significantly indebted to Rachel Carson's book *Silent Spring* [15].

*Embryology.*—Beginning about 1960 a drug known as "thalidomide" became an increasingly popular sedative in Europe. It seemed superior to all others in effectiveness and harmlessness. But by the end of 1961 a most painful disillusionment had set in. When taken during the early weeks of pregnancy, it frequently interfered with the development of the limb buds of the child, resulting in the birth of a child exhibiting *phocomelia*—seal-limbs, little flipper-like hands, without long arm bones. In addition, there were other variable defects of the ears, digestive tract, heart, and large blood vessels; strawberry marks were common [16]. Only a minority of the children whose mothers took thalidomide during the first trimester developed phocomelia, but so widespread was the use of the drug that the number of cases produced in West Germany alone in two years' time probably exceeded 6,000. This experience contributed to a reevaluation of the whole idea of therapy, particularly of newly pregnant women. The developing embryo is a set of cybernetic systems of the greatest complexity. Coupled with the high rate of change during the early weeks is a high sensitivity to foreign chemicals inserted into the system. To a growing extent, physicians are loath to permit a newly pregnant woman to take any drug if it can possibly be avoided.

When we think in terms of systems, we see that a fundamental misconception is embedded in the popular term "side effects" (as has been pointed out to me by James W. Wiggins). This phrase means roughly "effects which I hadn't foreseen, or don't want to think about." As concerns the basic mechanism, side-effects no more deserve the adjective "side" than does the principal" effect. It is hard to think in terms of systems, and we eagerly warp our language to protect ourselves from the necessity of doing so.

*Genetics.*—When a new gene is discovered, it must be named; this is accomplished by naming it for some conspicuous effect it has on the organism. But when a very careful study is made, it is found that a mutant gene has not one effect but many. For example, close analysis of one mutant gene in the laboratory rat has shown [17] no less than twenty-two well-defined effects, including effects on ribs, larynx, trachea, vertebrae, lungs, red blood cells, heart, teeth, and capillaries. Yet all these effects spring from a single chemical change in the genetic material of the fertilized egg. In the early days, geneticists often used the word "pleiotropy" to refer to the multiple effects of genes. Now it seems scarcely worth while to use this word because we are pretty sure that all genes are pleiotropic. The word "pleiotropy" is a fossil remnant of the days when geneticists failed to have sufficient appreciation of the developing organism as a system.

Pleiotropy presents animal and plant breeders with one of their most basic and persistent problems. The breeding performance of the St. Bernard dog will serve to illustrate the problem. Crosses between St. Bernard and other breeds of dogs produce a large proportion of stillborn or lethally malformed puppies. The trouble apparently lies in the pituitary gland, which is overactive. When we look closely at the adult St. Bernard, we see that its abnormally large head and paws correspond to "acromegaly" in humans, a condition also caused by an overactive pituitary. The St. Bernard breed is, in fact, standardized around this abnormality. Why are not the causative genes more deleterious to the breed? Undoubtedly because there are other, "modifier," genes which alter the whole genetic system so that it can tolerate the effects of the "principal" genes. The production of a new breed built about some distinctive gene often takes a long time because the breeder must find, and breed for, a multitude of modifier genes which create a genetic system favorable to the principal gene. This work is almost entirely trial and error; along the way the breeder must put up with large losses in the way of unsuccessful systems of genes.

## X. The Feasibility of Human Wishes

The dream of the philosopher's stone is old and well known and has its counterpart in the ideas of skeleton keys and panaceas. Each of these images is of a single thing which solves all problems within a certain class. The dream of such cure-alls is largely a thing of the past. We now look askance at anyone who sets out to find the philosopher's stone.

The mythology of our time is built more around the reciprocal dream— the dream of a highly specific agent *which will do only one thing*. It was this myth which guided Paul Ehrlich in his search for disease-specific therapeutic agents. "Antitoxins and antibacterial substances are, so to speak, charmed bullets which strike only those objects for whose destruction they have been produced," said Ehrlich in voicing this myth. Belief in the myth has inspired much fruitful research; but it *is* a myth, as the phenomena of allergies, anaphylaxis, auto-immunization, and other "side effects" show us. It is *our* myth, and so it is hard to see.

The tragic danger in the myth has been neatly uncovered by W. W. Jacobs in his classic short story, "The Monkey's Paw." In this story a man is allowed three wishes. He wishes first for money. He gets it. It is brought to his door as compensation for his son's death in the mill. Horrified, the father wishes his son alive again. He gets that wish too—his son comes to the door looking as he would after such an accident. In desperation, the father wishes everything back as it was before he was given the three wishes.

The moral of the myth can be put in various ways. One: wishing won't make it so. Two: every change has its price. Three (and this one I like the best): *we can never do merely one thing*. Wishing to kill insects, we may put an end to the singing of birds. Wishing to "get there" faster, we insult our lungs with smog. Wishing to know what is happening everywhere in the world at once, we create an information overload against which the mind rebels, responding by a new and dangerous apathy.

Systems analysis points out in the clearest way the virtual irrelevance of good intentions in determining the consequences of altering a system. For a particularly clear-cut example, consider the Pasteurian revolution—the application of bacteriology and sanitation to the control of disease. We embarked on this revolution because we wished to diminish loss of life by disease. We got our wish, but it looks now as though the price will be an ultimate increase in the amount of starvation in the world. We could have predicted this, had we taken thought, for Malthus came before Pasteur, and Malthus clearly described the cybernetic system that controls populations. The negative feedbacks Malthus saw were misery and vice—by which he meant disease, starvation, war, and (apparently) contraception. Whatever diminution in effect one of these feedbacks undergoes must be made up for by an increase in the others. War, it happens, is almost always a feeble demographic control; and contraception is not yet as powerful as we would like it to be; so, unless we exert ourselves extraordinarily in the next decade, starvation will have to take over. Like the father in "The Monkey's Paw," we wanted only one thing—freedom from disease. But, in the system of the world, we can never change merely one thing.

Suppose that at the time Pasteur offered us his gift of bacteriology—and I use the name "Pasteur" in a symbolic way to stand for a multitude of workers—suppose at that time that some astute systems analyst had drawn a Malthusian cybernetic diagram on the blackboard and had pointed out to us the consequences of accepting this gift. Would we have refused it? I cannot believe we would. If we were typically human, we would probably have simply called forth our considerable talent for denial and gone ahead, hoping for the best (which perhaps is what we actually did).

But suppose we had been what we like to dream we are—completely rational and honest, and not given to denial? Would we then have rejected the gift of disease control? Possibly; but I think not. It is not more likely that we would, instead, have looked around for another gift to combine with this one to produce a new, stable system? That other gift is well known, of course: it is the one Margaret Sanger gave us, to speak symbolically again. It is a gift we are now in the process of accepting.

In terms of systems, we can give this analysis:

| System | Stability |
|---|---|
| Malthusian | Yes |
| Pasteurian | No |
| Sangerian | Possibly |
| Pasteurian-Sangerian | Yes |

A systems analyst need not, when confronted with a new invention, reject it out of hand simply because "we can never do merely one thing." Rather, if he has the least spark of creativity in him, he says, "We can never do merely one thing, *therefore we must do several* in order that we may bring into being a new stable system." Obviously, in planning a new system he would have to examine many candidate-ideas and re-examine our value system to determine what it is we really want to maximize. Not easy work, to say the least.


## XI. Is Planning Possible?

Some of the most excruciating questions of our time hinge on feasibility of planning. Is good planning possible? Is it possible to devise a planned system that is at least as good as a free system? Can the free market be dispensed with without losing its desirable virtues?

There is no dearth of literature supporting and condemning planning. Rather than add to this double battery of polemic literature, I would like to take a different approach. I would prefer to adopt an agnostic attitude toward the principal question and ask a second question: *If* successful planning is possible, what are its preconditions? If we can see these clearly, we should be in a better position to answer the principal question. The major points at issue seem to me to be the following.

1. Can it be shown, before instituting a plan, that all significant factors have been taken account of? It is not easy to see what the nature of the proof would be; and in any case, the consequences of past planning attempts do not make us optimistic.

2. Are we sure that we can predict all possible interactions of factors, even when we have complete knowledge of them? This is not as disturbing a question now as it was in the past. Any system of equations that can be solved "in principle" can be turned over to computing machines, which are immensely faster, more patient, and more reliable than human beings; and all computing machines operate under the Magna Charta given them by A. M. Turing [18].

3. Granted that we can predict a new and better stable system, can we also devise an acceptable transition? The many social systems known to historians and anthropologists represent so many points in space and time. The transitions from one to another are usually obscure; or, when recorded, are known to involve great human suffering and immense wastage of human resources. In general, transitions seem more feasible for small populations than large—but will small populations ever again exist?

4. Can we take adequate account of the reflexive effect of knowledge and planning on the actions of the planned and the planners? I have argued elsewhere [19] that a satisfactory theory of the social sciences must be based on recognition of three classes of truth. No one, to my knowledge, has tackled this fundamental problem.

5. Can it be shown that programming, in the light of the reflexive effect of knowledge, does not lead to some sort of infinitive regress? Only so can solutions be achieved.

6. Can the calculations be carried out fast enough? Modern calculating machines, with their basic operations measured in micro-seconds, are marvelously speedy. But the number of operations required may be astronomical, and the $3.1557 \times 10^7$ seconds available in each year may not be enough.

7. Can we persuade men to accept change? A casual survey of important reforms effected in the recent past [20] shows that each of them took about seventy-five to one hundred years for completion. It is a general impression (and a correct one, I think) that the speed at which social problems *appear* is now accelerating. But is there any indication that the rate of solution is also accelerating? We seem to need some basic reform in people's reaction to proposed changes. Would this demand a new sort of faith? And in what? Science? Truth? Humanism?

8. Will any plan we adopt have adequate self-correcting mechanisms built into it? It is one of the virtues of a market economy that any error in judgment as to what people want is soon corrected for. Price fluctuations *communicate* needs to the managers. But in a planned economy, it has been often noted, planners who make errors are likely deliberately to interfere with the free flow of information in order to save their skins. Can a planned system include uncloggable channels of information?

Such seem to me to be the principal difficulties in the way of planning. Whether they will ultimately prove insuperable, who can say? But for the foreseeable future, I suggest there is much to be said for this analysis [21] by Kenneth Boulding:

. . . I believe the market, when it works well, is a true instrument of redemption, though a humble one, not only for individuals but for society. It gives the individual a sense of being wanted and gives him an opportunity of serving without servility. It gives society the opportunity of coordinating immensely diverse activities without coercion. The "hidden hand" of Adam Smith is not a fiction.

There are forces operating in society, as there are within the human organism, which make for health. The doctor is merely the cooperator with these great forces in the body. The doctor of society—who is equally necessary—must also be a humble cooperator with the great forces of ecological interaction, which often restore a society to health in spite of his medications. It is precisely this 'anarchy' which Professor Niebuhr deplores which saves us, in both the human and the social organism. If we really establish conscious control over the heartbeat and the white blood cells, how long would we last? Health is achieved by the cooperation of consciousness with a largely unconscious physiological process. Selfconsciousness is not always an aid to health, either in the individual or in society.

The problem of planning will not soon be disposed of, nor soon solved, but perhaps some false issues can be avoided if we make a distinction between "planning" and "designing." By *planning* I mean here what I think most people have in mind, the making of rather detailed, rather rigid plans. The word *designing* I would like to reserve for the much looser, less detailed, specification of a cybernetic system which includes negative feedbacks, self-correcting controls. The classical market economy is such a design. Kenneth Boulding when he speaks of "the market, *when it works well*" is, I believe, implicitly referring to the biologist's model of homeostasis shown in Figure 4. The classical market should not be called *natural,* for it is truly a human invention, however unconsciously made. It is not universal. It has been modified continually as men have groped toward better solutions. I would submit that the proper role for conscious action is the ethical evaluation of many possible homeostatic systems, the selection of the best *possible* one, and the refinement of its design so as to make the homeostatic plateau as broad as it can be, thus maximizing both social stability and human freedom.

# 22

## Population, Biology and the Law

*(1971)*

### Introduction

The problem of overpopulation and the degradation of the environment
has only recently come into the full consciousness of the general public,
but it will surely exercise the best minds we have for at least a generation. In the poor countries of the world overpopulation exhibits itself in
starvation and the threat of starvation, and in the social disruption created
by these threats. In the rich countries, the principal symptoms of overpopulation are pollution and the social disorganization resulting from congestion and the perception of the degradation of the quality of life. The
quality of life can diminish even under conditions of increasing economic
"prosperity." It is figuratively possible to drive to the poorhouse in a
Cadillac, surrounded by the automotive smog created by an excess of
private amenities coupled with a deficiency of public ones. As the economist John Kenneth Galbraith says, we have succeeded in combining
"private affluence and public penury."

From *Journal of Urban Law*, 48:563–578. Copyright © 1971.

The family which takes its mauve and cerise, air-conditioned, power-steered, and power-braked automobile out for a tour passes through cities that are badly paved, made hideous by litter, blighted buildings, billboards, and posts for wires that should long since have been put underground. They pass on into a countryside that has been rendered largely invisible by commercial art. (The goods which the latter advertise have an absolute priority in our value system. Such aesthetic considerations as a view of the countryside accordingly come second. On such matters we are consistent.) They picnic on exquisitely packaged food from a portable icebox by a polluted stream and go on to spend the night at a park which is a menace to public health and morals. Just before dozing off on an air mattress, beneath a nylon tent, amid the stench of decaying refuse, they may reflect vaguely on the curious unevenness of their blessings. Is this, indeed, the American genius?[1]

The problems posed by increasing population are only in small part soluble by technological means. They must also be attacked at the political level. We must evolve new methods of living together in relative peace under crowded conditions; or else we must devise and accept controls that will prevent us from creating crowded conditions in the first place. Either way, we face loss of freedom. We must voluntarily give up some freedoms to avoid losing even more precious ones because of inaction. What freedoms should we voluntarily give up? What political controls are most acceptable and least fraught with danger for the future? These questions are certainly not scientific questions, and not ones on which a scientist *per se* can speak with authority. But the answers to political and social questions must be consonant with basic scientific facts. A scientist may not know the legal answers, but he should be able to lay out the scientific framework into which political answers must be fitted.

## Population, an Earthly Problem

It all began when Malthus, in 1798, said that population, when unchecked, increases in a "geometric" fashion. Today, we would say that population increases "exponentially." Compound interest is a special case of exponential increase. The most important characteristic of compound interest is that a sum increasing by compound interest increases without limit—or "the limit is infinity," to put it another way. At three per cent compound interest, a sum doubles in 23 years. At one per cent, doubling takes 70 years; at 0.1 per cent the doubling period is 693 years, and at 0.01 per cent it is 6,930 years. But no matter how small the rate of increase, the limit is infinity. In a finite world, exponential increase must eventually come to a stop.

The earth is finite. Perhaps the universe is not, but the universe is not available to us as a way of solving terrestrial population problems. The difficulty of reaching so near a body as the moon is now surely apparent to everyone. The moon is quite unsatisfactory as a place for human existence, as are also all of the other planets of the solar system. Beyond the solar system the next possible stopping place would be at the planets (if such exist) of the star Alpha Centauri, which is 4.3 light-years away. At the speed of our present spaceships, it would require more than 100,000 years to reach Alpha Centauri. It is certainly possible to speed up our spaceships; but Alpha Centauri is very far away. More than a decade ago it was calculated[2] that with the most advanced technology conceivable the cost for exporting surplus human population to other solar systems would be some three million dollars per man—and no developments since this calculation was made indicate any need for revising the estimate downward. Space travel is no solution for the human population problem, which must be solved *here*. How shall we set about it?

## Consequences of Voluntary Controls

Those who fear population controls on earth often urge that there is no need for man to take a deliberate hand in this matter because population growth will automatically come to an end some day, without human intervention. *How right they are*—in a sense. In a finite world, any exponential function must eventually come to an end. If we do absolutely nothing, human population growth must eventually stop because of starvation, mass disease, or universal warfare and civil disorder. If the prospect of these "natural" controlling mechanisms does not disturb us, we have nothing to worry about. The population problem will solve itself.

But if we regard such natural controls as repugnant, if we think that they are more frightening than control mechanisms we might deliberately engineer into society, then we should examine the properties of positive, conscious controls. Each method of deliberate population control has its own advantages and disadvantages. We should try to estimate these in advance (though we shall probably not be completely successful). We should try to see what sorts of legislation are needed to meet the challenges posed by the facts of life.

At the present time many people react very emotionally to the mere suggestion that a government might take deliberate steps to control family size. Because of this resistance a not very courageous government might well elect to control population size by measures not specifically identified as population control measures. Following such a policy would give an illusion of individual freedom to the citizens, but the measures used would produce what the demographer Kingsley Davis refers to as "a catalogue of horrors." Trusting that individual families would use contraception when sufficiently motivated by external pressures, the government might:

> squeeze consumers through taxation and inflation; make housing very scarce by limiting construction; force wives and mothers to work outside the home to offset the inadequacy of male wages, yet provide few childcare facilities; encourage migration to the city by paying low wages in the country and providing few rural jobs; increase congestion in cities by starving the transit system; increase personal insecurity by encouraging conditions that produce unemployment and by haphazard political arrests.[3]

When these pressures occur "spontaneously," diminished family size is the response, as we saw during the great depression of the 1930's. But could such pressures be deliberately invoked as a means of population control? Would the citizenry acquiesce in such a governmental policy? It seems doubtful. The public would no doubt decide that overt means of population control would be more acceptable than covert means like these.

Population control in a finite world implies, sooner or later, zero population growth. Birth rate must equal death rate.[4] Those who are regarded as radicals in population matters these days[5] say that the human population is already past the optimum point and that our first goal should be to produce a negative population growth rate until we actually reduce the population to a lower level, at which point a policy of zero population growth could be safely instituted. A more conservative view might be that we should not worry about the exact position of the optimum population, but should seek a zero growth rate as soon as possible.

At the other extreme, even those[6] who maintain that the human population is below the optimum level now—a position they adopt without explaining the criteria on which they make this judgment—must, if they are rational, admit that a zero growth rate has to be achieved sooner or later; on the time scale of human history, the time must be soon.

In the past, it has been fashionable to say that population control can be achieved by family planning alone, that is, by adhering to the program laid out by some thirty members of the United Nations in 1967:

> The Universal Declaration of Human Rights describes the family as the natural and fundamental unit of society. It follows that any choice and decision with regard to the size of the family must irrevocably rest with the family itself, and cannot be made by anyone else.[7]

In the tradition of Western law this statement sounds innocent, even commendable. But scientifically it opens a hornet's nest. There are several things wrong with it. In the first place, insofar as it addresses itself to the population problem (which it does only indirectly, and partially by denial) the Universal Declaration presumes an exact congruence of family goals and national goals, and a perfect sensitivity of the family to what the nation needs. But has there ever been a wife who decided to discontinue the pill because her country needed more citizens? Or a husband who bought condoms at the drugstore because the word was out from Washington that we need no more children for a while? National pressures *might*, of course, produce parallel family pressures, but experience indicates that the linkage between the two is extremely dubious. Even if such a linked system existed it would probably produce wild fluctuations in reproductive rate, analogous to the "pig cycle" of earlier days in American agriculture, before price supports. Time delays in an information-and-response system produce fluctuations. This is a well-known principle in cybernetics.[8]

When we reject the natural controls of starvation, disease, and devastating social disorders, and when we likewise reject the indirect controls catalogued by Professor Davis, what is left? Only positive controls, deliberately invoked. At this point, there are various possibilities, each raising its own characteristic problems. We might elect to control population in a statistical fashion only. For example, by tax incentives or punishments we might reward those people who control the size of their family in the desired way. No one would be *forbidden* to reproduce as much as he cared to; his bread would merely be buttered on one side, and his attention called to which side. Retaining a measure of freedom of choice is always desirable, other things being equal. *But other things are not equal:* this assertion springs from a fundamental principle that was first discovered by biologists, but which has applications far beyond the purview of biology.

If some couples have more children than others when subjected to identical social pressures, what will be the consequences? "Philoprogenitive" couples will have more children—which is merely saying the same thing in other words. More important: This reproductive difference will have signal consequences if there is even the slightest *hereditary* quality to the philoprogenitiveness. In every animal that has been thoroughly studied, reproductivity is indeed affected by genetic determiners. To the biologist such a generalization strongly implies that man (who is also an animal) is governed by the same principle; but many non-biologists exhibit signs of acute anxiety when told that any human behavioral characteristic is genetically determined. Crucial experiments in the human species are not now available to settle the question, and they would take a long time to carry out. Fortunately, we do not have to wait for such a definitive settling of the "heredity versus environment" problem in the area of reproduction. All we need to know is whether human reproduction is "hereditary" *in the most general sense*—that is, whether the daughters of prolifically reproducing mothers have more children than the daughters of other mothers. Demographic analysis shows that this is indeed true.[9] At this point it does not matter whether the prolific quality that is handed down from mother to daughter is handed down through chromosomes and DNA, or whether it is exclusively a matter of social heredity, of the climate of opinion created in the home of the maturing daughter. In either case, the children of philoprogenitive parents will themselves produce a larger proportion of philoprogenitive parents in the next generation who will then produce a still larger proportion. In other words, the ratio of philoprogenitive to non-philoprogenitive individuals will increase in exponential fashion, like compound interest. In the limit, the ratio will approach infinity—that is, ultimately the entire population will be made up of philoprogenitive people to the exclusion of those whose needs to become parents—whether genetically or socially determined—are not so strong. It is interesting to note that this inescapable logical consequence was first pointed out by the grandson of Charles Darwin[10] on the centenary of the publication of the *Origin of Species*. It relies on the most general form of the reasoning involved in the idea of natural selection, but it does not depend on the secondary question of whether the selection is natural or not. Selection is selection. In the long run, the consequences of selection are momentous.

**Family Responsibility and the Welfare State**

Among non-human animals prolificness is adjusted to the demands of the environment and to the species' "recognition"—to speak metaphorically—of the realities of its situation. Different species, facing different realities, are prolific to different degrees. Condors, eagles, and Emperor Penguins lay only a single egg in a season, whereas a partridge lays a clutch of a dozen eggs or more. Why the difference? Because the physiology is different, certainly; but what we want to know is: why, functionally? Other things being equal, natural selection favors an indefinite increase in fertility—but, again, the key to the puzzle is found precisely in the fact that *other things are not equal*.

The waist-high Emperor Penguin, holding its egg hidden between its legs on a windswept and frigid ice shelf in the Antarctic, simply could not manage to keep two eggs warm, much less a dozen. Natural selection favors a very restricted fertility in this situation. But ground-running birds, such as partridges, pheasants, and quails, living in a gentler climate, need not take such care of their offspring; among them natural selection favors greater fertility. But no matter what the species, there is always an upper limit to the crude fertility that is favored. Temperance *in some degree* is always favored by natural selection.

The blind forces of evolution produce a type of behavior that would be called "responsible" were it brought about by conscious choice. Though usage may not justify this term in the non-human situation, in a deep sense it can be defended. The restricted fertility of the Emperor Penguin—indeed of every species, for no species invests all its biological capital in simple reproduction—is a selectively created response to environmental "messages." If the message is not "heard" and appropriately responded to the species becomes extinct.

Selective adjustment to environmental realities takes place within the species. Individuals vary in their fertility, as in other characteristics. Part of the individual variation is genetic. For natural selection to be operative it is enough if only a part of the variation is genetic. The end result is the same no matter how small the genetic component may be.[11] For a given species in a given environment any tendency to overbreed is automatically corrected for through the mechanism of family responsibility (to speak metaphorically, but truly). In the bird species *Apus apus* (swifts) the brood is habitually a small one. A three-year study[12] made in 1946–48 showed that swifts that had three eggs per clutch managed to raise only 90 per cent as many offspring as did birds that had only two eggs per clutch (instead of the 150 per cent one would expect, if there were no mortality between hatching and flying). For the swifts, the facts of life dictate that the clutch size should be small. Any genetic tendency to produce larger clutches is selected against and largely eliminated. In the swifts, and indeed in most wild birds and mammals, the unit of responsibility is the family. If the family does not take care of its young, nobody will. Under these circumstances, selection speedily punishes any unwise "decisions" in reproduction.

If mankind lived by the same rule of family responsibility there would be no reason for the community as a whole to be concerned about family size. Errors of judgment would be punished, and those making the errors would leave fewer descendants in subsequent generations to continue the maladaptive behavior. To a considerable extent during man's life on earth he has lived by a rule of family responsibility—to a considerable extent, but not entirely. And recently, scarcely at all.

A little less than 200 years ago, the naturalist Carl Linnaeus, writing about a famine in Sweden, said:

> I fear that I shall not have any under-gardeners this summer to do daily work, for they say they cannot work without food, and for many days they have not tasted a crust of bread. One or two widows here are said not to have had any bread for themselves or their children for 8 days, and are ashamed to beg. Today a wife was sent to the castle for having cut her own child's throat, having had no food to give it, that it might not pine away in hunger and tears.[13]

Charity existed in those days, but it was a fickle, changeable thing. You could not count on it. Poor people were well advised to assume complete family responsibility, and seek to limit their reproduction. The technology of birth control was not as good then as it is now, but birth control in one form or another has existed since the dawn of history.[14] If all else failed, one controlled the size of one's family by infanticide, which was far commoner than we like to think.[15] It is quite apparent from Linnaeus' letter that he had ambivalent feelings about the woman who had cut her child's throat. It is obvious that there are risks in permitting homicide to pass unchallenged in society; but *caritas* moved the naturalist to empathize with the unfortunate Swedish mother.

In a system that depends entirely on family responsibility for the survival of the children, population control may be attainable by family planning. But when family responsibility is overthrown by a social welfare system, family planning is no longer capable of producing population control. The family has the children, and the community feeds them. The undesired consequence is a particular example of the basic ecological principle that "We can never do merely one thing."[16] Adopting the philosophy of a welfare society does not merely ensure that children shall not starve; it also makes it certain that family planning cannot achieve population control.

Those who drafted the United Nations statement implying that parenthood is a right undoubtedly did not realize that if it is, population control is impossible. Only by making parenthood a privilege, to be enjoyed under specified conditions and to a specified extent, can society achieve population control.[17]

## Some Technical Aspects of Population Control

A privilege has limits. When society has thought through the implications of the welfare state, how will it limit the privilege of parenthood? In
the present climate of opinion it would be difficult to defend differentials
in this privilege, whether the differentials were based on income or merit,
however measured. When society first concludes that parenthood is a
privilege it will no doubt initially regard it as a privilege to be equally
distributed among all members of society.[18]

It is possible that in the not too distant future society may decide that
the number of children per family must be strictly controlled in order to
avoid the verifiable evils of overpopulation. When this decision is made,
it will raise a number of practical issues that deserve to be discussed in
advance.

In the first place, a formula must be found for dealing with the "fractional child." With the present mortality, achieving zero population
growth in the United States would require that each couple have about
2.11 children. Since a fraction of a child cannot be produced, how is stability to be achieved? One way would be by seeking stability only in the
long run—by allowing three children per family for a period of years, and
then allowing only two children per family for awhile, or only one. Such
a scheme would lead to fluctuations, and perhaps some complaints about
belonging to a "lost generation." The economist Kenneth Boulding has
proposed another method, which he calls the "green stamps" method.[19]
Each couple could be issued permits for 2.11 children, and then dispose
of the fraction by going into the marketplace. Just as stock rights are sold
on the stock exchange, so fractional children-rights could be auctioned
off in a national market. Strongly philoprogenitive parents would presumably purchase such rights; less strongly motivated persons would prefer to
sell them for cash. Boulding's scheme has all the virtues of the classical
market mechanism, but it is such a surprising extension that he has not,
to date, been able to get people to take him seriously.

A technically simple way to control the number of children would be to
sterilize the woman after the birth of her $n$th child. Is this a shocking
idea? If so, try this "thought experiment": let $n = 20$. Few would maintain that it would be good either for society, the mother, or the family for
a woman to bear more than 20 children; the extreme case persuades many

that control of breeding by sterilization is not inherently a shocking idea. The important practical question is this: What should $n$ be?

Of course, the male member of a couple might be sterilized instead. Male sterilization is cheaper and easier than female sterilization (although recent medical advances have diminished the difference). Many members of the Women's Liberation Movement feel quite strongly that it is the man who should be sterilized, that the woman has been saddled with the responsibility of birth control for too long. The sentiment is understandable, but facts do not support their position. If there were no such thing as divorce and breaking-up of families, and remarriage, and if no woman ever had intercourse with more than one man, this feminist position would be defensible. But under present and foreseeable marital conditions it would lead to perplexing administrative decisions.

Suppose that the legal limit on children is two per couple. If John and Mary get a divorce after having one child, and Mary takes the child with her, and both members get married to new partners who have not previously had children, how many children are they now entitled to? Can Mary have only one more, while her ex-husband can have two? Suppose John marries a woman who already has two children: Can he now have no more? Even more perplexing would be the problems posed by the new experimental group marriages. Suppose three women and five men are cohabiting. Suppose that one of the women has a child, but she hasn't the foggiest notion who the father is: What male should this child be charged to? There are blood tests, of course, but these can only *exclude* parenthood. With the most refined tests, paternity is *not* excluded in about one-third of the cases.

"It is a wise father that knows his own child."[20] When abortion is free, and readily available to all women, the system of birth control can be perfect, and women can be held strictly accountable for the birth of a child, as men cannot. Biology has made the women responsible. Women may regret this, but they should take heart in the fact that power comes with responsibility. Given a complete system of birth control and a more than ample supply of inseminators a woman can have complete control over her reproductive life, to the extent that society permits it.

## The Quis Custodiet Problem

One of the awkward consequences of increasing knowledge is that it forces us to enunciate qualified directives. In an earlier day, the unqualified biblical directive "increase and multiply" told the true believers exactly what their duty was. As long as they were increasing as fast as possible, the chosen people were behaving morally. Any excess they might produce would be taken care of by the "natural" processes of starvation and crowd diseases. There was no need to saddle the individual with the responsibility of determining the quantitative meaning of a qualified directive.

Increasing control of "natural" processes has loaded new responsibilities on mankind in moral matters. Absolute ethics must be replaced by situation ethics[21] (less happily called relative ethics). The essential doctrine of situation ethics is this: the morality of an act is a function of the state of the system at the time it is performed. In the present context, the situationist would say: if there is plenty of room in the world, go ahead and have another child. On the other hand, if your part of the world is already overcrowded, parents who produce yet one more child diminish the common store available to all.

The requirements of situation ethics cannot be satisfied by statute law. How many different situations are there? Perhaps an infinite number; in any case, a very large number that is undoubtedly beyond intelligent enumeration at any particular point in time. It is hardly conceivable that a legislative body could be wise enough to foresee all the particular situations that could arise and take account of them in a rigidly prescriptive law. The only intelligent alternative is to write a law that is explicit only in its intent, leaving the details of its application to an administrative body. The more complex society becomes, the greater is its need for administrative law. Such law can easily lead to evils because it violates John Adams' prescription for "a government of laws and not men." With administrative law mere men are charged with the determination of the morality of acts in a fluid situational nexus. A system of administrative law is singularly liable to corruption, producing a government by men, not laws.

*Quis custodiet ipsos custodes?*—"Who shall watch the watchers themselves?" This is a serious practical question, and one to which there is no overall theoretical answer. But the mere existence of peril is not sufficient reason for abandoning administrative law. In a complex and rapidly changing world, statute law cannot be changed fast enough to adapt to shifting reality. However great the hazards of corruption in the watchdog agencies—and they are great—we cannot do without such agencies. Our problem is to make them work.

Perhaps a scientist may be permitted to give a personal reaction to this difficult problem. The molecular biologist, Cy Levinthal, once remarked that: "There are two kinds of biologists, those who are looking to see if there is one thing that can be understood, and those who keep saying it is very complicated and that nothing can be understood."[22] Biologists of the second kind may be very scholarly, but they are not creative. To understand the world and to control it, one must have faith that understanding is possible, that solutions can be found, that control is attainable. The more creative spirits in science are engaged in a continuous internecine war with the less creative, who cherish their impotence.

Is not this same spiritual disjunction found in the realm of law and politics? Are there not lawyers and political scientists who so cherish impotence that they merely collect tales of the malfunction of administrative systems, making no effort to analyze the reason for the malfunction in order to prevent it in the future? Since an ever larger proportion of our legal directives must be filtered through administrative systems, we had jolly well better set about making these systems more flexible, more intelligent, and less corruptible. Inventiveness is called for.

## The Threat of Tribalism

Population control will be difficult enough to achieve peacefully if society has merely to deal with families that differ in their desire to have children. If groups larger than the family assert their intention to exceed community norms, the difficulty of achieving population control will be greatly compounded.

This vexing problem is often stated as a racial problem. Some exponents of "Black Power" identify all proposals to control population as "genocide" and call upon their brothers (and sisters!) to engage in a breeding war. With such an example before us there is a strong temptation to regard the question as a racial one, but this would be a mistake. The issue is far larger and should be called a *tribal* question, using the term as Beryl Crowe[23] has used it. The large, and largely sophistical, literature on race is almost irrelevant to the real issue.[24]

Any group of people that perceives itself as a distinct group, and which is so perceived by the outside world, may be called a tribe. The group might be a race, as ordinarily defined, but it need not be; it can just as well be a religious sect, a political group, or an occupational group. The essential characteristic of a tribe is that it should follow a double standard of morality—one kind of behavior for in-group relations, another for out-group.

It is one of the unfortunate and inescapable characteristics of tribalism that it eventually evokes counter-tribalism (or, to use a different figure of speech, it "polarizes" society). The members of a tribe (for example, the Mafia in the United States) have an immense competitive advantage *vis-à-vis* society in general if the rest of society does not think in tribal terms. This is true even if the members of the tribe violate no law of the encompassing society.[25] Merely by always (and perfectly legally) throwing business their own way the members of a self-conscious tribe have a competitive advantage over those outside the tribe if the latter (perhaps as a matter of principle) refuse to act in a tribal way, insisting on judging men on their own merits and not on a basis of tribal membership. When the world outside of a self-conscious tribe perceives what it is losing by its non-tribal behavior, it almost inevitably adopts the morality of the tribe. Tribalism is what the scientist would call a "behavioral sink"; you can easily slide into it, but escape is something of an unexplained miracle (if, indeed, it is possible).

The attempt to escape tribalism is called "integration"; to encourage tribalism is "separatism." These conflicting goals are at the heart of what we call "urban problems" today (though they transcend the urban locus). The alternatives of integration and separatism pose a multitude of serious practical and moral questions, which have by no means been completely explored. The analysis presented here is not a complete one: it is heavily biased in the direction of the biological aspects of the problem. The apparent implications of this analysis must, at some other time and in some other place, be balanced against non-biological issues.

Separatism raises the threat of the "competitive exclusion principle."

The meaning of this principle[26] can be easily explained in a strictly biological setting. Suppose that one introduces into the same region two different species that inhabit the same "ecological niche." An ecological niche is *not* the place where the species lives; the term is a shorthand way of indicating what the ecologist Elton[27] called the "profession" of the species—what sort of food the species eats, how it catches it, what hours of the day it works, what kind of environment it requires, etc. If, by hypothesis, two species occupy *exactly* the same ecological niche, then all that one needs to know to predict the ultimate outcome of their competition is the rates at which they reproduce in this ecological niche. If one of them reproduces at a rate of 2 per cent per year while the other reproduces at a rate of 3 per cent, the ratio of the numbers of the faster reproducing species to the numbers of the slower will increase year by year. In fact, since their rates of reproduction, like compound interest, are exponential functions, a little algebra shows that the ratio of the two exponential functions is itself an exponential function. The ratio of the faster species to the slower species increases without limit. If the environment is finite—and it always *is* finite—the total number of organisms that can be supported by this environment is also finite. Since the size of the population of a species can never be less than one individual, this means that ultimately the slower breeding species will be completely eliminated from the environment. This will be true no matter how slight the difference in the rate of reproduction of the two species. Only a mathematically exact equality in their rates would ensure their continued coexistence—and such an exact equality is inconceivable in the real world. As a consequence, two species that occupy exactly the same ecological niche cannot coexist indefinitely in the same geographical area. Or to put the matter another way: ecological differentiation with respect to niche requirements is a necessary condition for the coexistence of different species.

So much for the strictly biological aspects. What application does the competitive exclusion principle have to the human situation? *Homo sapiens* is generally conceded to be but a single species—certainly interbreeding among the various races is possible, insofar as the practical tests have been carried out.[28] Insofar as human beings act as members of a single species *in reproductive matters* the competitive exclusion principle is irrelevant. With complete integration no physiological or other differences would develop between groups, and hence there would be no opportunity for the exclusion principle to exert its effect.

However, if human beings consciously adopt a policy of separatism in breeding, at that point the competitive exclusion principle becomes relevant and operative. With complete reproductive isolation the mathematics of the exclusion principle take effect. It then becomes possible for one group to outbreed another—in fact, unless specific arrangements to avoid this eventuality are introduced, one breeding group *will* necessarily outbreed others, ultimately replacing them.

What alternatives are there to the exclusion of one competing tribe by another? One possibility is that the two tribes may become ecologically differentiated, that one may adopt one set of occupations while the other adopts another. If each tribe is involved in at least one occupation that is essential for the continuance of society, while the other tribe is forbidden to enter into that occupation, then indefinite coexistence is possible. Occupational differentiation, the human equivalent of ecological differentiation, is a way to achieve tribal coexistence.

Occupational specialization produces something that is formally analogous to an organism. In the human body, liver cells carry out one set of functions while kidney cells carry out another. Though they may reproduce at different rates neither group replaces the other because both are needed for the continuous existence of the whole organism of which they are part, and the whole organism has at its command various negative feedback processes that prevent each of its constituent populations of cells from overbreeding and displacing the other.

Another possible response to the threat of the competitive exclusion principle is to institute rigid geographic separation between different tribes. If tribe X is given the state of Mississippi, to which tribe Y is forbidden admittance, while Y lives in New York, where X is not allowed, then both tribes can continue to coexist in the same nation, because they do not exist in the same geographic area.

If there is neither ecological differentiation nor geographical separation then two self-conscious tribes can continue to coexist indefinitely only if society somehow establishes a mechanism of positive control of the tribal rates of breeding. Within limits society might allow the tribal ratio to vary, imposing no restrictions on breeding; but at certain limiting ratios the breeding of both tribes would be rigidly controlled to prevent the further relative diminution of the minority tribe. Such a social system (analogous to the organismal system in biology) is *conceivable*—though how it might be brought into being is almost beyond imagining at the present time.

To become sensitized to the tribal aspect of our pluralistic society is to become immensely impressed with the enormity of the difficulties ahead of us. A seductive dream of the automatic disappearance of tribal distinctions blinded us to the reality of separative processes in society for half a century after Israel Zangwill[29] coined the term "the melting pot." Then Nathan Glazer and Daniel Patrick Moynihan removed the blinders.[30] Now that we perceive the population component of the tribal problem the road into the future appears dark indeed. Though "the common man," i.e., the non-academic man, does not produce a literature, there is little doubt that many shrewd people in this category have an intuitive grasp of the interaction of tribalism and reproduction, of family responsibility and welfare economics. Such unvoiced intuitions probably account for much of the voter resistance to welfare programs that are almost universally praised in public. The incongruence of public praise and public rejection on the secret ballot should make us suspect that real issues are hidden under a taboo.

It is difficult to see how the law can respond to the mathematical and logical implications of tribalism in a world that is increasingly over-filled with people. When there was a low-density frontier to absorb the surplus and unplanned population increase, logically incompatible value assumptions could be safely left unchallenged. But the frontier has disappeared now, and the exhilerating population explosion of the past three hundred years has now become a painful *im*plosion. Social and political science must strip the taboo from the area where population control and welfare ideals intersect and respond creatively to the logical and human challenges if we are to find a way to make the coexistence of social variety and domestic peace possible.

# 23

## Population Skeletons in the Environmental Closet

### *(1972)*

First, Barry Commoner wrote a book, *"The Closing Circle"* (Knopf, 1971). Then Paul R. Ehrlich and John P. Holdren criticized the book; and then Commoner criticized their criticism (*Bulletin of the Atomic Scientists,* May 1972). The result: a sizable body of controversial literature. How is one to deal with it?

One might go through the antagonists' arguments point by point, carefully comparing and evaluating them. If a lawsuit were involved, with a million dollars at stake, this would be appropriate. But there is no such suit. Consideration for the reader dictates a much simpler approach.

I will try to plunge directly to the heart of the matter, bypassing some of the fascinating interplay of antagonistic rhetoric. I don't want this essay to swell to the length of Adam Sedgwick's scathing review of one of the controversial books of the Victorian age, Robert Chambers' *"Vestiges of Creation."* Sedgwick's review was 85 pages long! By comparison, Commoner's and Ehrlich and Holdren's contributions are mercifully short—but only by comparison.

The deep question at issue is the importance of the population component in pollution and other forms of environmental disruption (E.D.). In

From *The Bulletin of the Atomic Scientists,* 28(6):37–41. Copyright © June 1972.

both his book and his critique Commoner goes to great lengths to prove that the population component is minor. Two elements of his argument merit separate treatment: (a) the empirical data and (b) the algebraic procedure.

It is both a weakness and a strength that the data are empirical. On the one hand, they are true; but on the other, one may well ask how general is their significance? Many measures can be determined, but which are the most significant in accounting for E.D.? Beer bottles? Water heaters? Clothes dryers? Automobiles? When one presents some of the percentage increases over a span of years, bias enters in, as is apparent in the Commoner data brought together in Ehrlich and Holdren's Table 2. Nonreturnable soda bottles increased 53,000 percent in the postwar years for the simple reason that the initial production base used for the calculation was nearly zero. Even the most rabid "econut" would not claim that overall pollution increased by such a large percentage.

How should one weight the items assembled in such a table? What would a complete table look like? (Impossibly long, no doubt.) And how would the E.D. produced by each of the items compare with that produced by each of its many alternative materials or ways of meeting the same demand? (Environmentally minded activists all too easily forget to ask this critical question; they forget the basic rule of ethics and ecology that "We can never do nothing.")

Furthermore, neither the increase in use nor the increase in the resultant pollution over a particular time span can be assumed to be part of a universal law applicable forever into the indefinite future. But it is the future we are primarily concerned about. When first introduced into a wealthy country, a desirable product enjoys a population growth that is exponential by a factor many times greater than the exponent for human population growth. Ultimately the market is saturated with the product; thereafter production drops to some constant factor times the human population size.

As for the E.D. caused in the manufacture, use and ultimate disposal of the product, this clearly depends on the state of technology. On the whole, we may assume that technology will improve (particularly if we take care that it does), though at what rate there is no *a priori* way of knowing. A conservative view would be that E.D.-control approaches an asymptotic value, generally an unknown one.

From the past we get only empirical values, and little theory. We have little success in predicting the future of environmental disruption.

As for the algebra of determining what percentage of today's pollution is ''caused'' by technological growth and change in the recent past, and what percentage should be charged against population growth, this depends on what is to be compared with what. My own reading of the arguments gives the edge to Ehrlich and Holdren, but I will not linger to justify that opinion, for there are, I think, more important matters to take up.

### Population Asymptote

At a fixed level of population, the amount of environmental disruption is a function of the state and use of technology. For the sake of argument we may grant that the E.D. function could be caused to decrease in time, provided we face this question: Is the asymptote of the E.D. function zero, or something greater than zero? I suspect the latter; true believers in technology may believe in the former.

On the other hand, if we take the level of technology as fixed, then the amount of environmental disruption is a function of population size. Population growth, as Benjamin Franklin, Robert Wallace and T. R. Malthus emphasized, is a potentially limitless function—but only in a limitless world. In the real world, the maximum population achievable approaches an asymptote. What asymptote, depends on many factors including (most importantly) the ''amount of environment'' allocated to, or taken by, each unit of population. This defines the ''level of living.'' Escape from all asymptotes is not one of man's options; he can merely choose his asymptote.

A low population asymptote permits a high level of living as an option. Those who are ascetically minded need not choose this option; but only if a low population asymptote is adopted and enforced can men be free to enjoy, if they wish, Cadillacs, symphony orchestras, wooded wilderness—and meat with their meals. The highest possible population asymptote permits only one kind of life, namely the ascetic, which is then no longer an option but an inescapable fate.

It should be noted also that the highest possible asymptote can be achieved only by accepting a great deal of environmental disruption. Pollution control always bears a cost, which can be paid for only out of affluence. Even those who care nothing about Cadillacs and symphonies may resent emphysema.

Of course if technology can improve forever without limit, so that the E.D. curve has zero as its asymptote, the above argument is specious. But surely the burden of proof lies on those who assert so remarkable a theorem?

Barry Commoner is not entirely unaware of the relevance of population growth, but he acknowledges it grudgingly. Consider these sentences from page 113 of his book:

> It is easy to demonstrate that the changes in pollution level in the United States since World War II cannot be accounted for simply by the increased population, which in that period rose by only 42 per cent. Of course this is but a simplistic response to a simplistic proposal. It is conceivable that even a 40 or 50 per cent increase in population size *might* be the real cause of a much larger increase in pollution intensity.

The qualifications put Commoner on safe ground no matter what facts later turn up; but the thrust of the rhetoric is another matter. "Simplistic," "conceivable" and "might"—these are surely ways of denigrating the importance of population.

Like the theologian Richard J. Neuhaus, author of *"In Defense of People"* (Macmillan, 1972), Commoner is very much pro-people in the sense of "the more the merrier." On page 114 Commoner says:

> The earth has experienced not only a "population explosion," but also, and more meaningfully, a "civilization explosion." People, and indeed their growth in number, are the source of the vastly elaborated network of events that comprises the civilization of man: the new knowledge of nature generated by science, the power of technology to guide natural forces, the huge increase in material wealth, the rich elaboration of economic, cultural, social, and political processes.

**Forever Upward?**

There is much truth in this. Looking backward, it is difficult to believe that the same growth in technology (et cetera) could have taken place if the human population had never increased beyond the limit of a single tribe of two thousand people. But what if we look forward? Is it certain that the quality of life graphed against population is a curve that slopes forever upward? Is it not even possible that quality has already passed through a peak and is heading downward? Possible, at least?

I have previously discussed this question in a somewhat different context (S. Fred Singer, ed., *"Is There an Optimum Level of Population?"* [New York: McGraw-Hill, 1971], p. 263):

> Not even the merits of urbanization require a large population—only local concentrations of the artists, artisans, philosophers, and scientists who are capable, under peculiar political and social circumstances that are poorly understood, of creating a distinctive "civilization." Athens, in its Golden Age, consisted of only a quarter of a million people, of whom almost half were slaves and only 40,000 were full citizens. The substitution of machine slaves for human slaves has surely reduced the critical size required for a great center of culture (given the right attendant circumstances) to considerably less than a quarter of a million.

**New York and Athens**

Let me pose a related question. The "standard metropolitan statistical area" called New York had a population as of 1970 of 11,529,000 people. That's 46 times the total population of classical Athens, or 288 times the population of Athenians of full citizenship status. In civilization, in urbanity, or in the production of art, new intellectual discoveries, or what have you—is modern New York 288 times as great as classical Athens? Or even 46 times as great? No one, to my knowledge, has attempted to quantify an answer to this question. It hardly seems worth the effort. The answer is surely obvious, and lends no support to the conclusion implied by Commoner that more is always better. Beyond some undetermined, but not large, number the stimulation people give each other becomes more irritating and inhibiting than mind-expanding.

Commoner does not worry about population growth because he believes, with most demographers, that (p. 237): "tendencies for self-regulation are characteristic of human population systems"—a belief that can be comforting if one does not inquire closely into the meaning of the word "tendencies," or the level of living at which ZPG (zero population growth) might be effortlessly achieved. Commoner is confident that the "demographic transition" makes unnecessary any serious consideration of deliberate population control. So we had better look critically at the concept of the demographic transition.

For most of man's existence ZPG prevailed, on the average. (Diseases caused wide fluctuations.) Graphing birth rate and death rate against time for this long period gives two interlaced lines, both fluctuating about a single mean value. The average rate of growth for hundreds of thousands of years was only 0.001 per cent per year. About 300 years ago, in Europe, the death rate curve began to fall below the birth rate curve. This produced a gap between the two lines which is called the "demographic gap." The greater this gap, the greater the rate of population growth.

Somewhat later the birth rate started to drop, approaching the falling death rate curve. Ultimately, of course, the two curves must once more interweave about a single mean value. At that point, ZPG will be reestablished. If we are lucky, both birth and death rates will be lower than they were among primitive men, and the length of life correspondingly greater. The entire time during which there is a gap between the two curves is called the "demographic transition."

A mystique common among demographers holds that there is something automatic and benevolent about this process, that we need not lift a finger to alter the "natural" course of events. Against this comforting thought several cogent observations can be advanced.

1. The demographic transition has not proceeded to completion in even one country in the world. (Commoner erroneously states on page 118 that the transition "has occurred" already in most of the industrialized nations.) At one time we thought Ireland had safely passed through the transition, with the ambiguous help of the devastating Potato Famine. But we were wrong. Ireland is now off and running again, with a current growth rate of 0.5 per cent. The doubling time for

her population is now a mere 140 years; and the demographic gap is
widening.

2. There is absolutely no theory to indicate that the demographic gap
will close automatically at a level of population consonant with a quality of life that anybody would call good; and much experience and
theory supports the contrary expectation.

3. There is no reason to think that the poor countries of the world will
duplicate the population history of the rich. The still incomplete transition of the European countries took several centuries. Today's poor
countries may have only a few decades to complete their transition,
without catastrophe; and they are starting with a demographic gap three
times as wide as the one that afflicted Europe.

The superstitious aspects of demographic transition doctrine were
beautifully exposed by the sociologist Kingsley Davis in his article, "Population" (*Scientific American*, September 1963). The tragedy of basing
foreign aid on a belief in natural "development" (a metaphor that leans
dangerously on embryology) has been amply documented by the economist John M. Culbertson in his "Economic Development: An Ecological
Approach" (Knopf, 1971).


## Population Control

Commoner is apparently unaware of the shaky foundations of the benevolent demographic transition. In addition I suspect he has a genuine,
and understandable, fear of the possible consequences of acknowledging
the fictional character of the benevolent transition. If we must eschew this
pleasant superstition, and if we are unwilling to settle for the most
wretched equilibrium conditions conceivable, then we will have to think
about controlling population deliberately.

But who is "we"? Who is controlled? And by what means? It is quite
understandable that Commoner (and many others) are so frightened by
half-glimpsed answers that they do not seriously investigate the possibilities. "Population control," says Commoner near the end of his article,
". . . no matter how disguised, involves some measure of political repression . . ." and is, therefore, in his opinion, unthinkable.

Population control (as opposed to personal birth control), by whatever means, must involve either the law or informal (nonstatutory) communal mechanisms that possess the repressive force and universality of statutory law. Recognizing that population control within a sovereign country will be possible only when a large majority of its population can agree on both the aim and the methods, I once stated that such control—if it is ever achieved—will be achieved by "mutual coercion, mutually agreed upon." Commoner, like many others, bridles at this expression, not recognizing that it is, in fact, merely an operational definition of any law in a democracy. A community that rejects all such coercion is, in the strict and literal sense, a lawless community. A village of a hundred souls, insulated from all other peoples, can live happily in a lawless condition. But a nation of 205 million people ain't no village.

It is ironic that biologist Commoner's analysis fails most notably when the logic of the situation is most distinctively biological. On page 214 of his book he says (and the italics are his):

> If a majority of the United States population voluntarily practiced birth control adequate to population stabilization, there would be no need for coercion. The corollary is that *coercion is necessary only if a majority of the population refuses voluntarily to practice adequate birth control.* This means that the majority would need to be coerced by the minority. This is, indeed, political repression.

The truth is quite otherwise. To begin with, let us agree that mutual coercion in a democracy can successfully be brought about by law only if the majority of the population is in agreement. In fact, our experience with the Prohibition Law taught us that sometimes the acceptance of coercion requires an overwhelming majority.

Commoner maintains that if the majority accepts a program of voluntary population control there is no need for coercion. In a special case, he is right. If deviations from the approved number of children occur solely as a matter of chance, and if there is no causal continuity between the high deviants of one generation and the high deviants of the next then coercion is not necessary. All the community has to do is set the approved number low enough to allow for randomly occurring overbreeding, and successful population control by voluntary means will be achieved.

But this special case is not common, and it is not what creates the situation that can lead to coercive population control. Problems arise when

there is a causal continuity between the overbreeders of successive generations, when one group of people, as a matter of policy, decides to
outbreed another. When that happens, a purely voluntary system of population control is sure to fail.

Is this a purely theoretical example, of no practical importance now or
in the future? It is not. During the 1960s the government of Ceylon ac-
tively supported "family planning" in the hope that this voluntary
method would bring about population control. At the end of the decade
the government withdrew its support from the program. Why?

Because the ruling class, the Sinhalese, had become convinced that a
minority group, the politically less powerful Tamils, were not cooperating in the voluntary family limitation program. The Sinhalese, 70 per
cent of the population, perceived that if the Tamils (11 per cent) consis-
tently outbred them, the minority group would someday become the majority and might then seize political control.

Note the effect the new policy can be expected to have on population
growth. At present, the population of Ceylon is increasing by 2.4 per cent
per year. If the new policy of the Sinhalese results in more Sinhalese
being born, the overall rate of population increase will increase. On the
other hand, even if the call for more Sinhalese babies is ineffective, population still will increase faster as the faster-breeding Tamils come to constitute an ever larger fraction of the total population.

Thus we see that a purely voluntary system of population control can
fail even if (contrary to Commoner's supposition) it is only a minority
group that refuses to cooperate. Simple mathematical analysis shows that
it does not matter how small this minority is, so long as it exists.

### Tribalism Defined

We need not go as far as Ceylon to find illuminating examples of the
dangers of competition in reproduction. The competitive aspects of reproduction are appreciated also in Northern Ireland and in Belgium. The
reader may be able to think of other examples. Dangers arise whenever
"tribalism" displaces feelings of loyalty to the larger community. I have
defined tribalism in the following way (*Journal of Urban Law,* April
1971):

Any group of people that perceives itself as a distinct group, and which is so perceived by the outside world, may be called a tribe. The group might be a race, as ordinarily defined, but it need not be; it can just as well be a religious sect, a political group, or an occupational group. The essential characteristic of a tribe is that it should follow a double standard of morality—one kind of behavior for in-group relations, another for out-group.

It is one of the unfortunate and inescapable characteristics of tribalism that it eventually evokes counter-tribalism (or, to use a different figure of speech, it "polarizes" society).

When that point has been reached, population control becomes impossible. This may not be the worst of the consequences of tribalism.

The theoretical principle involved in making a shambles of a program of voluntary population control is known as the "competitive exclusion principle." The idea has figured in biological literature more or less explicitly, for more than a century. It was the basis of the microbiologist M. W. Beijerinck's "elective culture method," with which I am sure botanist Barry Commoner is acquainted. I first discussed its human implications in "Nature and Man's Fate" (Rinehart, 1959). The total literature on the human implications is miniscule, and for good reason: no one yet sees an acceptable way around some of its more frightening implications (or what appear to be its implications). Certainly I don't. The subject is, I suspect, under a bit of a taboo. Perhaps it is better so, for the present.

I can sympathize with a biologist who honors the taboo. I am willing to attribute his silence to commendable compassion and caution. Paul and Anne Ehrlich in their *"Population Resources Environment"* (2nd ed.; Freeman, 1972), do not so much as hint at either the problem or the principle. Neither do Ehrlich and Holdren in their critical article. I can only suppose that they are observing the taboo. I do not criticize them for that.

On the other hand, I think Barry Commoner can be justly criticized for entering the tabooed area and giving the wrong answer. Look once more at the quotation given above from page 214 of his book. If Dr. Commoner were called in to advise the Ceylonese government in matters of population control, what advice would he give, if he made it consistent with the passage quoted?

It would have to be something like this: "You have nothing to worry about. If the majority of the Ceylonese population voluntarily adopts family planning, guided by the ideal of a small enough family, there is no need for coercion. The noncooperating Tamils constitute only 11 per cent of the Ceylonese population and are hence no threat to a voluntary population control program."

In spite of this adverse comment, I regard "The Closing Circle" as a good book, for the present moment in history. (What more can a successful expositor ask?) Bernard de Fontenelle (1657–1757), the first great popularizer of science, wisely said that "Well established beliefs can be successfully attacked only by degrees." Barry Commoner is also a great popularizer of science, and the science he is explaining—ecology—is, as Paul Sears has said, a subversive one. It is subversive in its implications for human institutions and long established habits of thought. As a practical matter it is not only necessary, it is probably also best, that the full implications of so revolutionary a science as ecology not be fully revealed to the public in an instant. "The Closing Circle," with its overemphasis on the technological factor and its "protesting too much" about population, may well be all that the general public is ready for at this time. Commoner has advanced a few degrees in attacking well-established beliefs, and his powerful voice has been widely heard. For this he deserves praise. That which he has left undone should be regarded by others as an opportunity to continue with the unending work of public education.

# 24

## The Survival of Nations
## and Civilization

### (1971)

Is a vigorous pronatalist policy necessary for national survival in a competitive world? Over the centuries many men have thought so. In the 19th century Parson Weems (who created the legend of George Washington and the cherry tree) wrote:

> My friends, 'tis population, 'tis population *alone,* that can save our bacon. List, then ye Bachelors and ye Maidens fair, if truly ye do love your dear:
>
> > O list with rapture to the decree,
> > Which thus in Genesis you may see:
> > Marry, and raise up soldiers, might and main,
> > Then laugh ye may, at England, France, and Spain.

If national survival depends on winning a breeding race, what is the prognosis for America? As of 1970 the United States' population was 205 million out of a world total of 3632 million. That makes us just 5.6 per-

From *Science,* 172:1297. Copyright © 1971 American Association for the Advancement of Science.

cent of the world's population. One person out of 18 is an American. We are decidedly in the minority.

Everyday we are a smaller minority. We are increasing at only 1 percent per year; the rest of the word increases twice as fast. By the year 2000 one person in 24 will be an American; in 100 years, only one in 46. The projected figures assume that present trends will continue. They may not; but is there any better basis for a national policy?

What should we do? In the past, we might have used these facts to justify imperialism, conquest, and the extermination of other peoples. No more. We are not saints, but we are beyond the point of adopting an explicit national policy of this sort.

Should we, then, take Parson Weems's advice seriously and try to outbreed everybody else? Merely keeping up with the rest of the world would require American women to double the number of their children. Can a government of men persuade women that it is their patriotic duty to emulate the rabbits? Or force them?

If we renounce conquest and overbreeding, our survival in a competitive world depends on what kind of world it is: One World, or a world of national territories. If the world is one great commons, in which all food is shared equally, then we are lost. Those who breed faster will replace the rest. Sharing the food from national territories is operationally equivalent to sharing territories: in both cases a commons is established, and tragedy is the ultimate result. In the absence of breeding controls, a policy of "one mouth, one meal" ultimately produces one totally miserable world.

In a less than perfect world, the allocation of rights based on territory must be defended if a ruinous breeding race is to be avoided. It is unlikely that civilization and dignity can survive everywhere; but better in a few places than in none. Fortunate minorities must act as the trustees of a civilization that is threatened by uninformed good intentions.

[Some time after the publication of this editorial an answering one was contributed to *Science* by Dr. Mina Rees under the title "A Humane Approach to Population Problems." [1] Dr. Rees graciously spoke of "The Tragedy of the Commons" as a "distinguished article," and made no attempt to refute the argument of this essay or to show that it was irrelevant to the "Survival" editorial. [2] Nevertheless she concluded her remarks by saying that "Surely there are alternatives to the solution that Dr. Hardin proposed in his editorial, alternatives that will be more responsive to man's concern for his fellow men." She gave no hint as to what these alternatives might be. I believe I am no less desirous than my critics[3] to discover more easily acceptable alternatives; but how much good does it do to assert that "surely" such alternatives exist unless one can give at least an inkling as to what they might be?

I have said (see Chapter 1) that the stalker of taboos should consider himself a failure if he becomes a martyr. By that standard my editorial can be judged to be a substantial step towards failure. Though Dr. Rees very considerately identified herself at the foot of her editorial only by her university affiliation she was in fact at that time president of the American Association for the Advancement of Science whose official organ *Science* is. These facts were undoubtedly known to many of her readers. She also wrote: "However unrepresentative his conclusions, Professor Hardin is completely free to express his views, and the publication of these views is within the established traditon of *Science*." Operationally, what does this mean? I can only report that I turned out several more editorials for *Science* after "Survival", only to have all of them rejected without comment by the editor. Appropriately discouraged, I soon stopped submitting editorials, until the pejoristic threat of xerography moved me to try once more, six years later, with the result included as No. 19 in this collection.

I think I erred in my understanding of what an editorial is. Its brevity and lack of documentation make an editorial a dangerous place to expose minority views, for the refutation of which the conventional wisdom has a ready battery of knee-jerk responses of the sort so well described by George Orwell in his essay, "Politics and the English Language."[4] Like it or not, we must recognize that the editorial is really suitable only as a vehicle for views so conventional that the average reader murmurs "How true!" while his blood pressure rises by not so much as a millimeter.]

# PART FIVE:
# "NEED" AS SUPERSTITION

# 25

# Is This Trip Necessary?

## (1969)

To the Editors, Sirs:

William F. Hamilton II and Dana K. Nance's "Systems Analysis of Urban Transportation" [*Scientific American*, July 1969] should go far toward helping us shake ourselves loose from paralyzing presuppositions about acceptable solutions to the urban transportation problem. The question is: Does it go far enough?

No systems analysis exhausts all the possibilities. The authors say their goal "was to model all the significant modes, actual and potential, of transporting people in an urban area." They did not ask the wider question: *Is this trip necessary?*

Thoughtlessly, we seem to assume that our places of residence and work are *given* (By God? By Nature?), that they cannot be altered by a rational planner. Yet once we become aware of this silent assumption we begin to ask productive questions. Is it rational for an individual whose home is in *A* to travel to *B* to work each day, while someone in *B* travels to *A?* Is it rational to zone cities as we do now, with businesses in one area and homes in another, instead of intermixing the two? What is the optimum size of a city, and how is the solution affected by the kinds of business? What effect will TV-telephones have on commuting and business travel, and indeed on the centralization of employees in offices as we know them?

No intuitive answer to these questions is acceptable; the computer must be used. The cost of radically restructuring the city would be great, but it might not be greater than the cost of the radical transportation system proposed by Hamilton and Nance. Since most of our cities need to be rebuilt anyway, redesigning them might not add much to the expense.

Ancient Rome failed to solve the problem of the city, and the hardening of her arteries of transportation was not ameliorated by desperate attempts to control movement without giving attention to the whole system. As Lewis Mumford says in *The City in History: Its Origins, Its Transformations, Its Prospects* (page 219), the reason for Rome's failure "was precisely the same reason that makes present-day traffic regulations, with the widening and multiplication of traffic arteries, so futile and inept: namely, no attempt was made to control the congestion of the land itself, or to reduce the density of population housed in its buildings. Absurdly, the factors that generate traffic remained outside the scheme of control."

Is there any reason to think that our present efforts to solve this urban problem will be any more successful than the Romans'? New transportation "hardware" may not suffice; we may need the new "software" of a restructured community.

# 26

## The Trans-Science of "Necessity"

### (1976)

The debate over nuclear power is marred by an argument of the pro-nuclear scientists that does not rest on science at all, but which they fail to identify as something else. Many have put forward essentially the same argument; I will discuss only the form given to it by one of our most distinguished physicists, Hans Bethe.

Bethe's argument, which has been vigorously criticized,[1] was published in highly polished form in *Scientific American* for January 1976. An essential element of the argument was encased in Bethe's title, "The Necessity of Fission Power," and reiterated in the concluding two sentences: "This country needs power to keep its economy going. Too little power means unemployment and recession, if not worse."

Is the last sentence a scientific assertion? Plainly it is not; it is what Weinberg calls "trans-science."[2] The connection between energy flux, unemployment, economic health and social chaos is a matter that may fall within the purview of political theory, economics, sociology, anthropology or psychiatry. An atomic scientist who makes such a statement is speaking completely outside the area of his *professional* competence.

From *The Bulletin of the Atomic Scientists*, 32(9):24. Copyright © 1976.

Why, then, does Bethe insist on "the necessity of fission power"? This trans-scientific assertion comes from the arsenal of growthmanship economists who, until recently, have been almost the only visible breed.[3] It is an article of faith with such as these that no economic system can function well unless it is always growing—forever. This dogma is part of the conventional wisdom of our time—*but only in our part of the world*.

China, as near as we can make out, has four times the U.S. population and consumes perhaps one-twentieth as much energy per capita, and yet—if we can believe newspaper reports—China has *zero* unemployment. (Our recent unemployment rate has been around 8 percent. Some of our economists say that the unemployment problem would be "solved" if we got this rate down to 3 percent—an interesting example of "solving by definition.")

Introducing China into the discussion provokes an objection: "But that's under communism! We don't want that system here." Let us agree. But does such an objection not imply this hypothesis: *Capitalism can survive only in an energy-rich economy that is growing forever?* Is that a scientific hypothesis? Plainly, it is not. It may be true. Some political theorist should examine this critical hypothesis to see whether it is true or not. Our decision to use, or not to use, fission power would no doubt be affected by the results of such an analysis.

Humanity has lived more than a million years without atomic energy. I find it hard to believe that a species with the intelligence to tame fire, develop agriculture, invent writing, split the atom and perfect contraceptives is too stupid to be able to live within a fixed energy budget. Yet pro-nuclear scientists, when they call for an "inexhaustible" source of energy in the face of perpetual population growth, reveal that they think it impossible for humankind to live within an energy budget.

They may be right, of course; in which case, from a cosmic point of view, it might be said that we deserve the fate that awaits us.

# 27

# Nobody Ever Dies of Overpopulation

*(1971)*

Those of us who are deeply concerned about population and the environment—"Econuts," we're called—are accused of seeing herbicides in trees, pollution in running brooks, radiation in rocks, and overpopulation everywhere. There is merit in the accusation.

I was in Calcutta when the cyclone struck East Bengal in November, 1970. Early dispatches spoke of 15,000 dead, but the estimates rapidly escalated to 2,000,000 and then dropped back to 500,000. A nice round number; it will do as well as any, for we will never know. The nameless ones who died, "unimportant" people far beyond the fringes of the social power structure, left no trace of their existence. Pakistani parents repaired the population loss in just 40 days, and the world turned its attention to other matters.

What killed those unfortunate people? The cyclone, newspapers said. But one can just as logically say that overpopulation killed them. The Gangetic delta is barely above sea level. Every year several thousand people are killed in quite ordinary storms. If Pakistan were not overcrowded, no sane man would bring his family to such a place. Ecologically

From *Science,* 171:527. Copyright © 1971 by the American Association for the Advancement of Science.

speaking, a delta belongs to the river and the sea; man obtrudes there at his peril.

In the web of life every event has many antecendents. Only by an arbitrary decision can we designate a single antecedent as "cause." Our choice is biased—biased to protect our egos against the onslaught of unwelcome truths. As T. S. Eliot put it in *Burnt Norton:*

> Go, go, go, said the bird: human kind
> Cannot bear very much reality.

Were we to identify overpopulation as the cause of a half-million deaths, we would threaten ourselves with a question to which we do not know the answer: *How can we control population without recourse to repugnant measures?* Fearfully we close our minds to an inventory of possibilities. Instead, we say that a cyclone caused the deaths, thus relieving ourselves of responsibility for this and future catastrophes. "Fate" is *so* comforting.

Every year we list tuberculosis, leprosy, enteric diseases, or animal parasites as the "cause of death" of millions of people. It is well known that malnutrition is an important antecedent of death in all these categories; and that malnutrition is connected with overpopulation. But overpopulation is not called the cause of death. We cannot bear the thought.

People are dying now of respiratory diseases in Tokyo, Birmingham, and Gary, because of the "need" for more industry. The "need" for more food justifies overfertilization of the land, leading to eutrophication of the waters, and lessened fish production—which leads to more "need" for food.

What will we say when the power shuts down some fine summer on our eastern seaboard and several thousand people die of heat prostration? Will we blame the weather? Or the power companies for not building enough generators? Or the econuts for insisting on pollution controls?

One thing is certain: we won't blame the deaths on overpopulation. No one ever dies of overpopulation. It is unthinkable.

# 28

# *Gregg's Law*

## *(1975)*

No proposal to attack world population problems should be taken
seriously if it does not explicitly deal with Gregg's Law: *You can't cure a
cancer by feeding it.* One may either support or attack this law, but one
should not ignore it.

Alan Gregg (1890–1957), a wise and kindly physician, was for many
years vice president of the Rockefeller Foundation. In 1955 he wrote: "I
suggest, as a way of looking at the population problem, that there are
some interesting analogies between the growth of the human population
of the world and the increase of cells observable in neoplasms. . . . Cancerous growths demand food; but, so far as I know, they have never been
cured by getting it."

Malthus, of course, would have agreed with Gregg. Writing in 1798 he
said: "That population does invariably increase where there are the
means of subsistence, the history of every people that have ever existed
will abundantly prove." Such a clear statement was sure to evoke a contradiction. In 1842 Thomas Doubleday, in "The True Law of Population," stated that nutrition and fertility are *inversely* related. The way to

From *BioScience*, 25(7):415. Copyright 1975 American Institute of Biological Sciences.

stop population growth, he said, is to feed people well. This Anti-Gregg
Hypothesis was revived in 1952 by Josué de Castro. In "The Geography
of Hunger," de Castro asserted that population growth can be brought to
a halt by feeding everybody plenty of proteins.

Physiological evidence does not support the Anti-Gregg Hypothesis.
The supposition is, of course, very pleasing to our humanitarian impulses. The will to believe what is pleasant has, in the last generation, led
to another anti-Gregg position, the doctrine of the Benign Demographic
Transition. The latest mutation is favored by the most powerful demographers of our day, a group Kingsley Davis calls the "Population Establishment." Observing that rich countries have lower fertility than poor
countries, these demographers conclude that the way to reduce fertility is
to shower poor people with food *and* wealth; zero population growth will
then automatically ensue.

Unfortunately, too many historical facts contradict the latest anti-Gregg
position. Take the United States, for example. When income went down
in the 1930's, so also did fertility. Following the Second World War, income rose continuously until 1974, but fertility rose until 1957 and then
fell. Most perplexing. Now another depression threatens. Who would like
to bet that fertility will rise as times get tough? That is what the Anti-
Gregg Hypothesis predicts. If we won't bet on this hypothesis for our
own country, are we wise to bet on it elsewhere?

Our own foreign aid money is laid down on such a wager. Worse still,
we wager the well-being of poor foreigners also. Thus far, we—*and
they*—have lost in this gamble. In the last generation, our massive foreign
aid bets have not prevented poor populations from nearly doubling while
their growth rates have trebled. Their environments are more stressed
than ever. The prospects for their posterity become worse every day. It is
a mark of the compulsive gambler that he doubles the stakes when he
loses steadily. Those who call for still greater increases in foreign aid to
push poor people through the hypothetical demographic transition seem to
be in the grip of a compulsion. That it is a humanitarian compulsion does
not excuse actions that fly in the face of Gregg's Law.

# 29

# *Parenthood: Right or Privilege?*

*(1970)*

Birth control is not population control. Individual goals, not community needs, motivate individual actions. In every nation women want more children than the community needs.

How can we reduce reproduction? Persuasion must be tried first. Tomorrow's mothers must be educated to seek careers other than multiple motherhood. Community nurseries are needed to free women for careers outside the home. Mild coercion may soon be accepted—for example, tax rewards for reproductive nonproliferation.

But in the long run a purely voluntary system selects for its own failure: noncooperators outbreed cooperators. So what restraints shall we employ? A policeman under every bed? Jail sentences? Compulsory abortion? Infanticide? . . . Memories of Nazi Germany rise and obscure our vision.

We need not titillate our minds with such horrors, for we already have at hand an acceptable technology: sterilization. The taboo on this subject is fast dissolving, thanks to Arthur Godfrey and Paul Ehrlich, who have confessed their sterilizations in public. Fear (mostly unjustified) about the safety of the "pill" has motivated multitudes to follow in their footsteps.

It should be easy to limit a woman's reproduction by sterilizing her at the birth of her $n$th child. Is this a shocking idea? If so, try this "thought-experiment": let $n = 20$. Since this is not shocking, let $n$ diminish until population control is achievable. The Women's Liberation Movement may not like it, but control must be exerted through females. Divorce and remarriage play havoc with assigning responsibility to couples or to men. Biology makes women responsible.

Many who want no third child would fight resolutely for the freedom to have that which they do not want. But what is freedom? Hegel said that "Freedom is the recognition of necessity." People need to recognize that population control is needed to protect the quality of life for our children.

The "right" to breed implies *ownership* of children. This concept is no longer tenable. Society pays an ever larger share of the cost of raising and educating children. The idea of ownership is surely affected by the thrust of the saying that "He who pays the piper calls the tune." On a biological level the idea of ownership of children has not been defensible for almost a century, not since August Weismann drew his celebrated diagram of the relationship of germ plasm to somatoplasm.

Biologically, all that I give "my" child is a set of chromosomes. Are they *my* chromosomes? Hardly. Sequestered in the germinal area long before *my* birth, "my" gonadal chromosomes have lived a life of their own, beyond my control. Mutation has altered them. In reproduction, "my" germ plasm is assembled in a new combination and mixed with another assortment with a similar history. "My" child's germ plasm is not *mine;* it is really only part of the community's store. I was merely the temporary custodian of part of it.

If parenthood is a right, population control is impossible. If parenthood is only a privilege, and if parents see themselves as trustees of the germ plasm and guardians of the rights of future generations, then there is hope for mankind.

# 30

## Living on a Lifeboat

### (1974)

Susanne Langer (1942) has shown that it is probably impossible to approach an unsolved problem save through the door of metaphor. Later, attempting to meet the demands of rigor, we may achieve some success in cleansing theory of metaphor, though our success is limited if we are unable to avoid using common language, which is shot through and through with fossil metaphors. (I count no less than five in the preceding two sentences.)

Since metaphorical thinking is inescapable it is pointless merely to weep about our human limitations. We must learn to live with them, to understand them, and to control them. "All of us," said George Eliot in *Middlemarch*, "get our thoughts entangled in metaphors, and act fatally on the strength of them." To avoid unconscious suicide we are well advised to pit one metaphor against another. From the interplay of competitive metaphors, thoroughly developed, we may come closer to metaphor-free solutions to our problems.

No generation has viewed the problem of the survival of the human species as seriously as we have. Inevitably, we have entered this world of

From *BioScience*, 24(10):561–568. Copyright American Institute of Biological Sciences.

concern through the door of metaphor. Environmentalists have emphasized the image of the earth as a spaceship—Spaceship Earth. Kenneth
Boulding (1966) is the principal architect of this metaphor. It is time, he
says, that we replace the wasteful "cowboy economy" of the past with
the frugal "spaceship economy" required for continued survival in the
limited world we now see ours to be. The metaphor is notably useful in
justifying pollution control measures.

Unfortunately, the image of a spaceship is also used to promote measures that are suicidal. One of these is a generous immigration policy,
which is only a particular instance of a class of policies that are in error
because they lead to the tragedy of the commons (Hardin 1968). These
suicidal policies are attractive because they mesh with what we unthink-
ably take to be the ideals of "the best people." What is missing in the
idealistic view is an insistence that rights and responsibilities must go
together. The "generous" attitude of all too many people results in asserting inalienable rights while ignoring or denying matching responsibilities.

For the metaphor of a spaceship to be correct the aggregate of people
on board would have to be under unitary sovereign control (Ophuls
1974). A true ship always has a captain. It is conceivable that a ship
could be run by a committee. But it could not possibly survive if its
course were determined by bickering tribes that claimed rights without responsibilities.

What about Spaceship Earth? It certainly has no captain, and no executive committee. The United Nations is a toothless tiger, because the sig-
natories of its charter wanted it that way. The spaceship metaphor is used
only to justify spaceship demands on common resources without acknowledging corresponding spaceship responsibilities.

An understandable fear of decisive action leads people to embrace
"incrementalism"—moving toward reform by tiny stages. As we shall
see, this strategy is counterproductive in the area discussed here if it
means accepting rights before responsibilities. Where human survival is
at stake, the acceptance of responsibilities is a precondition to the acceptance of rights, if the two cannot be introduced simultaneously.

**Lifeboat Ethics**

Before taking up certain substantive issues let us look at an alternative metaphor, that of a lifeboat. In developing some relevant examples the following numerical values are assumed. Approximately two-thirds of the world is desperately poor, and only one-third is comparatively rich. The people in poor countries have an average per capita GNP (Gross National Product) of about $200 per year; the rich, of about $3,000. (For the United States it is nearly $5,000 per year.) Metaphorically, each rich nation amounts to a lifeboat full of comparatively rich people. The poor of the world are in other, much more crowded lifeboats. Continuously, so to speak, the poor fall out of their lifeboats and swim for a while in the water outside, hoping to be admitted to a rich lifeboat, or in some other way to benefit from the "goodies" on board. What should the passengers on a rich lifeboat do? This is the central problem of "the ethics of a lifeboat."

First we must acknowledge that each lifeboat is effectively limited in capacity. The land of every nation has a limited carrying capacity. The exact limit is a matter for argument, but the energy crunch is convincing more people every day that we have already exceeded the carrying capacity of the land. We have been living on "capital"—stored petroleum and coal—and soon we must live on income alone.

Let us look at only one lifeboat—ours. The ethical problem is the same for all, and is as follows. Here we sit, say 50 people in a lifeboat. To be generous, let us assume our boat has a capacity of 10 more, making 60. (This, however, is to violate the engineering principle of the "safety factor." A new plant disease or a bad change in the weather may decimate our population if we don't preserve some excess capacity as a safety factor.)

The 50 of us in the lifeboat see 100 others swimming in the water outside, asking for admission to the boat, or for handouts. How shall we respond to their calls? There are several possibilities.

*One.* We may be tempted to try to live by the Christian ideal of being "our brother's keeper," or by the Marxian ideal (Marx 1875) of "from each according to his abilities, to each according to his needs." Since the needs of all are the same, we take all the needy into our boat, making a total of 150 in a boat with a capacity of 60. The boat is swamped, and everyone drowns. Complete justice, complete catastrophe.

*Two*. Since the boat has an unused excess capacity of 10, we admit just 10 more to it. This has the disadvantage of getting rid of the safety factor, for which action we will sooner or later pay dearly. Moreover, *which* 10 do we let in? "First come, first served?" The best 10? The neediest 10? How do we *discriminate?* And what do we say to the 90 who are excluded?

*Three*. Admit no more to the boat and preserve the small safety factor. Survival of the people in the lifeboat is then possible (though we shall have to be on our guard against boarding parties).

The last solution is abhorrent to many people. It is unjust, they say. Let us grant that it is.

"I feel guilty about my good luck," say some. The reply to this is simple: *Get out and yield your place to others*. Such a selfless action might satisfy the conscience of those who are addicted to guilt but it would not change the ethics of the lifeboat. The needy person to whom a guilt-addict yields his place will not himself feel guilty about his sudden good luck. (If he did he would not climb aboard.) The net result of conscience-stricken people relinquishing their unjustly held positions is the elimination of their kind of conscience from the lifeboat. The lifeboat, as it were, purifies itself of guilt. The ethics of the lifeboat persist, unchanged by such momentary aberrations.

This then is the basic metaphor within which we must work out our solutions. Let us enrich the image step by step with substantive additions from the real world.


## Reproduction

The harsh characteristics of lifeboat ethics are heightened by reproduction, particularly by reproductive differences. The people inside the lifeboats of the wealthy nations are doubling in numbers every 87 years; those outside are doubling every 35 years, on the average. And the relative difference in prosperity is becoming greater.

Let us, for a while, think primarily of the U.S. lifeboat. As of 1973 the

United States had a population of 210 million people, who were increasing by 0.8% per year, that is, doubling in number every 87 years.

Although the citizens of rich nations are outnumbered two to one by the poor, let us imagine an equal number of poor people outside our lifeboat—a mere 210 million poor people reproducing at a quite different rate. If we imagine these to be the combined populations of Colombia, Venezuela, Ecuador, Morocco, Thailand, Pakistan, and the Philippines, the average rate of increase of the people "outside" is 3.3% per year. The doubling time of this population is 21 years.

Suppose that all these countries, and the United States, agreed to live by the Marxian ideal, "to each according to his needs," the ideal of most Christians as well. Needs, of course, are determined by population size, which is affected by reproduction. Every nation regards its rate of reproduction as a sovereign right. If our lifeboat were big enough in the beginning it might be possible to live *for a while* by Christian-Marxian ideals. *Might.*

Initially, in the model given, the ratio of non-Americans to Americans would be one to one. But consider what the ratio would be 87 years later. By this time Americans would have doubled to a population of 420 million. The other group (doubling every 21 years) would now have swollen to 3,540 million. Each American would have more than eight people to share with. How could the lifeboat possibly keep afloat?

All this involves extrapolation of current trends into the future, and is consequently suspect. Trends may change. Granted: but the change will not necessarily be favorable. If—as seems likely—the rate of population increase falls faster in the ethnic group presently inside the lifeboat than it does among those now outside, the future will turn out to be even worse than mathematics predicts, and sharing will be even more suicidal.

**Ruin in the Commons**

The fundamental error of the sharing ethic is that it leads to the tragedy of the commons. Under a system of private property the man (or group of men) who own property recognize their responsibility to care for it, for if they don't they will eventually suffer. A farmer, for instance, if he is intelligent, will allow no more cattle in a pasture than its carrying capacity justifies. If he overloads the pasture, weeds take over, erosion sets in, and the owner loses in the long run.

But if a pasture is run as a commons open to all, the right of each to use it is not matched by an operational responsibility to take care of it. It is no use asking independent herdsmen in a commons to act responsibly, for they dare not. The considerate herdsman who refrains from overloading the commons suffers more than a selfish one who says his needs are greater. (As Leo Durocher says, "Nice guys finish last.") Christian-Marxian idealism is counterproductive. That it *sounds* nice is no excuse. With distribution systems, as with individual morality, good intentions are no substitute for good performance.

A social system is stable only if it is insensitive to errors. To the Christian-Marxian idealist a selfish person is a sort of "error." Prosperity in the system of the commons cannot survive errors. If *everyone* would only restrain himself, all would be well; but it takes *only one less than everyone* to ruin a system of voluntary restraint. In a crowded world of less than perfect human beings—and we will never know any other—mutual ruin is inevitable in the commons. This is the core of the tragedy of the commons.

One of the major tasks of education today is to create such an awareness of the dangers of the commons that people will be able to recognize its many varieties, however disguised. There is pollution of the air and water because these media are treated as commons. Further growth of population and growth in the per capita conversion of natural resources into pollutants require that the system of the commons be modified or abandoned in the disposal of "externalities."

The fish populations of the oceans are exploited as commons, and ruin lies ahead. No technological invention can prevent this fate: in fact, all improvements in the art of fishing merely hasten the day of complete ruin. Only the replacement of the system of the commons with a responsible system can save oceanic fisheries.

The management of western range lands, though nominally rational, is in fact (under the steady pressure of cattle ranchers) often merely a government-sanctioned system of the commons, drifting toward ultimate ruin for both the rangelands and the residual enterprisers.

## World Food Banks

In the international arena we have recently heard a proposal to create a new commons, namely an international depository of food reserves to which nations will contribute according to their abilities, and from which nations may draw according to their needs. Nobel laureate Norman Borlaug has lent the prestige of his name to this proposal.

A world food bank appeals powerfully to our humanitarian impulses. We remember John Donne's celebrated line, "Any man's death diminishes me." But before we rush out to see for whom the bell tolls let us recognize where the greatest political push for international granaries comes from, lest we be disillusioned later. Our experience with Public Law 480 clearly reveals the answer. This was the law that moved billions of dollars worth of U.S. grain to food-short, population-long countries during the past two decades. When P.L. 480 first came into being, a headline in the business magazine *Forbes* (Paddock and Paddock 1970) revealed the power behind it: "Feeding the World's Hungry Millions: How it will mean billions for U.S. business."

And indeed it did. In the years 1960 and to 1970 a total of $7.9 billion was spent on the "Food for Peace" program, as P.L. 480 was called. During the years 1948 to 1970 an additional $49.9 billion were extracted from American taxpayers to pay for other economic aid programs, some of which went for food and food-producing machinery. (This figure does *not* include military aid.) That P.L. 480 was a give-away program was concealed. Recipient countries went through the motions of paying for P.L. 480 food—with IOU's. In December 1973 the charade was brought to an end as far as India was concerned when the United States "forgave" India's $3.2 billion debt (Anonymous 1974). Public announcement of the cancellation of the debt was delayed for two months: one wonders why.

"Famine—1974!" (Paddock and Paddock 1970) is one of the few publications that points out the commercial roots of this humanitarian attempt. Though all U.S. taxpayers lost by P.L. 480, special interest groups gained handsomely. Farmers benefited because they were not asked to contribute the grain—it was bought from them by the taxpayers. Besides the direct benefit there was the indirect effect of increasing demand and thus raising prices of farm products generally. The manufacturers of farm machinery, fertilizers, and pesticides benefited by the farmers' extra efforts to grow more food. Grain elevators profited from storing the grain for varying lengths of time. Railroads made money hauling it to port, and shipping lines by carrying it overseas. Moreover, once the machinery for P.L. 480 was established an immense bureaucracy had a vested interest in its continuance regardless of its merits.

Very little was ever heard of these selfish interests when P.L. 480 was defended in public. The emphasis was always on its humanitarian effects. The combination of multiple and relatively silent selfish interests with highly vocal humanitarian apologists constitutes a powerful lobby for extracting money from taxpayers. Foreign aid has become a habit that can apparently survive in the absence of any known justification. A news commentator in a weekly magazine (Lansner 1974), after exhaustively going over all the conventional arguments for foreign aid—self-interest, social justice, political advantage, and charity—and concluding that none of the known arguments really held water, concluded: "So the search continues for some logically compelling reasons for giving aid . . ." In other words, *Act now, Justify later*—if ever. (Apparently a quarter of a century is too short a time to find the justification for expending several billion dollars yearly.)

The search for a rational justification can be short-circuited by interjecting the word "emergency." Borlaug uses this word. We need to look sharply at it. What is an "emergency?" It is surely something like an accident, which is correctly defined as *an event that is certain to happen, though with a low frequency* (Hardin 1972a). A well-run organization prepares for everything that is certain, including accidents and emergencies. It budgets for them. It saves for them. It expects them—and mature decision-makers do not waste time complaining about accidents when they occur.

What happens if some organizations budget for emergencies and others do not? If each organization is solely responsible for its own well-being, poorly managed ones will suffer. But they should be able to learn from experience. They have a chance to mend their ways and learn to budget for infrequent but certain emergencies. The weather, for instance, always varies and periodic crop failures are certain. A wise and competent government saves out of the production of the good years in anticipation of bad years that are sure to come. This is not a new idea. The Bible tells us that Joseph taught this policy to Pharaoh in Egypt more than 2,000 years ago. Yet it is literally true that the vast majority of the governments of the world today have no such policy. They lack either the wisdom or the competence, or both. Far more difficult than the transfer of wealth from one country to another is the transfer of wisdom between sovereign powers or between generations.

"But it isn't their fault! How can we blame the poor people who are caught in an emergency? Why must we punish them?" The concepts of blame and punishment are irrelevant. The question is, what are the operational consequences of establishing a world food bank? If it is open to every country every time a need develops, slovenly rulers will not be motivated to take Joseph's advice. Why should they? Others will bail them out whenever they are in trouble.

Some countries will make deposits in the world food bank and others will withdraw from it: there will be almost no overlap. Calling such a depository-transfer unit a "bank" is stretching the metaphor of *bank* beyond its elastic limits. The proposers, of course, never call attention to the metaphorical nature of the word they use.

## The Ratchet Effect

An "international food bank" is really, then, not a true bank but a disguised one-way transfer device for moving wealth from rich countries to poor. In the absence of such a bank, in a world inhabited by individually responsible sovereign nations, the population of each nation would repeatedly go through a cycle of the sort shown in Figure 1. $P_2$ is greater than $P_1$, either in absolute numbers or because a deterioration of the food supply has removed the safety factor and produced a dangerously low ratio of resources to population. $P_2$ may be said to represent a state of overpopulation, which becomes obvious upon the appearance of an "accident," e.g., a crop failure. If the "emergency" is not met by outside help, the population drops back to the "normal" level—the "carrying capacity" of the environment—or even below. In the absence of population control by a sovereign, sooner or later the population grows to $P_2$ again and the cycle repeats. The long-term population curve (Hardin 1966) is an irregularly fluctuating one, equilibrating more or less about the carrying capacity.

A demographic cycle of this sort obviously involves great suffering in the restrictive phase, but such a cycle is normal to any independent country with inadequate population control. The third century theologian Tertullian (Hardin 1969a) expressed what must have been the recognition of many wise men when he wrote: "The scourges of pestilence, famine, wars, and earthquakes have come to be regarded as a blessing to overcrowded nations, since they serve to prune away the luxuriant growth of the human race."

Only under a strong and farsighted sovereign—which theoretically could be the people themselves, democratically organized—can a population equilibrate at some set point below the carrying capacity, thus avoiding the pains normally caused by periodic and unavoidable disasters. For this happy state to be achieved it is necessary that those in power be able to contemplate with equanimity the "waste" of surplus food in times of bountiful harvests. It is essential that those in power resist the temptation to convert extra food into extra babies. On the public relations level it is necessary that the phrase "surplus food" be replaced by "safety factor."

But wise sovereigns seem not to exist in the poor world today. The most anguishing problems are created by poor countries that are governed by rulers insufficiently wise and powerful. If such countries can draw on a world food bank in times of "emergency," the population *cycle* of Figure 1 will be replaced by the population *escalator* of Figure 2. The input

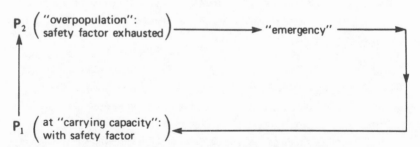

Fig. 1. The population cycle of a nation that has no effective, conscious population control, and which receives no aid from the outside. $P_2$ is greater than $P_1$.

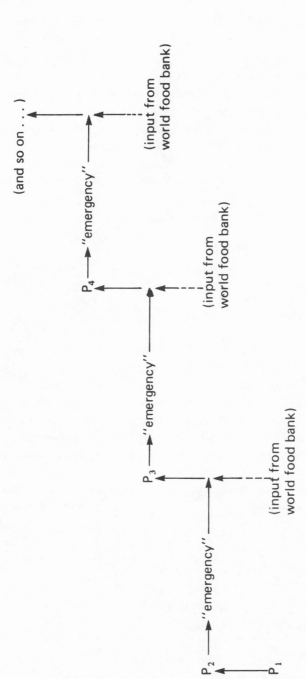

Fig. 2. The population escalator. Note that input from a world food bank acts like the pawl of a ratchet, preventing the normal population cycle shown in Figure 1 from being completed. $P_{n+1}$ is greater than $P_n$, and the absolute magnitude of the "emergencies" escalates. Ultimately the entire system crashes. The crash is not shown, and few can imagine it.

of food from a food bank acts as the pawl of a ratchet, preventing the population from retracing its steps to a lower level. Reproduction pushes the population upward, inputs from the world bank prevent its moving downward. Population size escalates, as does the absolute magnitude of "accidents" and "emergencies." The process is brought to an end only by the total collapse of the whole system, producing a catastrophe of scarcely imaginable proportions.

Such are the implications of the well-meant sharing of food in a world of irresponsible reproduction.

I think we need a new word for systems like this. The adjective "melioristic" is applied to systems that produce continual improvement; the English word is derived from the Latin *meliorare,* to become or make better. Parallel with this it would be useful to bring in the word *pejoristic* (from the Latin *pejorare,* to become or make worse). This word can be applied to those systems which, by their very nature, can be relied upon to make matters worse. A world food bank coupled with sovereign state irresponsibility in reproduction is an example of a pejoristic system.

This pejoristic system creates an unacknowledged commons. People have more motivation to draw from than to add to the common store. The license to make such withdrawals diminishes whatever motivation poor countries might otherwise have to control their populations. Under the guidance of this ratchet, wealth can be steadily moved in one direction only, from the slowly-breeding rich to the rapidly-breeding poor, the process finally coming to a halt only when all countries are equally and miserably poor.

All this is terribly obvious once we are acutely aware of the pervasiveness and danger of the commons. But many people still lack this awareness and the euphoria of the "benign demographic transition" (Hardin 1973) interferes with the realistic appraisal of pejoristic mechanisms. As concerns public policy, the deductions drawn from the benign demographic transition are these:

1) If the per capita GNP rises the birth rate will fall; hence, the rate of population increase will fall, ultimately producing ZPG (Zero Population Growth).

2) The long-term trend all over the world (including the poor countries) is of a rising per capita GNP (for which no limit is seen).

3) Therefore, all political interference in population matters is unnecessary; all we need to do is foster economic "development"—*note the metaphor*—and population problems will solve themselves.

Those who believe in the benign demographic transition dismiss the pejoristic mechanism of Figure 2 in the belief that each input of food from the world outside fosters development within a poor country thus resulting in a drop in the rate of population increase. Foreign aid has proceeded on this assumption for more than two decades. Unfortunately it has produced no indubitable instance of the asserted effect. It has, however, produced a library of excuses. The air is filled with plaintive calls for more massive foreign aid appropriations so that the hypothetical melioristic process can get started.

The doctrine of demographic laissez-faire implicit in the hypothesis of the benign demographic transition is immensely attractive. Unfortunately there is more evidence against the melioristic system than there is for it (Davis 1963). On the historical side there are many counter-examples. The rise in per capita GNP in France and Ireland during the past century has been accompanied by a rise in population growth. In the 20 years following the Second World War the same positive correlation was noted almost everywhere in the world. Never in world history before 1950 did the worldwide population growth reach 1% per annum. Now the average population growth is over 2% and shows no signs of slackening.

On the theoretical side, the denial of the pejoristic scheme of Figure 2 probably springs from the hidden acceptance of the "cowboy economy" that Boulding castigated. Those who recognize the limitations of a spaceship, if they are unable to achieve population control at a safe and comfortable level, accept the necessity of the corrective feedback of the population cycle shown in Figure 1. No one who knew in his bones that he was living on a true spaceship would countenance political support of the population escalator shown in Figure 2.

## Eco–Destruction Via the Green Revolution

The demoralizing effect of charity on the recipient has long been known. "Give a man a fish and he will eat for a day: teach him how to fish and he will eat for the rest of his days.'' So runs an ancient Chinese proverb. Acting on this advice the Rockefeller and Ford Foundations have financed a multipronged program for improving agriculture in the hungry nations. The result, known as the "Green Revolution," has been quite remarkable. "Miracle wheat" and "miracle rice" are splendid technological achievements in the realm of plant genetics.

Whether or not the Green Revolution can increase food production is doubtful (Harris 1972, Paddock 1970, Wilkes 1972), but in any event not particularly important. What is missing in this great and well-meaning humanitarian effort is a firm grasp of fundamentals. Considering the importance of the Rockefeller Foundation in this effort it is ironic that the late Alan Gregg, a much-respected vice president of the Foundation, strongly expressed his doubts of the wisdom of all attempts to increase food production some two decades ago. (This was before Borlaug's work—supported by Rockefeller—had resulted in the development of "miracle wheat.") Gregg (1955) likened the growth and spreading of humanity over the surface of the earth to the metastasis of cancer in the human body, wryly remarking that "Cancerous growths demand food; but, as far as I know, they have never been cured by getting it."

"Man does not live by bread alone"—the scriptural statement has a rich meaning even in the material realm. Every human being born constitutes a draft on all aspects of the environment—food, air, water, unspoiled scenery, occasional and optional solitude, beaches, contact with wild animals, fishing, hunting—the list is long and incompletely known. Food can, perhaps, be significantly increased: but what about clean beaches, unspoiled forests, and solitude? If we satisfy the need for food in a growing population we necessarily decrease the supply of other goods, and thereby increase the difficulty of equitably allocating scarce goods (Hardin 1969b, 1972b).

The present population of India is 600 million, and it is increasing by 15 million per year. The environmental load of this population is already great. The forests of India are only a small fraction of what they were three centuries ago. Soil erosion, floods, and the psychological costs of crowding are serious. Every one of the net 15 million lives added each year stresses the Indian environment more severely. *Every life saved this year in a poor country diminishes the quality of life for subsequent generations.*

Observant critics have shown how much harm we wealthy nations have already done to poor nations through our well-intentioned but misguided attempts to help them (Paddock and Paddock 1973). Particularly reprehensible is our failure to carry out postaudits of these attempts (Farvar and Milton 1972). Thus have we shielded our tender consciences from knowledge of the harm we have done. Must we Americans continue to fail to monitor the consequences of our external "do-gooding?" If, for instance, we thoughtlessly make it possible for the present 600 million Indians to swell to 1,200 millions by the year 2001—as their present growth rate promises—will posterity in India thank *us* for facilitating an even greater destruction of *their* environment? Are good intentions ever a sufficient excuse for bad consequences?

## Immigration Creates a Commons

I come now to the final example of a commons in action, one for which the public is least prepared for rational discussion. The topic is at present enveloped by a great silence which reminds me of a comment made by Sherlock Holmes in A. Conan Doyle's story, "Silver Blaze." Inspector Gregory had asked, "Is there any point to which you would wish to draw my attention?" To this Holmes responded:

"To the curious incident of the dog in the night-time."

"The dog did nothing in the night-time," said the Inspector.

"That was the curious incident," remarked Sherlock Holmes.

By asking himself what would repress the normal barking instinct of a watchdog Holmes realized that it must be the dog's recognition of his master as the criminal trespasser. In a similar way we should ask ourselves what repression keeps us from discussing something as important as immigration?

It cannot be that immigration is numerically of no consequence. Our government acknowledges a *net* inflow of 400,000 a year. Hard data are understandably lacking on the extent of illegal entries, but a not implausible figure is 600,000 per year (Buchanan 1973). The natural increase of the resident population is now about 1.7 million per year. This means that the yearly gain from immigration is at least 19%, and may be 37%, of the total increase. It is quite conceivable that educational campaigns like that of Zero Population Growth, Inc., coupled with adverse social and economic factors—inflation, housing shortage, depression, and loss of confidence in national leaders—may lower the fertility of American women to a point at which all of the yearly increase in population would be accounted for by immigration. Should we not at least ask if that is what we want? How curious it is that we so seldom discuss immigration these days!

Curious, but understandable—as one finds out the moment he publicly questions the wisdom of the status quo in immigration. He who does so is promptly charged with *isolationism, bigotry, prejudice, ethnocentrism, chauvinism,* and *selfishness.* These are hard accusations to bear. It is pleasanter to talk about other matters, leaving immigration policy to wallow in the cross-currents of special interests that take no account of the good of the whole—*or of the interests of posterity.*

We Americans have a bad conscience because of things we said in the past about immigrants. Two generations ago the popular press was rife with references to *Dagos, Wops, Pollacks, Japs, Chinks,* and *Krauts*—all pejorative terms which failed to acknowledge our indebtedness to Goya, Leonardo, Copernicus, Hiroshige, Confucius, and Bach. Because the implied inferiority of foreigners was *then* the justification for keeping them out, it is *now* thoughtlessly assumed that restrictive policies can only be based on the assumption of immigrant inferiority. *This is not so.*

Existing immigration laws exclude idiots and known criminals; future laws will almost certainly continue this policy. But should we also consider the quality of the average immigrant, as compared with the quality of the average resident? Perhaps we should, perhaps we shouldn't. (What is "quality" anyway?) But the quality issue is not our concern here.

From this point on, *it will be assumed that immigrants and native-born citizens are of exactly equal quality,* however quality may be defined. The focus is only on quantity. The conclusions reached depend on nothing else, so all charges of ethnocentrism are irrelevant.

World food banks move food to the people, thus facilitating the exhaustion of the environment of the poor. By contrast, unrestricted immigration moves people to the food, thus speeding up the destruction of the environment in rich countries. Why poor people should want to make this transfer is no mystery: but why should rich hosts encourage it? This transfer, like the reverse one, is supported by both selfish interests and humanitarian impulses.

The principal selfish interest in unimpeded immigration is easy to identify; it is the interest of the employers of cheap labor, particularly that needed for degrading jobs. We have been deceived about the forces of history by the lines of Emma Lazarus inscribed on the Statue of Liberty:

> *Give me your tired, your poor*
> *Your huddled masses yearning to*
> *  breathe free,*
> *The wretched refuse of your teeming*
> *  shore,*
> *Send these, the homeless, tempest-*
> *  tossed, to me:*
> *I lift my lamp beside the golden*
> *  door.*

The image is one of an infinitely generous earth-mother, passively opening her arms to hordes of immigrants who come here on their own initiative. Such an image may have been adequate for the early days of colonization, but by the time these lines were written (1886) the force for immigration was largely manufactured inside our own borders by factory and mine owners who sought cheap labor not to be found among laborers already here. One group of foreigners after another was thus enticed into the United States to work at wretched jobs for wretched wages.

At present, it is largely the Mexicans who are being so exploited. It is particularly to the advantage of certain employers that there be many illegal immigrants. Illegal immigrant workers dare not complain about their working conditions for fear of being repatriated. Their presence reduces the bargaining power of all Mexican-American laborers. Cesar Chavez has repeatedly pleaded with congressional committees to close the doors to more Mexicans so that those here can negotiate effectively for higher wages and decent working conditions. Chavez understands the ethics of a lifeboat.

The interests of the employers of cheap labor are well served by the silence of the intelligentsia of the country. WASPS—White Anglo-Saxon

Protestants—are particularly reluctant to call for a closing of the doors to immigration for fear of being called ethnocentric bigots. It was, therefore, an occasion of pure delight for this particular WASP to be present at a meeting when the points he would like to have made were made better by a non-WASP speaking to other non-WASPS. It was in Hawaii, and most of the people in the room were second-level Hawaiian officials of Japanese ancestry. All Hawaiians are keenly aware of the limits of their environment, and the speaker had asked how it might be practically and constitutionally possible to close the doors to more immigrants to the islands. (To Hawaiians, immigrants from the other 49 states are as much of a threat as those from other nations. There is only so much room in the islands, and the islanders know it. Sophistical arguments that imply otherwise do not impress them.)

Yet the Japanese-Americans of Hawaii have active ties with the land of their origin. This point was raised by a Japanese-American member of the audience who asked the Japanese-American speaker: "But how can we shut the doors now? We have many friends and relations in Japan that we'd like to bring to Hawaii some day so that they can enjoy this beautiful land."

The speaker smiled sympathetically and responded slowly: "Yes, but we have children now and someday we'll have grandchildren. We can bring more people here from Japan only by giving away some of the land that we hope to pass on to our grandchildren some day. What right do we have to do that?"

To be generous with one's own possessions is one thing; to be generous with posterity's is quite another. This, I think, is the point that must be gotten across to those who would, from a commendable love of distributive justice, institute a ruinous system of the commons, either in the form of a world food bank or that of unrestricted immigration. Since every speaker is a member of some ethnic group it is always possible to charge him with ethnocentrism. But even after purging an argument of ethnocentrism the rejection of the commons is still valid and necessary if we are to save at least some parts of the world from environmental ruin. Is it not desirable that at least some of the grandchildren of people now living should have a decent place in which to live?

## The Asymmetry of Door-Shutting

We must now answer this telling point: "How can you justify slamming the door once you're inside? You say that immigrants should be kept out. But aren't we all immigrants, or the descendants of immigrants? Since we refuse to leave, must we not, as a matter of justice and symmetry, admit all others?"

It is literally true that we Americans of non-Indian ancestry are the descendants of thieves. Should we not, then, "give back" the land to the Indians; that is, give it to the now-living Americans of Indian ancestry? As an exercise in pure logic I see no way to reject this proposal. Yet I am unwilling to live by it; and I know no one who is. Our reluctance to embrace pure justice may spring from pure selfishness. On the other hand, it may arise from an unspoken recognition of consequences that have not yet been clearly spelled out.

Suppose, becoming intoxicated with pure justice, we "Anglos" should decide to turn our land over to the Indians. Since all our other wealth has also been derived from the land, we would have to give that to the Indians, too. Then what would we non-Indians do? Where would we go? There is no open land in the world on which men without capital can make their living (and not much unoccupied land on which men with capital can either). Where would 209 million putatively justice-loving, non-Indian, Americans go? Most of them—in the persons of their ancestors—came from Europe, but they wouldn't be welcomed back there. Anyway, Europeans have no better title to their land than we to ours. They also would have to give up their homes. (But to whom? And where would *they* go?)

Clearly, the concept of pure justice produces an infinite regress. The law long ago invented statutes of limitations to justify the rejection of pure justice, in the interest of preventing massive disorder. The law zealously defends property rights—but only *recent* property rights. It is as though the physical principle of exponential decay applies to property rights. Drawing a line in time may be unjust, but any other action is practically worse.

We are all the descendants of thieves, and the world's resources are inequitably distributed, but we must begin the journey to tomorrow from the point where we are today. We cannot remake the past. We cannot, without violent disorder and suffering, give land and resources back to the ''original'' owners—who are dead anyway.

We cannot safely divide the wealth equitably among all present peoples, so long as people reproduce at different rates, because to do so would guarantee that our grandchildren—everyone's grandchildren—would have only a ruined world to inhabit.

## Must Exclusion Be Absolute?

To show the logical structure of the immigration problem I have ignored many factors that would enter into real decisions made in a real world. No matter how convincing the logic may be it is probable that we would want, from time to time, to admit a few people from the outside to our lifeboat. Political refugees in particular are likely to cause us to make exceptions: We remember the Jewish refugees from Germany after 1933, and the Hungarian refugees after 1956. Moreover, the interests of national defense, broadly conceived, could justify admitting many men and women of unusual talents, whether refugees or not. (This raises the quality issue, which is not the subject of this essay.)

Such exceptions threaten to create runaway population growth inside the lifeboat, i.e., the receiving country. However, the threat can be neutralized by a population policy that includes immigration. An effective policy is one of flexible control.

Suppose, for example, that the nation has achieved a stable condition of ZPG, which (say) permits 1.5 million births yearly. We must suppose that an acceptable system of allocating birth-rights to potential parents is in effect. Now suppose that an inhumane regime in some other part of the world creates a horde of refugees, and that there is a widespread desire to admit some to our country. At the same time, we do not want to sabotage our population control system. Clearly, the rational path to pursue is the following. If we decide to admit 100,000 refugees this year we should compensate for this by reducing the allocation of birth-rights in the following year by a similar amount—that is, downward to a total of 1.4 million. In that way we could achieve both humanitarian and population control goals. (And the refugees would have to accept the population controls of the society that admits them. It is not inconceivable that they might be given proportionately fewer rights than the native population.)

In a democracy, the admission of immigrants should properly be voted on. But by whom? It is not obvious. The usual rule of a democracy is votes for all. But it can be questioned whether a universal franchise is the most just one in a case of this sort. Whatever benefits there are in the admission of immigrants presumably accrue to everyone. But the costs would be seen as falling most heavily on potential parents, some of whom would have to postpone or forego having their (next) child because of the influx of immigrants. The double question *Who benefits? Who pays?* suggests that a restriction of the usual democratic franchise would be appropriate and just in this case. Would our particular quasi-democratic form of government be flexible enough to institute such a novelty? If not, the majority might, out of humanitarian motives, impose an unacceptable burden (the foregoing of parenthood) on a minority, thus producing political instability.

Plainly many new problems will arise when we consciously face the immigration question and seek rational answers. No workable answers can be found if we ignore population problems. And—if the argument of this essay is correct—so long as there is no true world government to control reproduction everywhere it is impossible to survive in dignity if we are to be guided by Spaceship ethics. Without a world government that is sovereign in reproductive matters mankind lives, in fact, on a number of sovereign lifeboats. For the foreseeable future survival demands that we govern our actions by the ethics of a lifeboat. Posterity will be ill served if we do not.

# 31

## Trouble in the Lifeboat

Opposition to "lifeboat ethics" was prompt and vigorous. Much of it was unnecessary, and I am afraid I was to blame for that. When I presented my paper orally before a meeting of the American Association for the Advancement of Science in San Francisco, an editor of *Psychology Today* asked if he could publish it. I agreed to prepare a shortened version, which I did, under the title "Lifeboat Ethics." [1] Unfortunately the editor, without consulting me, added a subtitle: "The Case Against Helping the Poor." The best that can be said for this subtitle is that it certainly catches people's attention.

How can anybody be against helping the poor? I'm not; and I know no one who is. Human beings are social animals. We want to help one another whenever we can (provided the effort doesn't cost too much trouble or expense). The key question is this: what constitutes help? Building dams—if these increase disease? Bringing in the "Green Revolution"—if this increases unemployment? Helping people in the highlands cut wood for fuel—if this increases flooding in the lowlands? The words "help" and "aid" are prejudicial. To be objective we should initially use only the word "intervention" and then constantly ask, "Will the proposed intervention actually help the people subjected to it, without hurting their neighbors or their posterity?'' U.S. AID—a clever, prejudicial acronym for the Agency for International Development—should really be called the U.S. Intervention Agency; but this yields no usefully prejudicial acronym with which to wheedle Congress out of money.

I suspect that many people who might have accepted the argument of "Living on a Lifeboat" were inflexibly turned against it by their conviction that the author was opposed to helping the poor. The list of my opponents includes some distinguished names. For a second time I was honored with an attack by a president of the American Association for the Advancement of Science in the editorial column of *Science*.[2] This time it was Dr. Roger Revelle, Director of the Center for Population Studies at Harvard; he dismissed lifeboat ethics as "this obscene doctrine." Dr. Revelle may be right of course:

> The American Heritage Dictionary defines the word ["obscene"] as follows: "Offensive to accepted standards of decency or modesty." Obscenity is, then, a relational term: it defines the relation of an idea to the standards of the speaker. It is an unacceptable relation, so we must always ask, which needs changing—the idea or the standards?
>
> Half a century ago D. H. Lawrence challenged the obscenity of sex. "Decent" people tried to suppress *"Lady Chatterley's Lover"*: in the end they lost and we changed our standards. Now there are those who regard rational discussion of survival as an obscenity. Should we repress open and rational discussion, or should we tackle the very real problems of survival in an overcrowded world?[3]

Those who regard an idea as obscene will naturally try to prevent discussion—or at any rate, dispassionate discussion. Their behavior ostensively defines the area of a taboo. In a society like ours that esteems freedom of discussion, a taboo on words or ideas has two layers: the first is the primary taboo on the forbidden thing; the second is the taboo against mentioning that there is a taboo. Faced with what he regards as the necessity of suppressing discussion, a person who praises discussion in the abstract may have recourse to the word "obscene." The stalker of taboos becomes, in such a society, an obscenity-stalker.

As many of my critics have pointed out, there are rhetorical dangers in the lifeboat metaphor. ''We in the U.S. don't live on a lifeboat; we live on a luxury liner'' is the most frequent comment. This raises difficult questions of the meaning and limits of necessity, luxury, temperance and waste, all puzzling and important matters quite apart from the lifeboat situation. Such critics raise, perhaps unwittingly, the spectre of sumptuary laws, which most of us in the European culture thought we had seen the last of in the 17th century. *Plus ça change, plus c'est la même chose?*

In February 1975 a symposium on "Triage in Medicine and Society" was held at the Texas Medical Center's Institute of Religion and Human Development in Houston. Though I was unable to attend I was invited to contribute the concluding essay when time came to publish the proceedings in a scholarly journal. Since the lifeboat metaphor evoked such strong emotional reactions I de-emphasized it in my essay, laying stress instead on the more fundamental idea of carrying capacity. This concept, both simple and profound, is one that real "dirt farmers" understand almost intuitively, but which seems to be almost beyond the grasp of many economists, who assume that every shortage can be cured by raising the price. The ratio of economists to farmers is highest in the richest countries, from which I deduce that the more prosperous a nation is the more difficult will it be for its citizenry to take in the ethical implications of carrying capacity. This limitation on understanding among the rich is unfortunate for the poor of the world, most especially for their posterity.

Then it was decided to republish the symposium as a book, under the title *Lifeboat Ethics: The Moral Dilemmas of World Hunger*.[4] The other contributors, not wanting to benefit from a discussion of other people's misery, wished to assign all the royalties to some international organization devoted to sending food abroad to starving people. That was a reasonable course of action for those who believe that every gift of food is synonymous with aid, but it posed a moral dilemma for me, being unwilling as I am to equate intervention with aid. I did not want to be selfish, but neither did I want to harm others (as I saw the matter) by a gift of food. What to do? As an alternative I suggested that we assign the royalties to the Hastings Institute for Society, Ethics and the Life Sciences. The money would then neither help nor harm the present poor of the world, but by financing some fundamental thinking (such as indeed goes on at the Hastings) it might ultimately decrease the misery in the world at least a little bit. The suggestion was accepted. What follows in the next chapter is my contribution to the book.

# 32

# *Carrying Capacity as an Ethical Concept*

## *(1976)*

Lifeboat Ethics is merely a special application of the logic of the commons.[1] The classic paradigm is that of a pasture held as common property by a community and governed by the following rules: first, each herdsman may pasture as many cattle as he wishes on the commons; and second, the gain from the growth of cattle accrues to the individual owners of the cattle. In an underpopulated world the system of the commons may do no harm and may even be the most economic way to manage things, since management costs are kept to a minimum. In an overpopulated (or overexploited) world a system of the commons leads to ruin, because each herdsman has more to gain individually by increasing the size of his herd than he has to lose as a single member of the community guilty of lowering the carrying capacity of the environment. Consequently he (with others) overloads the commons.

Even if an individual fully perceives the ultimate consequences of his actions he is most unlikely to act in any other way, for he cannot count on the restraint *his* conscience might dictate being matched by a similar restraint on the part of *all* the others. (Anything less than all is not

From *Soundings*, 59(1):120–137. Copyright © 1976 The Society for Values in Higher Education and Vanderbilt University.

enough.) Since mutual ruin is inevitable, it is quite proper to speak of the *tragedy* of the commons.

Tragedy is the price of freedom in the commons. Only by changing to some other system (socialism or private enterprise, for example) can ruin be averted. In other words, in a crowded world survival requires that some freedom be given up. (We have, however, a choice in the freedom to be sacrificed.) Survival is possible under several different politico-economic systems—but not under the system of the commons. When we understand this point, we reject the ideal of distributive justice stated by Karl Marx a century ago, "From each according to his ability, to each according to his needs." [2] This ideal might be defensible if "needs" were defined by the larger community rather than by the individual (or individual political unit) *and if "needs" were static.* [3] But in the past quarter-century, with the best will in the world, some humanitarians have been asserting that rich populations must supply the needs of poor populations even though the recipient populations increase without restraint. At the United Nations conference on population in Bucharest in 1973 spokesmen for the poor nations repeatedly said in effect: "We poor people have the right to reproduce as much as we want to; you in the rich world have the responsibility of keeping us alive."

Such a Marxian disjunction of rights and responsibilities inevitably tends toward tragic ruin for all. It is almost incredible that this position is supported by thoughtful persons, but it is. How does this come about? In part, I think, because language deceives us. When a disastrous loss of life threatens, people speak of a "crisis," implying that the threat is temporary. More subtle is the implication of quantitative stability built into the pronoun "they" and its relatives. Let me illustrate this point with quantified prototype statements based on two different points of view.

*Crisis analysis:* "*These* poor people (1,000,000) are starving, because of a crisis (flood, drought, or the like). How can we refuse *them* (1,000,000)? Let us feed *them* (1,000,000). Once the crisis is past those who are still hungry are few (say 1,000) and there is no further need for our intervention."

*Crunch analysis:* "*Those* (1,000,000) who are hungry are reproducing. We send food to *them* (1,010,000). *Their* lives (1,020,000) are saved. But since the environment is still essentially the same, the next year *they*

(1,030,000) ask for more food. We send it to *them* (1,045,000); and the next year *they* (1,068,000) ask for still more. Since the need has not gone away, it is a mistake to speak of a passing crisis: it is evidently a permanent crunch that this growing 'they' face—a growing disaster, not a passing state of affairs."

"They" increases in size. Rhetoric makes no allowance for a ballooning pronoun. Thus we can easily be deceived by language. We cannot deal adequately with ethical questions if we ignore quantitative matters. This attitude has been rejected by James Sellers, who dismisses prophets of doom from Malthus[4] to Meadows[5] as "chiliasts." Chiliasts (or millenialists, to use the Latin-derived equivalent of the Greek term) predict a catastrophic end of things a thousand years from some reference point. The classic example is the prediction of Judgment Day in the year 1000 anno Domini. Those who predicted it were wrong, of course; but the fact that this specific prediction was wrong is no valid criticism of the use of numbers in thinking. Millenialism is numerology, not science.

In science, most of the time, it is not so much exact numbers that are important as it is the relative size of numbers and the direction of change in the magnitude of them. Much productive analysis is accomplished with only the crude quantitation of "order of magnitude" thinking. First and second derivatives are often calculated with no finer aim than to find out if they are positive or negative. Survival can hinge on the crude issue of the sign of change, regardless of number. This is a far cry from the spurious precision of numerology. Unfortunately the chasm between the "two cultures," as C. P. Snow called them,[6] keeps many in the nonscientific culture from understanding the significance of the quantitative approach. One is tempted to wonder also whether an additional impediment to understanding may not be the mortal sin called Pride, which some theologians regard as the mother of all sins.

Returning to Marx, it is obvious that the *each* in "to each according to his needs" is not—despite the grammar—a unitary, stable entity: "each" is a place-holder for a ballooning variable. Before we commit ourselves to saving the life of *each* and every person in need we had better ask this question: *"And then what?"* That is, what about tomorrow, what about posterity? As Hans Jonas has pointed out,[7] traditional ethics has almost entirely ignored the claims of posterity. In an overpopulated world humanity cannot long endure under a regime governed by posterity-blind ethics. It is the essence of ecological ethics that it pays attention to posterity.

Since "helping" starving people requires that we who are rich give up some of our wealth, any refusal to do so is almost sure to be attributed to selfishness. Selfishness there may be, but focusing on selfishness is likely to be non-productive. In truth, a selfish motive can be found in all policy proposals. The selfishness of *not* giving is obvious and need not be elaborated. But the selfishness of giving is no less real, though more subtle.[8] Consider the sources of support for Public Law 480, the act of Congress under which surplus foods were given to poor countries, or sold to them at bargain prices ("concessionary terms" is the euphemism). Why did we give food away? Conventional wisdom says it was because we momentarily transcended our normal selfishness. Is that the whole story?

It is not. The "we" of the above sentence needs to be subdivided. The farmers who grew the grain did not give it away. They sold it to the government (which then gave it away). Farmers received selfish benefits in two ways: the direct sale of grain, and the economic support to farm prices given by this governmental purchase in an otherwise free market. The operation of P. L. 480 during the past quarter-century brought American farmers to a level of prosperity never known before.

Who else benefited—in a selfish way? The stockholders and employees of the railroads that moved grain to seaports benefited. So also did freight-boat operators (U.S. "bottoms" were specified by law). So also did grain elevator operators. So also did agricultural research scientists who were financially supported in a burgeoning but futile effort "to feed a hungry world."[9] And so also did the large bureaucracy required to keep the P.L. 480 system working. In toto, probably several million people personally benefited from the P.L. 480 program. Their labors cannot be called wholly selfless.

Who *did* make a sacrifice for P.L. 480? The citizens generally, nearly two hundred million of them, paying directly or indirectly through taxes. But each of these many millions lost only a little: whereas each of the million or so gainers gained a great deal. The blunt truth is that *philanthropy pays*—if you are hired as a philanthropist. Those on the gaining side of P.L. 480 made a great deal of money and could afford to spend lavishly to persuade Congress to continue the program. Those on the sacrificing side sacrificed only a little bit per capita and could not afford to spend much protecting their pocketbooks against philanthropic inroads. And so P.L. 480 continued, year after year.

Should we condemn philanthropy when we discover that some of its roots are selfish? I think not, otherwise probably no philanthropy would be possible. The secret of practical success in large-scale public philanthropy is this: see to it that the losses are widely distributed so that the per capita loss is small, but concentrate the gains in a relatively few people so that these few will have the economic power needed to pressure the legislature into supporting the program.

I have spent some time on this issue because I would like to dispose once and for all of condemnatory arguments based on "selfishness." As a matter of principle we should always assume that selfishness is *part* of the motivation of every action. But what of it? If Smith proposes a certain public policy, it is far more important to know whether the policy will do public harm or public good than it is to know whether Smith's motives are selfish or selfless. Consequences ("ends") can be more objectively determined than motivations ("means"). Situational ethics wisely uses consequences as the measure of morality. "If the end does not justify the means, what does?" asks Joseph Fletcher.[10] The obsession of older ethical systems with means and motives is no doubt in part a consequence of envy, which has a thousand disguises.[11] (Though I am sure this is true, the situationist should not dwell on envy very long, for it is after all only a motive, and as such not directly verifiable. In any case public policy must be primarily concerned with consequences.)

Even judging an act by its consequences is not easy. We are limited by the basic theorem of ecology, "We can never do merely one thing."[12] The fact that an act has many consequences is all the more reason for deemphasizing motives as we carry out our ethical analyses. Motives by definition apply only to intended consequences. The multitudinous unintended ones are commonly denigrated by the term "side effects." But "The road to hell is paved with good intentions," so let's have done with motivational evaluations of public policy.

Even after we have agreed to eschew motivational analysis, foreign aid is a tough nut to crack. The literature is large and contradictory, but it all points to the inescapable conclusion that a quarter of a century of earnest effort has not conquered world poverty. To many observers the threat of future disasters is more convincing now than it was a quarter of a century ago—and the disasters are not all in the future either.[13] Where have we gone wrong in foreign aid?

We wanted to do good, of course. The question, "How can we help a poor country?" seems like a simple question, one that should have a simple answer. Our failure to answer it suggests that the question is not as simple as we thought. The variety of contradictory answers offered is disheartening.

How can we find our way through this thicket? I suggest we take a cue from a mathematician. The great algebraist Karl Jacobi (1804–1851) had a simple stratagem that he recommended to students who found themselves butting their heads against a stone wall. *Umkehren, immer umkehren*—"Invert, always invert." Don't just keep asking the same old question over and over: turn it upside down and ask the opposite question. The answer you get then may not be the one you want, but it may throw useful light on the question you started with.

Let's try a Jacobian inversion of the food/population problem. To sharpen the issue, let us take a particular example, say India. The question we want to answer is, "How can we help India?" But since that approach has repeatedly thrust us against a stone wall, let's pose the Jacobian invert, "How can we *harm* India?" After we've answered this perverse question we will return to the original (and proper) one.

As a matter of method, let us grant ourselves the most malevolent of motives: let us ask, "How can we harm India—*really* harm her?" Of course we might plaster the country with thermonuclear bombs, speedily wiping out most of the 600 million people. But, to the truly malevolent mind, that's not much fun: a dead man is beyond harming. Bacterial warfare could be a bit "better," but not much. No: we want something that will really make India suffer, not merely for a day or a week, but on and on and on. How can we achieve this inhumane goal?

Quite simply: by sending India a bounty of food, year after year. The United States exports about 80 million tons of grain a year. Most of it we sell: the foreign exchange it yields we use for such needed imports as petroleum (38 percent of our oil consumption in 1974), iron ore, bauxite, chromium, tin, etc. But in the pursuit of our malevolent goal let us "un-selfishly" tighten our belts, make sacrifices, and do without that foreign exchange. Let us *give* all 80 million tons of grain to the Indians each year.

On a purely vegetable diet it takes about 400 pounds of grain to keep one person alive and healthy for a year. The 600 million Indians need 120 million tons per year; since their nutrition is less than adequate presumably they are getting a bit less than that now. So the 80 million tons we give them will almost double India's per capita supply of food. With a surplus, Indians can afford to vary their diet by growing some less efficient crops; they can also convert some of the grain into meat (pork and chickens for the Hindus, beef and chickens for the Moslems). The entire nation can then be supplied not only with plenty of calories, but also with an adequate supply of high quality protein. The people's eyes will sparkle, their steps will become more elastic; and they will be capable of more work. "Fatalism" will no doubt diminish. (Much so-called fatalism is merely a consequence of malnutrition.) Indians may even become a bit overweight, though they will still be getting only two-thirds as much food as the average inhabitant of a rich country. Surely—we think—surely a well-fed India would be better off?

Not so: *ceteris paribus,* they will ultimately be worse off. Remember, "We can never do merely one thing." A generous gift of food would have not only nutritional consequences: it would also have political and economic consequences. The difficulty of distributing free food to a poor people is well known. Harbor, storage, and transport inadequacies result in great losses of grain to rats and fungi. Political corruption diverts food from those who need it most to those who are more powerful. More abundant supplies depress free market prices and discourage native farmers from growing food in subsequent years. Research into better ways of agriculture is also discouraged. Why look for better ways to grow food when there is food enough already?

There are replies, of sorts, to all the above points. It may be maintained that all these evils are only temporary ones; in time, organizational sense will be brought into the distributional system and the government will crack down on corruption. Realizing the desirability of producing more food, for export if nothing else, a wise government will subsidize agricultural research in spite of an apparent surplus. Experience does not give much support to this optimistic view, but let us grant the conclusions for the sake of getting on to more important matters. Worse is to come.

The Indian unemployment rate is commonly reckoned at 30 percent, but it is acknowledged that this is a minimum figure. *Under*employment is rife. Check into a hotel in Calcutta with four small bags and four bearers will carry your luggage to the room—with another man to carry the key. Custom, and a knowledge of what the traffic will bear, decree this practice. In addition malnutrition justifies it in part. Adequately fed, half as many men would suffice. So one of the early consequences of achieving a higher level of nutrition in the Indian population would be to increase the number of unemployed.

India needs many things that food will not buy. Food will not diminish the unemployment rate (quite the contrary); nor will it increase the supply of minerals, bicycles, clothes, automobiles, gasoline, schools, books, movies, or television. All these things require energy for their manufacture and maintenance.

Of course, food is a form of energy, but it is convertible to other forms only with great loss; so we are practically justified in considering energy and food as mutually exclusive goods. On this basis the most striking difference between poor and rich countries is not in the food they eat but in the energy they use. On a per capita basis rich countries use about three times as much of the primary foods—grains and the like—as do poor countries. (To a large extent this is because the rich convert much of the grain to more "wasteful" animal meat.) But when it comes to energy, rich countries use ten times as much per capita. (Near the extremes Americans use 60 times as much per person as Indians.) By reasonable standards much of this energy may be wasted (e.g., in the manufacture of "exercycles" for sweating the fat off people who have eaten too much), but a large share of this energy supplies the goods we regard as civilized: effortless transportation, some luxury foods, a variety of sports, clean space-heating, more than adequate clothing, and energy-consuming arts—music, visual arts, electronic auxiliaries, etc. Merely giving food to a people does almost nothing to satisfy the appetite for any of these other goods.

But a well-nourished people is better fitted to try to wrest more energy from its environment. The question then is this: Is the native environment able to furnish more energy? And at what cost?

In India energy is already being gotten from the environment at a fearful cost. In the past two centuries millions of acres of India have been deforested in the struggle for fuel, with the usual environmental degradation. The Vale of Kashmir, once one of the garden spots of the world, has been denuded to such an extent that the hills no longer hold water as they once did, and the springs supplying the famous gardens are drying up. So desperate is the need for charcoal for fuel that the Kashmiri now make it out of tree leaves. This wasteful practice denies the soil of needed organic mulch.

Throughout India, as is well known, cow dung is burned to cook food. The minerals of the dung are not thereby lost, but the ability of dung to improve soil tilth is. Some of the nitrogen in the dung goes off into the air and does not return to Indian soil. Here we see a classic example of the "vicious circle": because Indians are poor they burn dung, depriving the soil of nitrogen and making themselves still poorer the following year. If we give them plenty of food, as they cook this food with cow dung they will lower still more the ability of their land to produce food.

Let us look at another example of this counter-productive behavior. Twenty-five years ago western countries brought food and medicine to Nepal. In the summer of 1974 a disastrous flood struck Bangladesh, killing tens of thousands of people, by government admission. (True losses in that part of the world are always greater than admitted losses.) Was there any connection between feeding Nepal and flooding Bangladesh? Indeed there was, and is.[14]

Nepal nestles amongst the Himalayas. Much of its land is precipitous, and winters are cold. The Nepalese need fuel, which they get from trees. Because more Nepalese are being kept alive now, the demand for timber is escalating. As trees are cut down, the soil under them is washed down the slopes into the rivers that run through India and Bangladesh. Once the absorption capacity of forest soil is gone, floods rise faster and to higher maxima. The flood of 1974 covered two-thirds of Bangladesh, twice the area of "normal" floods—which themselves are the consequence of deforestation in preceding centuries.

By bringing food and medicine to Nepal we intended only to save lives. But we can never do merely one thing, and the Nepalese lives we saved created a Nepalese energy-famine. The lives we saved from starvation in Nepal a quarter of a century ago were paid for in our time by lives lost to flooding and its attendant evils in Bangladesh. The saying, ''Man does not live by bread alone,'' takes on new meaning.

Still we have not described what may be the worst consequence of a food-only policy: revolution and civil disorder. Many kindhearted people who support food aid programs solicit the cooperation of ''hard-nosed'' doubters by arguing that good nutrition is needed for world peace. Starving people will attack others, they say. Nothing could be further from the truth. The monumental studies of Ancel Keys and others have shown that starving people are completely selfish.[15] They are incapable of cooperating with others; and they are incapable of laying plans for tomorrow and carrying them out. Moreover, modern war is so expensive that even the richest countries can hardly afford it.

The thought that starving people can forcefully wrest subsistence from their richer brothers may appeal to our sense of justice, *but it just ain't so*. Starving people fight only among themselves, and that inefficiently.

So what would happen if we brought ample supplies of food to a population that was still poor in everything else? They would still be incapable of waging war at a distance, but their ability to fight among themselves would be vastly increased. With vigorous, well-nourished bodies and a keen sense of their impoverishment in other things, they would no doubt soon create massive disorder in their own land. Of course, they might create a strong and united country, but what is the probability of that? Remember how much trouble the thirteen colonies had in forming themselves into a United States. Then remember that India is divided by two major religions, many castes, fourteen major languages and a hundred dialects. A partial separation of peoples along religious lines in 1947, at the time of the formation of Pakistan and of independent India, cost untold millions of lives. The budding off of Bangladesh (formerly East Pakistan) from the rest of Pakistan in 1971 cost several million more. All these losses were achieved on a low level of nutrition. The possibilities of blood-letting in a population of 600 million well-nourished people of many languages and religions and no appreciable tradition of cooperation stagger the imagination. Philanthropists with any imagination at all should be stunned by the thought of 600 million well-fed Indians seeking to meet their energy needs from their own resources.

So the answer to our Jacobian question, "How can we harm India?" is clear: send food *only*. Escaping the Jacobian by reinverting the question we now ask, "How can we *help* India?" Immediately we see that we must *never* send food without a matching gift of non-food energy. But before we go careening off on an intoxicating new program we had better look at some more quantities.

On a per capita basis, India uses the energy equivalent of one barrel of oil per year; the U.S. uses sixty. The world average of all countries, rich and poor, is ten. If we want to bring India only up to the present world average, we would have to send India about $9 \times 600$ million bbl. of oil per year (or its equivalent in coal, timber, gas or whatever). That would be more than five billion barrels of oil equivalent. What is the chance that we will make such a gift?

Surely it is nearly zero. For scale, note that our total yearly petroleum use is seven billion barrels (of which we import three billion). Of course we use (and have) a great deal of coal too. But these figures should suffice to give a feeling of scale.

More important is the undoubted psychological fact that a fall in income tends to dry up the springs of philanthropy. Despite wide disagreements about the future of energy it is obvious that from now on, for at least the next twenty years and possibly for centuries, our per capital supply of energy is going to fall, year after year. The food we gave in the past was "surplus." By no accounting do we have an energy surplus. In fact, the perceived deficit is rising year by year.

India has about one-third as much land as the United States. She has about three times as much population. If her people-to-land ratio were the same as ours she would have only about seventy million people (instead of 600 million). With the forested and relatively unspoiled farmlands of four centuries ago, seventy million people was probably well within the carrying capacity of the land. Even in today's India, seventy million people could probably make it in comfort and dignity—provided they didn't increase!

To send food only to a country already populated beyond the carrying capacity of its land is to collaborate in the further destruction of the land and the further impoverishment of its people.

Food plus energy is a recommendable policy; but for a large population under today's conditions this policy is defensible only by the logic of the old saying, ''If wishes were horses, beggars would ride.'' The fantastic amount of energy needed for such a program is simply not in view. (We have mentioned nothing of the equally monumental ''infrastructure'' of political, technological, and educational machinery needed to handle unfamiliar forms and quantities of energy in the poor countries. In a short span of time this infrastructure is as difficult to bring into being as is an abundant supply of energy.)

In summary, then, here are the major foreign-aid possibilities that tender minds are willing to entertain:

a. Food plus energy—a conceivable, but practically impossible program.

b. Food alone—a conceivable and possible program, but one which would destroy the recipient.

In the light of this analysis the question of triage[8] shrinks to negligible importance. If *any* gift of food to overpopulated countries does more harm than good, it is not necessary to decide which countries get the gift and which do not. For posterity's sake we should never send food to any population that is beyond the realistic carrying capacity of its land. The question of triage does not even arise.

Joseph Fletcher neatly summarized this point when he said, ''We should give if it helps but not if it hurts.'' We would do well to memorize his aphorism, but we must be sure we understand the proper object of the verb, which is the recipient. Students of charity have long recognized that an important motive of the giver is to help himself, the giver.[16] Hindus give to secure a better life in the next incarnation; Moslems, to achieve a richer paradise at the end of this life; and Christians in a simpler day no doubt hoped to shorten their stay in purgatory by their generosity. Is there anyone who would say that contemporary charity is completely free of the self-serving element?

To deserve the name, charity surely must justify itself primarily, perhaps even solely, by the good it does the recipient, not only in the moment of giving but in the long run. That every act has multiple consequences was recognized by William L. Davison, who grouped the consequences of an act of charity into two value-classes, positive and negative.[17] True charity, he said,

> confers benefits, and it refrains from injuring. . . . Hence, charity
> may sometimes assume an austere and even apparently unsympa-
> thetic aspect toward its object. When that object's real good cannot
> be achieved without inflicting pain and suffering, charity does not
> shrink from the infliction. . . . Moreover, a sharp distinction must
> be drawn between charity and amiability or good nature—the latter
> of which is a weakness and may be detrimental to true charity, al-
> though it may also be turned to account in its service.

To the ecologically-minded student of ethics, most traditional ethics
looks like mere amiability, focusing as it does on the manifest misery of
the present generation to the neglect of the more subtle but equally real
needs of a much larger posterity. It is amiability that feeds the Nepalese
in one generation and drowns Bangladeshi in another. It is amiability
that, contemplating the wretched multitudes of Indians asks, "How can
we let them starve?" implying that we, and only we, have the
power to end their suffering. Such an assumption surely springs from
hubris.

Fifty years ago India and China were equally miserable, and their future prospects equally bleak. During the past generation we have given
India "help" on a massive scale; China, because of political differences
between her and us, has received no "help" from us and precious little
from anybody else. Yet who is better off today? And whose future prospects look brighter? Even after generously discounting the reports of the
first starry-eyed Americans to enter China in recent years, it is apparent
that China's 900 million are physically better off than India's 600 million.

All that has come about without an iota of "help" from us.

Could it be that a country that is treated as a responsible agent does
better in the long run than one that is treated as an irresponsible parasite
which we must "save" repeatedly? Is it not possible that robust repon-
sibility is a virtue among nations as it is among individuals? Can we tolerate a charity that destroys responsibility?

Admittedly, China did not reach her present position of relative prosperity without great suffering, great loss of life. Did millions die? Tens of millions? We don't know. If we had enjoyed cordial relations with the new China during the birth process no doubt we would, out of a rich store of amiability, have seen to it that China remained as irresponsible and miserable as India. Our day-to-day decisions, with their delayed devastation, would have been completely justified by our traditional, posterity-blind ethics which seems incapable of asking the crucial question, *"And then what?"*

Underlying most ethical thought at present is the assumption that human life is the *summum bonum*. Perhaps it is; but we need to inquire carefully into what we mean by "human life." Do we mean the life of each and every human being now living, all 4,000,000,000 of them? Is each presently existing human being to be kept alive (and breeding) regardless of the consequences for future human beings? So, apparently, say amiable, individualistic, present-oriented, future-blind Western ethicists.

An ecologically-oriented ethicist asks, "And then what?" and insists that the needs of posterity be given a weighting commensurate with those of the present generation. The economic prejudice that leads to a heavy discounting of the future must be balanced by a recognition that the population of posterity vastly exceeds the population of the living.[18] We know from experience that the environment can be irreversibly damaged and the carrying capacity of a land permanently lowered.[14] Even a little lowering multiplied by an almost limitless posterity should weigh heavily in the scales against the needs of those living, once our charity expands beyond the limits of simple amiability.

We can, of course, increase carrying capacity somewhat. But only hubris leads us to think that our ability to do so is without limit. Despite all our technological accomplishments—and they are many—there is a potent germ of truth in the saying of Horace (65–8 B.C.): *Naturam expelles furca, tamen usque recurret.* "Drive nature off with a pitchfork, nevertheless she will return with a rush." This is the message of Rachel Carson,[19] which has been corroborated by many others.[20]

*The morality of an act is a function of the state of the system at the time the act is performed*—this is the foundation stone of situationist, ecological ethics.[12] A time-blind absolute ethical principle like that implied by the shibboleth, "the sanctity of life," leads to greater suffering than its situationist, ecological alternative—and ultimately and paradoxically, even to a lesser quantity of life over a sufficiently long period of time. The interests of posterity can be brought into the reckoning of ethics if we abandon the idea of the sanctity of (present) life as an absolute ethical ideal, replacing it with the idea of the sanctity of the carrying capacity.

Those who would like to make the theory of ethics wholly rational must look with suspicion on any statement that includes the word "sanctity." There is a whole class of terms whose principal (and perhaps sole) purpose seems to be to set a stop to inquiry: "self-evident" and "sanctity" are members of this class. I must, therefore, show that "sanctity" is used as something more than a discussion-stopper when it occurs in the phrase "the sanctity of the carrying capacity."

Some there are who so love the world of Nature (that is, Nature *sine* Man) that they regard the preservation of a world without humankind as a legitimate objective of human beings. It is difficult to argue this ideal dispassionately and productively. Let me only say that I am not one of this class of nature-lovers; my view is definitely anthropocentric. Even so I argue that we would do well to accept "Thou shalt not exceed the carrying capacity of any environment" as a legitimate member of a new Decalogue. When for the sake of momentary gain by human beings the carrying capacity is transgressed, the long-term interests of the same human beings—"same" meaning themselves and their successors in time—are damaged. I should not say that the carrying capacity is something that is *intrinsically* sacred (whatever *that* may mean) but that the rhetorical device "carrying capacity" is a shorthand way of dealing time and posterity into the game. A mathematician would, I imagine, view "carrying capacity" as an algorithm, a substitute conceptual element with a different grammar from the elements it replaces. Algorithmic substitutions are made to facilitate analysis; when they are well chosen, they introduce no appreciable errors. I think "carrying capacity" meets significant analytical demands of a posterity-oriented ethics.

In an uncrowded world there may be no ethical need for the ecological concept of the carrying capacity. But ours is a crowded world. We need this concept if we are to minimize human suffering in the long run (and not such a very long run at that). How Western man has pretty well succeeded in locking himself into a suicidal course of action by developing and clinging to a concept of the absolute sanctity of life is a topic that calls for deep inquiry. Lacking the certain knowledge that might come out of such a scholarly investigation, I close this essay with a personal view of the significance of—

CARRYING CAPACITY *
(To Paul Sears)
*A man said to the universe:*
*"Sir, I exist!"*
*"However," replied the universe,*
*"The fact has not created in me*
*A sense of obligation."*
*—Stephen Crane, 1899.*

So spoke the poet, at century's end;
And in those dour days when schools displayed the world,
"Warts and all," to their reluctant learners,
These lines thrust through the layers of wishfulness,
Forming the minds that later found them to be true.

All that is past, now.
Original sin, then mere personal ego,
Open to the shafts of consciousness,
Now flourishes as an ego of the tribe
Whose battle cry (which none dare question) is
"Justice!"—But hear the poet's shade:

A tribe said to the universe,
"Sir, We exist!"
"So I see," said the universe,
"But your multitude creates in me
No feeling of obligation.

"Need creates right, you say? Your need, your right?
Have you forgot we're married?

* Copyright © 1975 Garrett Hardin.

Humanity and universe—Holy, indissoluble pair!
Nothing you can do escapes my vigilant response.

"Dam my rivers and I'll salt your crops;
Cut my trees and I'll flood your plains.
Kill 'pests' and, by God, you'll get a silent spring!
Go ahead—save every last baby's life!
I'll starve the lot of them later,
When they can savor to the full
The exquisite justice of truth's retribution.
Wrench from my earth those exponential powers
No wobbling Willie should e'er be trusted with:
Do this, and a million masks of envy shall create
A hell of blackmail and tribal wars
From which civilization will never recover.

"Don't speak to me of shortage. My world is vast
And has more than enough—for no more than enough.
There is a shortage of nothing, save will and wisdom;
But there is a longage of people.

"Hubris—that was the Greeks' word for what ails you.
Pride fueled the pyres of tragedy
Which died (some say) with Shakespeare.
O, incredible delusion! That potency should have no limits!
'We believe no evil 'til the evil's done'—
Witness the deserts' march across the earth,
Spawned and nourished by men who whine, 'Abnormal weather.'
Nearly as absurd as crying, 'Abnormal universe!' . . .
But I suppose you'll be saying that, next."

Ravish capacity: reap consequences.
Man claims the first a duty and calls what follows
Tragedy.
Insult—Backlash. Not even the universe can break
This primal link. Who, then, has the power
To put an end to tragedy? Only those who recognize
Hubris in themselves.

# 33

## *The Economics of Wilderness*

### *(1969)*

To some it may seem anathema to mention wilderness and economics in the same breath. Certainly, in the past, some of the most dangerous enemies of wilderness have been men who spoke the economic lingo. Despite this historic tar I think the brush of economics is a proper one for painting a picture of wilderness as a problem in human choice.

Economics may be defined as the study of choice necessitated by scarcity. There is something odd, and even improper, in speaking of the "economics of abundance" as Stuart Chase once did. With true abundance all economics ceases, except for the ultimately inescapable economics of time. Of the economics of time there is no general theory, and perhaps cannot be. But for the *things* of the world there is an economics, something that can be said.

Although there really is no such thing as an economics of abundance, the belief that there is, is one of the suppurating myths of our time. This belief had its origin partly in a genuine economic phenomenon, "the economy of scale." For complex artifacts in general the unit cost goes

Based on a talk given at the Sierra Club Wilderness Conference, San Francisco, 15 March 1969. Reprinted by permission from *Natural History,* **78**(6):20–27. © 1969 The American Museum of Natural History.

down as the scale of manufacture increases. In general, the more complex the artifact, the more striking the economy of scale: the cost per unit to build a million automobiles per year is far, far less than the cost per unit when only one is manufactured. Because artifacts are so pervasive in modern life, most of us unconsciously assume "the bigger the better," and "the more the cheaper." It takes a positive effort of imagination to realize that there are things the supply of which cannot be multiplied indefinitely. Natural resources in general, and wilderness in particular, fall in this group.

This is obvious enough to Sierra Club members. It should be obvious to everyone, but it is not. Not long ago, for example, discussing some proposed improvements in a national park, the *Toronto Financial Post* said: "During 1968 and early 1969, campsites will be expanded and roads paved to enable the visitor to enjoy the wilderness atmosphere that was nearly inaccessible only a few years ago." This is an astonishing sentence, but I will bet that one would have to argue with the writer of it for quite a while before he could be made to see the paradox involved in speaking of building a road into the wilderness.

Wilderness cannot be multiplied, and it can be subdivided only a little. It is not increasing; we have to struggle to keep it from decreasing as population increases. Were we to divide up the wilderness among even a small fraction of the total population, there would be no real wilderness available to anyone. So what should we do?

The first thing to do is to see where we stand, to make a list of possibilities without (initially) making any judgment of their desirability. On the first level of analysis there are just three possibilities.

1. The wilderness can be opened to everyone. The end result of this is completely predictable: absolute destruction. Only a nation with a small population, perhaps no greater than one percent of our present population, a nation that does not have at its disposal our present means of transportation could maintain a wilderness that was open to all.

2. We can close the wilderness to everyone. In a limited sense, this action would preserve the wilderness. But it would be a wilderness like Bishop Berkeley's "tree in the quad" when no one is there: does wilderness really exist if no one experiences it? Such an action would save wilderness for the future, but it would do no one any good now.

3. We can allow only limited access to the wilderness. This is the only

course of action that can be rationally defended. Only a small percentage
of a large population can ever enjoy wilderness. By suitably defining our
standards, and by studying the variables in the situation, we can (in principle) work out a theory for maximizing the enjoyment of wilderness
under a system of limited access. Whatever our theory, we shall have to
wrestle with the problem of choice, the problem of determining what
small number among a vast population of people shall have the opportunity to enjoy this scarce good, wilderness. It is this problem of choice
that I wish to explore here.

What I have to say applies not only to wilderness in the sense in which
that term is understood by all good outdoorsmen but also to all other
kinds of outdoor recreational areas—to national parks, to ski areas, and
the like. All of these can be destroyed by localized overpopulation. They
differ in their "carrying capacity." The carrying capacity of a Coney
Island (for those who like it, and there are such people) is very high; the
carrying capacity of wilderness, in the sense defined by Howard Zahniser, is very low. In the Wilderness Bill of 1964 Zahniser's felicitous
definition stands for all to admire:

"A wilderness, in contrast with those areas where man and his own
works dominate the landscape is hereby recognized as an area where the
earth and its community of life are untrammeled by man, where man
himself is a visitor who does not remain."

The carrying capacity of Coney Island is, I suppose, something like
100 people per acre; the carrying capacity of a wilderness is perhaps one
person per square mile. But whatever the carrying capacity, as population
inexorably increases, each type of recreational area sooner or later comes
up against the problem of allocation of this scarce resource among the
more than sufficient number of claimants to it. It is at this point that the
problem of limited access must be faced.

How shall we limit access? How shall we choose from among the too-
abundant petitioners those few who shall be allowed in? Let's run over
the various possibilities.

*First:* By the marketplace. We can auction off the natural resource,
letting those who are richest among the sufficiently motivated buy. In our
part of the world and in our time most of us unhesitatingly label this
method of allotment "unfair." Perhaps it is. But don't forget that many

an area of natural beauty available to us today has survived unspoiled precisely because it was preserved in an estate of the wealthy in past times.
This method of allotment has at least the virtue that it preserves natural
treasures until a better, or perhaps we should merely say a more acceptable, method of distribution can be devised. The privilege of wealth has
in the past carried many of the beauties of nature through the first, destructive eras of nascent democracy to the more mature, later stages that
were capable of appreciating and preserving them.

*Second:* By queues. Wilderness could be made available on a first-
come, first-served basis, up to the extent of the carrying capacity. People
would simply line up each day in a long queue and a few would be
allowed in. It would be a fatiguing and wasteful system, but while it
would be "fair," it might not be stable.

*Third:* By lottery. This would be eminently "fair," and it would not be
terribly fatiguing or wasteful. In earlier days, the decision of a lottery was
regarded as the choice of God. We cannot recapture this consoling belief
(now that "God is dead"), but we are still inclined to accept the results
of a lottery. Lotteries serve well for the allocation of hunting rights in
some of our states where big game abounds.

*Fourth:* By merit. Whether one regards this as "unfair" or "fair"
depends on the complexion of one's political beliefs. Whether it is fair or
not, I will argue that it is the best system of allocation. Anyone who
argues for a merit system of determining rights immediately raises an
*argumentum ad hominem*. He immediately raises the suspicion that he is
about to define merit in such a way as to include himself in the meri-
torious group.

The suspicion is justified, and because it is justified it must be met. To
carry conviction, he who proposes standards must show that his argument
is not self-serving. What I hereby propose as a criterion for admission to
the wilderness is great physical vigor. I explicitly call your attention to
this significant fact: I myself cannot pass the test I propose. I had polio at
the age of four, and got around moderately well for more than 40 years,
but now I require crutches. Until today, I have not traded on my infir-
mity. But today I must, for it is an essential part of my argument.

I am not fit for the wilderness I praise. I cannot pass the test I propose.
I cannot enter the area I would restrict. Therefore I claim that I speak

with objectivity. The standard I propose is not an example of special pleading in my own interest. I can speak loudly where abler men would have to be hesitant.

To restrict the wilderness to physically vigorous people is inherently sensible. What is the experience of wilderness? Surely it has two major components. The first is the experience of being there, of (in Thoreau's words) being refreshed "by the sight of inexhaustible vigor, vast and titanic features," of seeing "that nature is so rife with life that myriads can afford to be sacrificed and suffered to prey on one another; that tender organizations can be so serenely squashed out of existence like pulp. . . ."

The experience of being there is part of the experience of wilderness, but only a part. If we were dropped down from a line by helicopter into the middle of this experience we would miss an important part of the total experience, namely the experience of getting there. The exquisite sight, sound, and smell of wilderness is many times more powerful if it is earned through physical achievement, if it comes at the end of a long and fatiguing trip for which vigorous good health is a necessity.

Practically speaking, this means that no one should be able to enter a wilderness by mechanical means. He should have to walk many miles on his own two feet, carrying all his provisions with him. In some cases, entrance might be on horse or mule back, or in a canoe, or by snowshoes; but there should be no automobiles, no campers, no motorcycles, no totegoats, no outboard motors, no airplanes. Just unmechanized man and nature—this is a necessary ingredient of the prescription for the wilderness experience.

That mechanical aids threaten wilderness is already recognized by managers of our wildernesses. Emergency roads, it is said, should be used sparingly. I submit that this cautious policy is not cautious enough. I submit that there should be *no* emergency roads, that the people who go into the wilderness should go in without radio transmitters, that they should know for certain that if an emergency arises they can get no help from the outside. If injured, they must either somehow struggle to the outside under their own power or (if lucky) catch the attention of another rare wanderer in the wilderness and get him to help. For people who are physically prepared for it, the wilderness is not terribly dangerous—but such danger as there is, is a precious part of the total experience. The knowledge that one is really on one's own is a powerful tonic. It would be cruelly sentimental to take this away from the wilderness adventurer.

There is not even a public interest in making the wilderness safe. Making great and spectacular efforts to save the life of an individual makes sense only when there is a shortage of people. I have not lately heard that there is a shortage of people.

There is, however, a public interest in making the wilderness as difficult and dangerous as it legitimately can be. There is, I think, a well-founded suspicion that our life has become, if anything, too safe for the best psychological health, particularly among the young. The ever greater extension of the boundaries of legal liability has produced a controlled and fenced-in environment in which it is almost impossible to hurt oneself—unless one tries. The behavior of the young clearly indicates that they really try. Drag races, road races, "rumbles," student sit-ins, marches, and tauntings of the police—all these activities look like the behavior of people looking for danger. I do not wish to deny that some of the activities may arise from other motivations also, e.g., idealistic political beliefs. I am only saying that it looks like deliberate seeking of danger is part of the motivation of our obstreperous young. I think it is an important part. I think we would do well to tear down some of the fences that now deprive people of the possibility of danger. A wilderness without rescue services would contribute to the stability of society.

There is a second way in which the interest of society is furthered by a rigorous wilderness. From time to time a president of the United States endeavors to improve the physical condition of the average citizen by resorting to a rhetorical bombardment. The verbal ammunition consists principally of the words "responsibility," "duty," and "patriotism." These rhetorical duds no longer move the young. The negative motivation of shame is, in general, not as effective as the positive motivation of prestige. A wilderness that can be entered only by a few of the most physically fit of the population will act as an incentive to myriads more to improve their physical condition. The motivation will be more effective if we have (as I think we should) a graded series of wilderness and park areas. Areas in which the carrying capacity is reckoned at one person per thousand acres should be the most difficult to enter; those with a capacity of one per hundred acres should be easier, those with one per ten, still easier, and so on. Yosemite Valley should, I suggest, be assigned a carrying capacity of about one per acre which might mean that it could be opened to anyone who could walk ten miles. At first, of course, the ten-mile walkers would be a very small class, but once the prestige factor took effect more and more people would be willing to walk such a distance. Then the standard should be made more rigorous.

I am sure other details of such a system would eventually have to be faced and worked out. It might be necessary to combine it with a lottery. Or some independent, easily administered test of physical fitness might be instituted. These are details, and in principle can be solved, so I will not spend time on them. But whatever the details, it is clear that many of our present national parks and national forests and other recreation areas should be forever closed to people on crutches, to small children, to fat people, to people with heart conditions, and to old people in the usual state of physical disrepair. On the basis of their lack of merit, such people (and remember, I am a member of this deprived group) should give up all claim of right to the wilderness experience.

The poet Goethe once said, "We must earn again for ourselves what we have inherited," recognizing that only those things that are earned can be precious. To be precious the heritage of wilderness must be open only to those who can earn it again for themselves. The rest, since they cannot gain the genuine treasury by their own efforts, must relinquish the shadow of it.

We need not be so righteous as to deny the excluded ones all experience of the out-of-doors. There is no reason in the world why we cannot expand our present practice of setting up small outdoor areas where we permit a high density of people to get a tiny whiff of nature. Camping cheek by jowl with thousands of others in an outdoor slum does not appeal to me personally—I have not visited Yosemite Valley in thirty years—but there are people who simply love this slummy togetherness, a fact that Sierra Clubbers sometimes forget or find hard to believe. By all means, let us create some al fresco slums for the people, but not in the likes of Yosemite Valley, which is too good for this purpose. But there will be little loss if some of the less attractive forest areas are turned into outdoor slums to relieve the pressure on the really good areas. We must have lakes that fairly pullulate with water skiers in order that we may be able to set aside other lakes for quiet canoeing. We must have easily reached beaches that fairly writhe with oily bodies and vibrate to a steady cacophony of transistor radios, in order to keep up other beaches, difficult of access, on which we can forbid all noise makers.

The idea of wilderness is a difficult one, but it is precisely because it is difficult that clarifying it is valuable. In discovering how to justify a restricted good to a nation of 200 million people that is still growing, we find a formula that extends beyond wilderness to a whole spectrum of recreational activities in the national commons. The solution of the difficult case erects a framework into which other cases can be easily fitted.

# NOTES

The citations of the notes to the chapters are set in several different styles. They have been copied without change from the original publications, which followed different "style books." The differences are not adaptive, but idiosyncratic.

In biology, the speciation process includes the "fixation" of non-adaptive genes (non-adaptive so far as we can tell). Isolation automatically produces differentiation, adaptive or not. In the publishing business something of this sort seems to have happened in bibliographic citations. There are many different systems, an abomination to the author of an interdisciplinary paper, who may have to submit his work to journals following different style-books.

The diversity of citation styles serves little real purpose beyond giving employment to typists. What are the chances of reducing the variety? Surely *nil*. This is something every reformer should ponder over; in miniature, this situation exhibits characteristics of more important malfunctioning units of society.

## 1

1. Garrett Hardin, 1969. *Population, Evolution, and Birth Control*, 2nd edition. San Fancisco: W. H. Freeman & Co. (p. 278).
2. Mary Steichen Calderone, ed., 1958. *Abortion in the United States*. New York: Hoeber-Harper.

# 2

Reprinted with permission from *ETC.*, **24**:263–281. 1967.
1. Karl Heinz Mehlan, 1965. Legal abortions in Roumania. *Journal of Sex Research*, **1**:31.
2. Christopher Tietze and Hans Lehfeldt, 1961. Legal abortion in Eastern Europe, *Journal of the American Medical Association*, **175**:1149.
3. Garrett Hardin, 1966. Abortion and human dignity. *Per/Se*, **1**:16. Edwin M. Schur, 1965. *Crimes Without Victims*. Englewood Cliffs, N.J.: Prentice-Hall. Lawrence Lader, 1966. *Abortion*. Indianapolis: Bobbs-Merrill.
4. Mary Steichen Calderone, ed., 1958. *Abortion in the United States*. New York: Hoeber-Harper,. (p. 157).
5. *Ibid.*, p. 178.
6. Luman H. Long, ed., 1966. *The World Almanac, 1966*. New York: World-Telegram. (p. 307)
7. Christopher Tietze, 1960. *Fertility and Sterility*, **11**:485.
8. Santa Barbara *News-Press*, 8 February 1965.
9. Eugene Quay, 1960. Justifiable abortion. *Georgetown Law Journal*, **49**:399.
10. Garrett Hardin, 1956. Meaninglessness of the word protoplasm. *Scientific Monthly*, **82**:112.
11. Karl R. Popper, 1959. *The Logic of Scientific Discovery*. London: Hutchinson. (p. 40)
12. Assembly Interim Committee on Criminal Procedure, Abortion Hearing (continued), AB 2614, December 17 and 18, 1962. San Diego, California. (p. 213)
13. *Ibid.*, p. 278.
14. *Ibid.*, p. 92.
15. *Ibid.*, p. 189.
16. Norman St. John-Stevas, 1963. *The Right to Life*. London: Hodder and Stoughton.
17. P. W. Bridgman, 1927. *The Logic of Modern Physics*. New York: Macmillan.
18. Mary Steichen Calderone, ed., 1958. *Abortion in the United States*. New York: Hoeber-Harper. (Chapter 11)
19. Rolando Armijo and Tegualdo Monreal, 1965. Epidemiology of provoked abortion in Santiago, Chile. *Journal of Sex Research*, **1**:143.
20. George H. Dunne, S.J., 1949. *Religion and American Democracy*. New York: America Press. (p. 31)
21. E. S. Turner, 1950. *Roads to Ruin: the Shocking History of Social Reform*. London: Michael Joseph.
22. V. P. Ring, 1966. *The Wall Street Journal*, 9 March, p. 12.
23. Rudolph Ehrensing, 1966. When is it really abortion? *The National Catholic Reporter*, 25 May, p. 4.

# 3

Reprinted with permission from *Journal of Marriage and the Family*, **30**:246–251. 1968.
1. Mary Steichen Calderone, ed., 1958. *Abortion in the United States*. New York: Hoeber-Harper. (p. 178)

2. Anthony C. Beilenson, 1966. Abortion and common sense. *Per/Se*, **1**:24.

3. Garrett Hardin, 1967. Semantic aspects of abortion. *ETC.*, **24**:263.

4. Lee Rainwater, 1960. *And the Poor Get Children*. Chicago: Quadrangle Books. (p. *ix* and Chapter 1)

5. Alice S. Rossi, 1966. Abortion laws and their victims. *Trans-Action*, **3** (Sept.-Oct.):7.

6. Calderone, *op. cit.*, p. 103.

7. *Ibid.*, p. 123.

8. Hans Forssman and Inga Thuwe, 1966. One hundred and twenty children born after application for therapeutic abortion refused. *Acta Psychiatrica Scandinavica*, **42**:71.

9. Lawrence Lader, 1966. *Abortion*. Indianapolis: Bobbs-Merrill.

10. Alan F. Guttmacher, ed., 1967. *The Case for Legalized Abortion*. Berkeley: Diablo Press.

11. Garrett Hardin, 1967. A scientist's case for abortion. *Redbook* (May), p. 62.

12. Garrett Hardin, 1967. Blueprints, DNA, and abortion: a scientific and ethical analysis. *Medical Opinion & Review*, **3**(2):74.

13. H. Curtis Wood, 1967. Letter to the editor. *Medical Opinion & Review*, **3**(11):19.

14. David T. Smith, ed., 1967. *Abortion and the Law*. Cleveland: Western Reserve University. (p. 179)

15. Anonymous, 1967. *Association for the Study of Abortion Newsletter*, **2**(3):6.

# 4

1. Garrett Hardin, 1972. *Exploring New Ethics for Survival. The Voyage of the Spaceship Beagle*. New York: Viking Press. (p. 107*n*)

2. Victor E. Shelford, 1956. Obituary of Charles Manning Child. *Bulletin of the Ecological Society of America*, **37**:32.

# 5

Reprinted with permission of the publisher from Garrett Hardin, ed., 1969. *Population, Evolution and Birth Control*, 2nd ed. San Francisco: W. H. Freeman and Co. Only the second half is here included.

# 7

1. Harold W. Helfrich, ed., 1970. *The Environmental Crisis*. New Haven, Conn.: Yale University Press. (p. 160)

2. J.A.M.H. Damoiseaux, 1960. Result of the international contest on population problems in underdeveloped areas. *Social Compass*, **7**(3):267–272.

# 10

The Letters to the Editor were printed in *New Scientist*, **39**(615):616. 1968.

The book *Objections to Roman Catholicism*, edited by Michael de la Bedoyere, was published by Constable of London in 1964.

# 11

Wylie's poem was originally published in *Scientific Monthly*, **67**:63 (1948).

# 12

Reprinted with permission of the publisher from *ETC.*, **23**:167–171. 1966.
1. Vernon Van Dyke, 1964. *Pride and Power: The Rationale of the Space Program*. Urbana: University of Illinois Press. (p. 155)
2. Garrett Hardin, 1956. Meaninglessness of the word protoplasm. *ETC.*, **13**:193–208.
3. Van Dyke, *op. cit.*, p. 151.
4. George Eliot, 1872. *Middlemarch*.
5. Van Dyke, *op. cit.*, p. 34.
6. *Ibid.*, p. 61.
7. *Ibid.*, p. 90.
8. Garrett Hardin, 1961. Three classes of truth. *ETC.*, **18**:5–20.
9. Van Dyke, *op. cit.*, p. 157.
10. Eugen Sänger, 1965. *Space Flight: Countdown for the Future*. New York: McGraw-Hill. (p. 8)
11. Sigmund Freud, 1925. Negation. In *Collected Papers*, **5**,181. London: Inst. of Psycho-Analysis, 1950.
12. Arthur C. Clarke, 1963. *Profiles of the Future*. New York: Harper & Row. (Chapter 8)
13. Dennis Gabor, 1963. *Inventing the Future*. London: Secker and Warburg. (p. 162)
14. Clarke, *op. cit.*, p. 116.
15. Fred J. Gruenberger, 1965. A measure for crackpots. *Science*, **145**:1413–1415.

# 13

1. L. R. Shepherd, "The Distant Future," in L. J. Carter (ed.), *Realities of Space Travel*, London: Putnam, 1957.
2. A. V. Cleaver, "The Development of Astronautics," in L. J. Carter, *op. cit.*, 1957.
3. *Time* magazine, 1 August 1955, p. 13.
4. *Science*, **127** (1958):691.
5. *Population Bulletin*, **13** (1957):133.
6. *Science*, **127** (1958):1038.

# 20

1. Stephen Risch and Douglas Boucher, 1976. What ecologists look for. *Bulletin of the Ecological Society*, **57**(3):8–9.
2. Peter L. Berger and Brigitte Berger, 1972. *Sociology*. New York: Basic Books. (pp. 172–173).

# 21

This article is based on a paper first presented to the Symposium on Central Planning and National Goals, at Sea Island, Georgia, in September, 1962. An earlier version of this article was published in *Central Planning and Neomercantilism,* Helmut Schoeck and James W. Wiggins, editors; New York: Van Nostrand, 1964. The present version was published in *Perspectives in Biology and Medicine,* **7**:58–84 (1963); two minor corrections, one mathematical the other bibliographic, have been made in the text.

1. M. Polanyi. Personal knowledge. London: Routledge & Kegan Paul, 1958.
2. W. Paley. Natural theology: or evidences of the existence and attributes of the diety collected from the appearances of nature. London: R. Faulder, 1802.
3. G. Hardin. Nature and man's fate. New York: Rinehart, 1959.
4. D. Ricardo. The principles of political economy and taxation (1817), p. 53. London: J. M. Dent (Everyman's Library), 1911.
5. S. Potter. Lifemanship. New York: Holt, 1950.
6. P. Sraffa (ed.). The works and correspondence of David Ricardo, I, 93. Cambridge: Cambridge University Press, 1951.
7. G. Hardin. Science, **131**:1292, 1960.
8. J. Von Neumann and O. Morgenstern. Theory of games and economic behavior. Princeton: Princeton University Press, 1944.
9. G. Hardin. Biology: its principles and implications, p. 489. San Francisco: W. H. Freeman, 1961.
10. S. Barr. The will of Zeus, p. 78. Philadelphia: Lippincott, 1961.
11. A. Gregg. J. Nerv. Mental Dis., **126**:3, 1958.
12. E. H. Chamberlin. The theory of monopolistic competition, 6th ed. Cambridge, Mass.: Harvard University Press, 1948.
13. L. Von Bertalanffy and A. Rapoport (eds.). Yearbook of the Society for the Advancement of General Systems Theory, Volume I. Ann Arbor, Mich.: Mental Health Research Institute, 1956.
14. C. Elton. Animal ecology, pp. 54–55. New York: Macmillan, 1927.
15. R. Carson. Silent spring. Boston: Houghton Mifflin, 1962.
16. H. B. Taussig. Sci. Amer., **207**:29, 1962.
17. H. Grüneberg. Animal genetics and medicine. New York: Paul B. Hoeber, 1947.
18. A. M. Turing. Proc. London Math. Soc., **42**:230, 1937.
19. G. Hardin. ETC., **18**:5, 1961.
20. E. S. Turner. Roads to ruin: the shocking history of social reform. London: Michael Joseph, 1950.
21. K. E. Boulding. The organizational revolution. New York: Harper, 1953.

# 22

This article was first published in the *Journal of Urban Law,* **48**(3):563–578, 1971. I am indebted to the editor for permission to reprint.

This paper, which was requested by the editor of the journal, had to be prepared only once, so the citations were couched in legal style at the outset. I have left the citations in that style rather than risk introducing new errors by recasting them. In one respect only do I consider the legal style superior: by writing "158 Science 730" legalists automatically distinguish between the volume (158, here) and the page of the article, without recourse to different type-fonts.

1. J. K. Galbraith, The Affluent Society, 253 (1958).

2. G. Hardin, 50 Jour. Heredity 68 (1959).

3. K. Davis, 158 Science 730 (1967).

4. In 1969, according to the Population Reference Bureau, the birth rate in the U.S. was 17.4 per thousand population, while the death rate was 9.6 producing a net growth rate of 7.8 per mil. or 0.78 per cent. Additions from immigration brought the population increase close to 1 per cent per year. At the same time, Costa Rica enjoyed (?) a birth rate of 45 per mil and a death rate of 7, producing a net growth rate of 3.8 per cent. Every one of the 137 countries routinely studied by the Bureau now has a positive growth rate, even Ireland, which had a zero, or even a negative, growth rate for many decades after the potato famine of the 1840's.

5. E.g. Paul R. Ehrlich, whose book The Population Bomb (1968) has attracted wide attention. He is not alone: Kenneth E. Boulding, Kingsley Davis, Raymond B. Cowles, J. J. Spengler, William and Paul Paddock, P. K. Whelpton, Paul B. Sears and many others are also on record as believing that we have long since passed the optimum point.

6. This is almost a "null class." The English economist Colin Clark is virtually the only outspoken proponent of this position.

7. U. Thant, 168 Intern. Planned Parenthood News 3 (1968).

8. See R. R. Wilkins, Regulation and Control in Living Systems 20 (H. Kalmus ed. 1966). Any time delay in a negative feedback system is potentially capable of producing fluctuations that can destroy the system, whether it is a natural system or a political system. For this reason, attempting to control population through individual decisions actuated by individual perceptions, with the time delays incurred by wishful thinking as well as the irreducible nine months of gestation, must always be suspect.

9. F. Godley in an unpublished Master's thesis, "Relationship of size of family of origin to the fertility of contemporary American women," University of Maryland (1969).

10. C. G. Darwin, 2 Evolution After Darwin 469 (S. Tax ed. 1960).

11. If the non-hereditary component is larger the process of evolution takes longer, but the direction is the same. See R. A. Fisher, Chap. 1, The Genetical Theory of Natural Selection (1929).

12. D. & E. Lack, 93 Ibis 501 (1951).

13. K. Hagberg, Carl Linnaeus 118 (1953).

14. N. E. Himes, Medical History of Contraception (1936).

15. W. L. Langer, 69 Amer. Hist. Rev. 1 (1963).

16. G. Hardin, Diversity and Stability in Ecological Systems 151 (1969).

17. G. Hardin, 169 Science 427 (1970).

18. At least among all normal, "legally competent" members. Even now, the denial of reproduction to those with marked mental deficiencies is widely accepted. As a matter of principle, some extreme equalitarians disapprove of even this restriction; but as a matter of political realism they do not often make this a political issue.

19. K. E. Boulding, The Meaning of the 20th Century (1964).
20. W. Shakespeare, The Merchant of Venice, Act II, Scene 2 (1600).
21. J. Fletcher, Situation Ethics (1966).
22. J. R. Platt, 146 Science 347 (1964).
23. B. L. Crowe, 166 Science 1103 (1969).
24. For typical examples of this sterile literature *see* M. F. A. Montague, 32 Jour. Heredity 243 (1941); and M. H. Fried, Science and the Concept of Race (M. Mead *et. al* ed. 1968).
25. Mario Puzo, the author of the novel The Godfather (1969) almost, but not quite, saw this point—and by that failure of insight greatly weakened the thrust of his tale.
26. G. Hardin, 131 Science 1292 (1960); and 7 Persp. Biol. & Med. 58 (1963). *See also* R. S. Miller, Advances in Ecological Research, Vol. 4 (L. B. Craig ed. 1967).
27. C. Elton, Animal Ecology (1927).
28. Probably not all conceivable matings have been tried, *e.g.,* the mating of a Laplander with a Hottentot, but there is no reason to think that any such mating would be sterile, or that the extremes among human beings should be assigned to different species.
29. I. Zangwill, The Melting Pot (1908).
30. N. Glazer & D. P. Moynihan, Beyond the Melting Pot (1963).

# 23

Reprinted from *Science and Public Affairs* (*Bulletin of the Atomic Scientists*) **28**(6):37–41, 1972.

The controversy between Ehrlich and Holdren on one side and Commoner on the other falls outside the province of the present book, but students of the ethical behavior of scientists are well advised to read the complete exchange in the *Bulletin:* **28**(5):16, 18–27; **28**(5):17, 42–56; and **28**(6):6. My contribution was written at the request of the editor, Richard S. Lewis, following the receipt of the first two manuscripts of the protagonists.

# 24

1. *Science,* **173**:381 (1971).
2. "The Tragedy of the Commons" was originally published in *Science,* **162**:1243–1248 (1968). Much as it is disliked, it has been reprinted in some fifty anthologies. For a thorough development of the implications of the commons by many authors see *Managing the Commons,* Garrett Hardin and John Baden, editors; San Francisco: Freeman, 1977. The original essay is included in that volume.
3. See for instance the Letters published in *Science,* **174**:1077–1078 (1971).
4. *Shooting an Elephant and Other Essays,* by George Orwell. New York: Harcourt, Brace (1950).

# 26

1. Philip M. Boffey, "Nuclear Power Debate: Signing Up the Pros and Cons," *Science,* **192** (1976), 120–122.
2. Alvin M. Weinberg, "Science and Trans-Science," *Minerva* **10:**2 (April 1972), 209–222.
3. Herman E. Daly, ed., *Toward a Steady-State Economy* (San Francisco, Calif.: W. H. Freeman, 1973).

# 30

Anonymous. 1974. *Wall Street Journal* 19 Feb.

Borlaug, N. 1973. Civilization's future: a call for international granaries. *Bull. At. Sci.* **29:**7–15.

Boulding, K. 1966. The economics of the coming Spaceship earth. *In* H. Jarrett, ed. Environmental Quality in a Growing Economy. Johns Hopkins Press, Baltimore.

Buchanan, W. 1973. Immigration statistics. *Equilibrium* **1**(3):16–19.

Davis, K. 1963. Population. *Sci. Amer.* **209**(3):62–71.

Farvar, M. T., and J. P. Milton. 1972. The Careless Technology. Natural History Press, Garden City, N.Y.

Gregg, A. 1955. A medical aspect of the population problem. *Science* **121:**681–682.

Hardin, G. 1966. Chap. 9 *in* Biology: Its Principles and Implications, 2nd ed. Freeman, San Francisco.

———. 1968. The tragedy of the commons. *Science* **162:**1243–1248.

———. 1969a Page 18 *in* Population, Evolution, and Birth Control, 2nd ed. Freeman, San Francisco.

———. 1969b. The economics of wilderness. *Nat. Hist.* **78**(6):20–27.

———. 1972a. Pages 81–82 *in* Exploring New Ethics for Survival: The Voyage of the Spaceship *Beagle.* Viking, N.Y.

———. 1972b. Preserving quality on Spaceship Earth. *In* J. B. Trefethen, ed. Transactions of the Thirty-Seventh North American Wildlife and Natural Resources Conference. Wildlife Management Institute, Washington, D.C.

———. 1973. Chap. 23 *in* Stalking the Wild Taboo. Kaufmann, Los Altos, Cal.

Harris, M. 1972. How green the revolution. *Nat. Hist.* **81**(3):28–30.

Langer, S. K. 1942. Philosophy in a New Key. Harvard University Press, Cambridge.

Lansner, K. 1974. Should foreign aid begin at home? *Newsweek,* 11 Feb., p. 32.

Marx, K. 1875. Critique of the Gotha program. Page 388 *in* R. C. Tucker, ed. The Marx-Engels Reader. Norton, N.Y., 1972.

Ophuls, W. 1974. The scarcity society. *Harpers* **248**(1487):47–52.

Paddock, W. C. 1970. How green is the green revolution? *BioScience* **20:**897–902.

Paddock, W., and E. Paddock. 1973. We Don't Know How. Iowa State University Press, Ames, Iowa.

Paddock, W., and P. Paddock. 1967. Famine—1975! Little, Brown, Boston.

Wilkes, H. G. 1972. The green revolution. *Environment* 14(8):32–39.

# 31

1. Garrett Hardin, 1974. Lifeboat ethics: the case against helping the poor. *Psychology Today,* 8(4):38ff.
2. Roger Revelle, 1974. The ghost at the feast. *Science,* 186:589.
3. Garrett Hardin, 1975. [Letter to the Editor.] *BioScience,* 25(3):148.
4. George R. Lucas, Jr., and Thomas V. Ogletree, eds., 1976. *Lifeboat Ethics: The Moral Dilemmas of World Hunger.* New York: Harper & Row.

# 32

1. Garrett Hardin, 1968: "The Tragedy of the Commons," *Science,* 162:1243–48.
2. Karl Marx, 1875: "Critique of the Gotha program." (Reprinted in *The Marx-Engels Reader,* Robert C. Tucker, editor. New York: Norton, 1972).
3. Garrett Hardin and John Baden, 1977. *Managing the Commons.* (San Francisco: W. H. Freeman.)
4. Thomas Robert Malthus, 1798: *An Essay on the Principle of Population, as it affects the Future Improvement of Society.* (Reprinted, *inter alia,* by the University of Michigan Press, 1959, and The Modern Library, 1960).
5. Donella H. Meadows, Dennis L. Meadows, Jorgen Randers, and William H. Behrens, 1972: *The Limits to Growth* (New York: Universe Books).
6. C. P. Snow, 1963: *The Two Cultures; and a Second Look* (New York: Mentor).
7. Hans Jonas, 1973: "Technology and Responsibility: Reflections on the New Task of Ethics," *Social Research,* 40:31–54.
8. William and Paul Paddock, 1967: *Famine–1975!* (Boston: Little, Brown & Co.).
9. Garrett Hardin, 1975: "Gregg's Law," *BioScience,* 25:415.
10. Joseph Fletcher, 1966: *Situation Ethics* (Philadelphia: Westminster Press).
11. Helmut Schoeck, 1969: *Envy* (New York: Harcourt, Brace & World).
12. Garrett Hardin, 1972: *Exploring New Ethics for Survival* (New York: Viking).
13. Nicholas Wade, 1974: "Sahelian Drought: No Victory for Western Aid," *Science,* 185:234–37.
14. Erik P. Eckholm, 1975: "The Deterioration of Mountain Environments," *Science,* 189:764–70.
15. Ancel Keys, et al., 1950: *The Biology of Human Starvation.* 2 vols. (Minneapolis: University of Minnesota Press).
16. A. S. Geden, 1928: "Hindu charity (almsgiving)," *Encyclopaedia of Religion and Ethics,* Vol. III, pp. 387–89 (New York: Scribner's).

17.  William L. Davidson, 1928: "Charity," *Encyclopaedia of Religion and Ethics,* Vol. III. p. 373 (New York: Scribner's).
18.  Garrett Hardin, 1974: "The Rational Foundation of Conservation," *North American Review,* **259**(4):14–17.
19.  Rachel Carson, 1962: *Silent Spring* (Boston: Houghton Mifflin).
20.  M. Taghi Farvar and John P. Milton, editors, 1969: *The Careless Technology,* (Garden City, N.Y.: Natural History Press).

# Index